First World War
and Army of Occupation
War Diary
France, Belgium and Germany

20 DIVISION
Divisional Troops
Royal Army Medical Corps
62 Field Ambulance
24 July 1915 - 30 May 1919

WO95/2109/3

The Naval & Military Press Ltd
www.nmarchive.com
Published in association with The National Archives

Published by

The Naval & Military Press Ltd

Unit 10 Ridgewood Industrial Park,

Uckfield, East Sussex,

TN22 5QE England

Tel: +44 (0) 1825 749494

www.naval-military-press.com

www.nmarchive.com

This diary has been reprinted in facsimile from the original. Any imperfections are inevitably reproduced and the quality may fall short of modern type and cartographic standards.

© Crown Copyright
Images reproduced by permission of The National Archives, London, England, 2015.

Contents

Document type	Place/Title	Date From	Date To
Miscellaneous	2109/3		
Heading	20th Division 62nd Field Ambulance Jly 1915-1919 May		
Heading	20th Division 62nd Field Ambulance 24th-30th July 1915 Vol. I		
War Diary	S S Conought	24/07/1915	24/07/1915
War Diary	Le. Havre	25/07/1915	25/07/1915
War Diary	Setques	26/07/1915	26/07/1915
War Diary	Ebblinghem	28/07/1915	28/07/1915
War Diary	Sec Bois Near Hazebrouck	29/07/1915	29/07/1915
War Diary	Sec Bois	29/07/1915	29/07/1915
War Diary	Vieux Berquin	30/07/1915	30/07/1915
Heading	20th Division 62nd F.A. Vol: 2 Aug 15		
Heading	War Diary of 62nd Field Ambce. Vol II From Aug 1/15 To Aug 30/15		
War Diary	Vieux Berquin	01/08/1915	16/08/1915
War Diary	Nouveau Monde	17/08/1915	30/08/1915
Heading	20th Division 62nd F.A. Vol. 4 Dec 1915		
Heading	War Diary of 62nd Field Ambce From Dec 2/15 To Dec 30/15 Vol. IV		
War Diary	Nouveau Monde	02/12/1915	30/12/1915
Heading	20th Div 62nd F.A. Jan 1916 Vol 5		
Heading	War Diary of 62nd Field Ambce From Jan 1/16 To Jan 31/16		
War Diary	Nouveau Monde	01/01/1916	17/01/1916
War Diary	Morbecque	18/01/1916	22/01/1916
War Diary	Arneke	23/01/1916	31/01/1916
Heading	62nd F. Amb. Feb 1916		
Heading	62nd F.A. Vol 6		
War Diary	Arneke	01/02/1916	03/02/1916
War Diary	Wormhout	05/02/1916	15/02/1916
War Diary	Hilhoek	17/02/1916	28/02/1916
Heading	20th Div. March April 1916 No. 62 F. Amb.		
Heading	62 F Amb Vol 7		
War Diary	Hilhoek Nr Poperinghe	01/03/1916	30/03/1916
War Diary	Hilhoek	01/04/1916	17/04/1916
War Diary	Wormhout	18/04/1916	30/04/1916
Heading	20th Div. No. 62 F. Amb. May 1916		
War Diary	In The Field	01/05/1916	28/05/1916
Heading	War Diary of Lieut. Colonel J.G. Gill. Officer Commanding. 62nd Field Ambulance R.A.M.C. 20th (Light) Division. 1st July 1916 To 31st July 1916		
War Diary	Red House Vlamertinghe-Poperinghe Road	01/07/1916	11/07/1916
War Diary	Red Farm	12/07/1916	16/07/1916
War Diary	Watou	17/07/1916	19/07/1916
War Diary	Bailleul	20/07/1916	21/07/1916
War Diary	Handinghem	22/07/1916	24/07/1916
War Diary	Halloy	24/07/1916	24/07/1916
War Diary	Bus Les Artois	26/07/1916	27/07/1916
War Diary	Couin	28/07/1916	31/07/1916

Heading	War Diary of O.C. 62nd Field Ambulance R.A.M.C. 20th (Light) Division 1st August 1916 To 31st August 1916		
War Diary	Couin	01/08/1916	16/08/1916
War Diary	Sarton	17/08/1916	17/08/1916
War Diary	Gezaincourt	18/08/1916	20/08/1916
War Diary	Happy Valley	21/08/1916	22/08/1916
War Diary	Carnoy	22/08/1916	31/08/1916
Heading	War Diary of The Officer Commanding 62nd Field Ambulance 20th (Light) Division. 1st September 1916 To 30th September 1916		
War Diary	Carnoy	01/09/1916	06/09/1916
War Diary	Meulte	07/09/1916	08/09/1916
War Diary	Mericourt	09/09/1916	11/09/1916
War Diary	Sand Pits	12/09/1916	13/09/1916
War Diary	Citadel	14/09/1916	16/09/1916
War Diary	Carnoy	17/09/1916	19/09/1916
War Diary	Citadel	20/09/1916	21/09/1916
War Diary	Meaulte	22/09/1916	25/09/1916
War Diary	Dublin Post Nr Montauban	26/09/1916	26/09/1916
War Diary	Dublin Post	26/09/1916	30/09/1916
Heading	War Diary of O.C. 62 Field Ambulance 20th Division 1st October 1916 To 31st October 1916		
War Diary	Montauban	01/10/1916	08/10/1916
War Diary	Meaulte	09/10/1916	13/10/1916
War Diary	Corbie	15/10/1916	16/10/1916
War Diary	Allonville	18/10/1916	18/10/1916
War Diary	Fremont	19/10/1916	21/10/1916
War Diary	St Sauveur	22/10/1916	31/10/1916
Heading	War Diary of The Officer Commanding 62nd Field Ambulance, R.A.M.C. 20th (Light) Division. 1st November 1916 To 30th November 1916 Vol 15		
War Diary	St Sauveur	01/11/1916	01/11/1916
War Diary	Molliens Vidame	02/11/1916	14/11/1916
War Diary	L'arbre 'a Mouche	14/11/1916	14/11/1916
War Diary	S/Airaines	15/11/1916	15/11/1916
War Diary	Allery	18/11/1916	24/11/1916
War Diary	Yzeux	25/11/1916	27/11/1916
War Diary	Sailly-Le-Sec	28/11/1916	30/11/1916
Heading	War Diary of The Officer Commanding 62nd Field Ambulance R.A.M.C. 20th (Light) Division 1st December 1916 To 31st December 1916 Vol 16		
War Diary	Sailly-Le-Sec	01/12/1916	01/12/1916
War Diary	Bussy-Les-Daours	02/12/1916	08/12/1916
War Diary	Ville-Sous-Corbie	09/12/1916	09/12/1916
War Diary	Carnoy	10/12/1916	31/12/1916
Heading	War Diary of The Officer Commanding 62nd Field Ambulance R.A.M.C. 20th (Light) Division 1st January 1917 To 31st January 1917		
War Diary	Carnoy	01/01/1917	25/01/1917
War Diary	Meaulte	26/01/1917	26/01/1917
War Diary	Corbie	27/01/1917	27/01/1917
War Diary	Cardonnette	28/01/1917	31/01/1917
Heading	War Diary of The Officer Commanding 62nd F. Ambulance R.A.M.C. 20th (Light) Division 1st February 1917 To 28th February 1917 Vol 18		

War Diary	Cardonnette	01/02/1917	07/02/1917
War Diary	Meaulte	07/02/1917	07/02/1917
War Diary	Carnoy	08/02/1917	28/02/1917
Heading	War Diary of The Officer Commanding 62nd Field Ambulance R.A.M.C. 20th (Light) Division 1st March 1917 To 31st March 1917 Vol 19		
War Diary	Carnoy	01/03/1917	31/03/1917
Heading	20th Div. 62nd F. A. April 1917		
Heading	War Diary of 62nd Field Ambulance From 1st April 1917 To 30th April 1917 Vol 20		
War Diary	Carnoy	01/04/1917	03/04/1917
War Diary	Rocquigny	04/04/1917	08/04/1917
War Diary	Lechelle	09/04/1917	28/04/1917
War Diary	Neuville	29/04/1917	30/04/1917
Heading	20th Div. No. 62. F. A. May 1917		
Heading	War Diary of 62nd Field Ambulance From 1st May 1917 To 31st May 1917 Vol 21		
War Diary	Neuville	01/05/1917	23/05/1917
War Diary	Beaulencourt	24/05/1917	24/05/1917
War Diary	Favreuil	26/05/1917	31/05/1917
Heading	No. 62 F. A. June 1917		
Heading	War Diary of 62nd Field Ambulance R.A.M.C. From 1st June 1917 To 30th June 1917 Vol 22		
War Diary	Favreuil	01/06/1917	01/06/1917
War Diary	Avesnes Les Bapaume	03/06/1917	27/06/1917
War Diary	Bihucourt	28/06/1917	30/06/1917
Heading	No. 62 F. A. July 1917		
Heading	War Diary of 62nd Field Ambulance R.A.M.C. From 1st July 1917 To 31st July 1917 Vol 23		
War Diary	Bihucourt	01/07/1917	01/07/1917
War Diary	Le Meillard	02/07/1917	21/07/1917
War Diary	Proven Area	22/07/1917	22/07/1917
War Diary	Handekot	24/07/1917	31/07/1917
Heading	B.E.F. Summary of Medical War Diaries For 62nd F.A., 20th Divn. 14th Corps, 5th Army. From 21.7.17		
War Diary	Headquarters	21/07/1917	21/07/1917
War Diary	Moves And Transfer	21/07/1917	21/07/1917
War Diary	Medical Arrangements	26/07/1917	26/07/1917
War Diary	Operations	31/07/1917	31/07/1917
War Diary	Casualties Evacuation	31/07/1917	31/07/1917
War Diary	Headquarters	21/07/1917	21/07/1917
War Diary	Moves And Transfer	21/07/1917	21/07/1917
War Diary	Medical Arrangements	26/07/1917	26/07/1917
War Diary	Operations	31/07/1917	31/07/1917
War Diary	Casualties Evacuation	31/07/1917	31/07/1917
Heading	B.E.F. Summary of Medical War Diaries For 62nd F.A., 20th Divn. 14th Corps, 5th Army.		
War Diary	Evacuation Casualties	01/08/1917	01/08/1917
War Diary	Operations Enemy	03/08/1917	10/08/1917
War Diary	Operations	15/08/1917	15/08/1917
War Diary	Casualties Evacuation	16/08/1917	16/08/1917
War Diary	Medical Arrangements	17/08/1917	17/08/1917
War Diary	Moves Detachment	18/08/1917	18/08/1917
War Diary	Operations Enemy	20/08/1917	23/08/1917
War Diary	Moves	24/08/1917	24/08/1917
War Diary	Operations Evacuation	27/08/1917	27/08/1917

War Diary	Medical Arrangements	28/08/1917	28/08/1917
War Diary	Decorations	30/08/1917	30/08/1917
War Diary	Operations Enemy	31/08/1917	31/08/1917
War Diary	Evacuations Casualties	01/08/1917	01/08/1917
War Diary	Operations Enemy	03/08/1917	10/08/1917
War Diary	Operations	15/08/1917	15/08/1917
War Diary	Casualties Evacuation	16/08/1917	16/08/1917
War Diary	Medical Arrangements	17/08/1917	17/08/1917
War Diary	Moves Detachment	18/08/1917	18/08/1917
War Diary	Operations Enemy	20/08/1917	23/08/1917
War Diary	Moves	24/08/1917	24/08/1917
War Diary	Operations Evacuation	27/08/1917	27/08/1917
War Diary	Medical Arrangements	28/08/1917	28/08/1917
War Diary	Decorations	30/08/1917	30/08/1917
War Diary	Operations Enemy	31/08/1917	31/08/1917
Heading	War Diary of 62nd Field Ambulance R.A.M.C. From 1st August 1917 To 31st August 1917 Vol 24		
Heading	No. 62. F.A. Aug 1917		
War Diary	Mouton Farm B 14.a.3.8 Sheet 28 N.W.	01/08/1917	01/08/1917
War Diary	Elverdinghe	01/08/1917	02/08/1917
War Diary	Mouton Farm Elverdinghe	03/08/1917	06/08/1917
War Diary	Mouton Farm B 14.a.2.8 Sheet 28 N.W.	07/08/1917	10/08/1917
War Diary	Elverdinghe	10/08/1917	11/08/1917
War Diary	Mouton Farm	11/08/1917	11/08/1917
War Diary	B 14.a.2.8 Sheet 28 N.W.	11/08/1917	13/08/1917
War Diary	Elverdinghe	14/08/1917	14/08/1917
War Diary	Mouton Farm	14/08/1917	16/08/1917
War Diary	Elverdinghe Mouton Farm B 14.a.3.8 Sheet 28 N.W.	16/08/1917	23/08/1917
War Diary	Panama Camp E 18 b 2.8 Sheet 27 Proven Area	24/08/1917	28/08/1917
War Diary	Panama Camp 27/E.18.b.2.8	29/08/1917	29/08/1917
War Diary	Proven Area	29/08/1917	31/08/1917
Diagram etc	Mouton Farm XIVth C.W. W.C.P.		
Heading	No. 62. F.A. Sept 1917		
War Diary	Decorations	01/09/1917	03/09/1917
War Diary	Operations Enemy	03/09/1917	03/09/1917
War Diary	Decorations	06/09/1917	06/09/1917
War Diary	Moves	09/09/1917	09/09/1917
War Diary	Moves Detachment	09/09/1917	09/09/1917
War Diary	Operations Enemy	09/09/1917	12/09/1917
War Diary	Moves	18/09/1917	18/09/1917
War Diary	Operations	20/09/1917	20/09/1917
War Diary	Evacuations Casualties	20/09/1917	21/09/1917
War Diary	Operations Enemy	21/09/1917	21/09/1917
War Diary	Moves	28/09/1917	28/09/1917
War Diary	Decorations	01/09/1917	03/09/1917
War Diary	Operations Enemy	03/09/1917	03/09/1917
War Diary	Decorations	06/09/1917	06/09/1917
War Diary	Moves	09/09/1917	09/09/1917
War Diary	Moves Detachment	09/09/1917	09/09/1917
War Diary	Operations Enemy	09/09/1917	12/09/1917
War Diary	Moves	18/09/1917	18/09/1917
War Diary	Operations	20/09/1917	20/09/1917
War Diary	Evacuations Casualties	20/09/1917	21/09/1917
War Diary	Moves	28/09/1917	28/09/1917
Heading	War Diary of 62nd Field Ambulance R.A.M.C. From 1st September 1917 To 30th September 1917 Vol 25		

War Diary	Panama Camp E 18.b.2.8 Sheet 27	01/09/1917	08/09/1917
War Diary	X 30 C Central XIV Sheet 19 X Corps Seek Distributing Centre	09/09/1917	16/09/1917
War Diary	X 30 C Central Sheet 19 C.S.D.O.	17/09/1917	17/09/1917
War Diary	Mouton Farm XIV Corps W.W.C.P. 28/ B14.a.2.8.	18/09/1917	20/09/1917
War Diary	Mouton Farm 28/B.14.a.2.8	21/09/1917	22/09/1917
War Diary	Mouton Farm C.W.W.C.P. B.14.a.2.8 Sheet 28 N W	23/09/1917	26/09/1917
War Diary	Mouton Farm XIV Corps. W.W.C.P. B.14.a.2.8 Sheet 28 N W	26/09/1917	27/09/1917
War Diary	Panama Camp Proven P5 Area	28/09/1917	28/09/1917
War Diary	Panama Camp Proven P5 Area 27/E.18.b.2.8	28/09/1917	30/09/1917
Heading	War Diary of 62nd Field Ambulance From 1st Oct 1917 To 31st Oct 1917 Vol 26		
Heading	B.E.F. Summary of Medical War Diaries of 62nd F.A., 20th Divn. 14th Corps, 5th Army.		
War Diary	Headquarters	02/10/1917	02/10/1917
War Diary	Moves And Transfer	02/10/1917	02/10/1917
Heading	B.E.F. Summary of Medical War Diaries of 62nd F.A., 20th Divn. 14th Corps, 5th Army.		
War Diary	Headquarters	02/10/1917	02/10/1917
War Diary	Moves And Transfer	02/10/1917	02/10/1917
War Diary	Panama Camp Proven Area E18.b.2.8 Sheet 27	01/10/1917	01/10/1917
War Diary	Bapaume	02/10/1917	04/10/1917
War Diary	Haut Allaines C29 B. (Sheet 62c)	06/10/1917	07/10/1917
War Diary	III Corps C.R.S. Moislains C.12.d.0.5 (Sheet 62c)	08/10/1917	19/10/1917
Miscellaneous	VII Corps Rest Station	20/10/1917	20/10/1917
War Diary	Moislains C.12.d.0.5 Sheet 62 C	21/10/1917	31/10/1917
War Diary	III Corps Rest Station	31/10/1917	31/10/1917
Heading	No. 62. F. A. Nov 1917		
Heading	War Diary of 62nd Field Ambulance From 1st Nov 1917 To 30 Nov 1917 Vol 27		
War Diary	III Corps Rest Station	01/11/1917	01/11/1917
War Diary	Moislains 62/C. C.12.d.0.5	02/11/1917	05/11/1917
War Diary	III Corps Rest Station	06/11/1917	06/11/1917
War Diary	Moislains 62c/C.12.d.0.5	07/11/1917	13/11/1917
War Diary	III Corps Rest Station	14/11/1917	16/11/1917
War Diary	Moislains C.12.d.0.5	18/11/1917	20/11/1917
War Diary	III Corps Rest Station	20/11/1917	20/11/1917
War Diary	Moislains C.12.d.0.5 62.C. Sheet	20/11/1917	21/11/1917
War Diary	III Corps Rest Station	21/11/1917	21/11/1917
War Diary	Moislains C 12.d.0.5 Sheet	22/11/1917	26/11/1917
War Diary	III Corps Rest Station	27/11/1917	27/11/1917
War Diary	Moislains C.12.d.0.5	27/11/1917	30/11/1917
Heading	No. 62 F. A. Dec 1917		
Heading	War Diary of 62nd Field Ambulance From 1 Dec 1917 To 31st Dec 1917 Vol 28		
War Diary	III Corps Rest Station	01/12/1917	01/12/1917
War Diary	Moislains C.12.d.0.5 62 C.	02/12/1917	05/12/1917
War Diary	Bouzincourt W. 16 Central Sheet 57D.	05/12/1917	06/12/1917
War Diary	Coupelle Neuve Lens Sheet 1.100,000	07/12/1917	11/12/1917
War Diary	Wallon Cappel Hazebrouck Sheet 1/100000	12/12/1917	28/12/1917
Heading	War Diary of 62nd Field Ambulance From 1st January 1918 To 31st January 1918 Vol 29		
War Diary	Wallon Cappel Sheet 5 A Hazebrouck 1/100000	03/01/1918	06/01/1918
War Diary	Woodcote House 28/I 20. C4.3	06/01/1918	08/01/1918
War Diary	Woodcote House I 20.C.4.3 Sheet 28	08/01/1918	16/01/1918

War Diary	Woodcote House I 20.C.4.3 Sheet 28 1/40,000	17/01/1918	31/01/1918
Heading	War Diary of 62nd Field Ambulance From 1st February 1918 To 28th February 1918 Vol 30		
War Diary	Woodcote House I 20.C.4.3. Sheet/28 1/40,000	01/02/1918	13/02/1918
War Diary	Ebblinghem T 22.b.8.3 Sheet 27 1/40,000	14/02/1918	22/02/1918
War Diary	Le Plessis 66 D 1/40000 W 1 C 9.1.	23/02/1918	23/02/1918
War Diary	Plessis W.I.C.9. 1/66 D.	24/02/1918	28/02/1918
Heading	War Diary of 62nd Field Ambulance From 1st March 1918 To 31st March 1918 Vol 31		
War Diary	Le Plessis W.1.C.9.1 Sheet 66D 1/40,000	01/03/1918	11/03/1918
War Diary	Le Plessis W.1.C.9.1.	12/03/1918	16/03/1918
War Diary	Le Plessis W.1.C.9.1. Sheet 66D 1/40,000	17/03/1918	22/03/1918
War Diary	Brouchy	23/03/1918	23/03/1918
War Diary	Guiscard	24/03/1918	26/03/1918
War Diary	Villers Aux Erables	27/03/1918	27/03/1918
War Diary	Sains-En-Amienois	28/03/1918	29/03/1918
War Diary	Warlus	30/03/1918	30/03/1918
War Diary	Abbeville	31/03/1918	31/03/1918
Heading	War Diary of 62nd Field Ambulance From 1st April 1918 To 30th April 1918 Vol 32		
War Diary	Abbeville	01/04/1918	03/04/1918
War Diary	Sorel	04/04/1918	05/04/1918
War Diary	La Boissiers	06/04/1918	09/04/1918
War Diary	Morival	10/04/1918	10/04/1918
War Diary	Ault	11/04/1918	17/04/1918
War Diary	Marquay Lens 11	18/04/1918	19/04/1918
War Diary	Marquay	20/04/1918	27/04/1918
War Diary	Le Quesnel	28/04/1918	29/04/1918
War Diary	Les Vents	30/04/1918	30/04/1918
Heading	62nd F.A. May 1918		
Heading	War Diary of 62nd Field Ambulance From 1st May 1918 To 31st May 1918 Vol 33		
War Diary	Quartre Vents	01/05/1918	01/05/1918
War Diary	S.2.c.8.3 Sheet 36c Jenks Siding	02/05/1918	15/05/1918
War Diary	S.2.c.8.3 Jenks Siding	16/05/1918	20/05/1918
War Diary	S.2.c.8.3 36c Jenks Siding	21/05/1918	27/05/1918
War Diary	S.2.c.8.3 Jenks Siding	28/05/1918	29/05/1918
War Diary	Carency X.17.c.6.2 Sheet 36 B	30/05/1918	31/05/1918
Miscellaneous	Addendum No. 2 To Operation Order No. 109 (39th Infantry Bde.)	18/05/1918	18/05/1918
Operation(al) Order(s)	61st. Infantry Brigade Order No. 6	17/05/1918	17/05/1918
Miscellaneous	Table of Reliefs. (Issued With 61st Infantry Brigade Order No. of 17th. May, 1918		
Operation(al) Order(s)	61st. Infantry Brigade Order No. 7	22/05/1918	22/05/1918
Operation(al) Order(s)	59th Infantry Brigade Operation Order No. 109	15/05/1918	15/05/1918
Operation(al) Order(s)	59th Infantry Brigade Operation Order No. 111	17/05/1918	17/05/1918
Miscellaneous	Table "A" Issued With 59th Infantry Brigade Operation Order No. 111		
Operation(al) Order(s)	59th Infantry Brigade Operation Order No. 108	12/05/1918	12/05/1918
Operation(al) Order(s)	59th Infantry Brigade Operation Order No. 110	15/05/1918	15/05/1918
Operation(al) Order(s)	61st. Infantry Brigade Order No. 4	09/05/1918	09/05/1918
Miscellaneous	Table of Reliefs (Issued With 61st Infantry Brigade Order No. 4, 9/5/18)	09/05/1918	09/05/1918
Miscellaneous	Addendum No. 1 To 20th (Light) Division Order No. 240	03/05/1918	03/05/1918

Type	Description	Date From	Date To
Operation(al) Order(s)	R.A.M.C. Operation Order No. 1. by Colonel B.F. Wingate, DSO, Commanding R.A.M.C. 20th Division.	01/05/1918	01/05/1918
Miscellaneous	Table "A" To Accompany 20th Divisional Order No. 240 Of 30.4.18	30/04/1918	30/04/1918
Operation(al) Order(s)	Medical Arrangements in Connection With 20th Division O.O. No. 240	01/05/1918	01/05/1918
Operation(al) Order(s)	20th Divisional R.A.M.C. Operation Order No. 2 by Colonel B.F. Wingate, D.S.O., A.D.M.C.	01/05/1918	01/05/1918
Operation(al) Order(s)	59th Infantry Brigade Operation Order No. 115	26/05/1918	26/05/1918
Miscellaneous	War Diary		
Heading	War Diary of 62nd Field Ambulance From 1st June 1918 To 30th June 1918 Vol 34		
War Diary	Carency X.17.c.6.2 36.B.	01/06/1918	20/06/1918
War Diary	Carency X.17.c.6.2. 44 B.	21/06/1918	29/06/1918
Miscellaneous	Amendment No. 1 To 61st Bde Order No. 11	18/06/1918	18/06/1918
Operation(al) Order(s)	61st. Brigade Order No. 11	16/06/1918	16/06/1918
Miscellaneous	61 Inf Bde Raid 19/20 June 18		
Miscellaneous	Amendment No. 2 To Disposition And Location Report No. 8	05/06/1918	05/06/1918
Miscellaneous	20th (Light) Division. Disposition And Location Report No. 8	29/05/1918	29/05/1918
Miscellaneous	Reference O.O. 9. Of 5th June, 1918	05/06/1918	05/06/1918
Operation(al) Order(s)	61st. Infantry Brigade Operation Order No. 9	05/06/1918	05/06/1918
Miscellaneous	Table-of-Reliefs. (Issued With 61st Infantry Brigade Order No. 9 Of 5/6/18)	05/06/1918	05/06/1918
Operation(al) Order(s)	59th Infantry Brigade Operation Order No. 118	10/06/1918	10/06/1918
Operation(al) Order(s)	59th Infantry Brigade Operation Order No. 119	12/06/1918	12/06/1918
Miscellaneous	Administrative Instructions Issued In Connection With 61st. Inf. Bde. Order No. 10, Dated 15. June. 1918	15/06/1918	15/06/1918
Operation(al) Order(s)	59th Infantry Brigade Operation Order No. 120	15/06/1918	15/06/1918
Miscellaneous	Table "A" Issued With 59th Infantry Bde. Operation Order No. 120		
Operation(al) Order(s)	61st. Infantry Brigade Order No. 10	13/06/1918	13/06/1918
Miscellaneous	Table of Reliefs. Issued With 61st. Infantry Brigade Order No. 10 Of 13th June, 1918	13/06/1918	13/06/1918
Heading	War Diary of The Officer Commanding, 62nd Field Ambulance. 20th (Light) Division. 1st July, 1918-31st July, 1918 Vol 35		
War Diary	X.15.c.6.2 Sheet 44B	01/07/1918	12/07/1918
War Diary	X.15.c.6.2 Sheet 44B Carency	13/07/1918	31/07/1918
Heading	War Diary of 62nd. Field Ambulance. 1st August, 1918 To 31st August 1918. Vol 36		
War Diary	X.15.c.6.2 44B Carency	01/08/1918	31/08/1918
Heading	War Diary of 62nd Field Ambulance From 1st September 1918 To 30th September 1918 Vol 37		
War Diary	X.16.c.6.2 Sheet 44B (Carency)	01/09/1918	30/09/1918
Heading	War Diary of 62nd Field Ambulance From 1st October 1918 To 31st October 1918 Vol 38		
War Diary	X.16.c.6.2 Sheet 44.B. Carency	01/10/1918	06/10/1918
War Diary	Marquay	07/10/1918	30/10/1918
War Diary	Cambrai	31/10/1918	31/10/1918
Heading	War Diary of 62nd Field Ambulance From 1st November 1918 To 30th November 1918 Vol 39		
War Diary	Cambrai	01/11/1918	03/11/1918
War Diary	Cagnoncles	04/11/1918	04/11/1918
War Diary	St. Aubert	05/11/1918	06/11/1918

War Diary	Vendegies	07/11/1918	08/11/1918
War Diary	La. Bois Crette	09/11/1918	10/11/1918
War Diary	St. Waast. La Vallee	11/11/1918	12/11/1918
War Diary	Taisnieres	13/11/1918	26/11/1918
War Diary	Bavay	27/11/1918	30/11/1918
Heading	War Diary of 62nd Field Ambulance From 1st December 1918. To 31st December 1918. Vol 40		
War Diary	Bavay	01/12/1918	05/12/1918
War Diary	Villers Pol	06/12/1918	06/12/1918
War Diary	Saulzoir	07/12/1918	07/12/1918
War Diary	Cambrai	08/12/1918	08/12/1918
War Diary	Grevillers	09/12/1918	09/12/1918
War Diary	Bertrancourt	10/12/1918	31/12/1918
Heading	20th Div. Box 1835 War Diary of 62nd Field Ambulance R.A.M.C. 1st January 1919-31st January 1919 Vol 41		
War Diary	Bertrancourt	01/01/1919	31/01/1919
Heading	War Diary of 62nd Field Ambulance From 1st Feb. 1919 To 28th Feb. 1919 Vol 42		
War Diary	Bertrancourt	01/02/1919	20/02/1919
War Diary	Mondicourt	20/02/1919	28/02/1919
Heading	War Diary of 62nd, Field Ambulance, From: 1st. March, 1919 To: 31st, March, 1919 Vol 43		
War Diary	Mondicourt	01/03/1919	19/03/1919
War Diary	Mondicourt France	19/03/1919	30/03/1919
Heading	War Diary of 62nd Field Ambulance From 1st. April, 1919. To 30th. April, 1919 Vol 44		
War Diary	Mondicourt	01/04/1919	18/04/1919
Heading	No. 62 Field Ambulance. May 1919		
War Diary	Mondicourt France	03/05/1919	30/05/1919
Diagram etc			
Heading	62nd F. Amb. Taren of Bertrancourt France February 1919		

2109/3

20TH DIVISION

62ND FIELD AMBULANCE
JLY 1915 - DEC 1918
1919/MAY

121/6242

20th Division.

127/6242

62nd Field Ambulance
Vol. I.

24th – 30th July/15

amb

Army Form C. 2118

WAR DIARY
or
INTELLIGENCE SUMMARY
(Erase heading not required.)

Place	Date	Hour	Summary of Events and Information	Remarks and references to Appendices
SS Connaught	July 24th	6.30 pm	This afternoon the 62nd Field Ambulance embarked on H.M.H.T. Connaught at Southampton en route for France. The Officers & transport reached on the 22nd in H.M.H.T. Princess to LE HAVRE.	
LE HAVRE	25th	9.30 am	The F.A. Amb. personnel disembarked at the port of LE HAVRE this morning at 8 a.m. and marched to No.5 Rest Camp where they joined their transport. The Unit is now reunited and complete.	
SETQUES	26th	4 pm	Arrived at WIZANES having left HAVRE by troop train at 3.pm 25th. No casualties nothing of moment to note. marched to SETQUES where the men have been billeted in a comfortable barn. J.O. & men and the Officers in houses in the village.	
EBBLINGHAM	29th	3 pm	Marched from SETQUES this morning at 9 am. After a good march & fine weather we arrived at the Chateau EBBLINGHAM at 3.30 pm together. Found small detention hospital station in one of the rooms of the house and men billeted in the farmyard. The Officers billeted in the house and where we received a few patients.	
SEC BOIS 29th HAZEBROUCK			Left about 5.15. The above billet & marched with 34th Brigade to SEC BOIS	

Army Form C. 2118

WAR DIARY
or
INTELLIGENCE SUMMARY
(Erase heading not required.)

Place	Date	Hour	Summary of Events and Information	Remarks and references to Appendices
S Ee BOIS	July 29	7 pm	A large number of men fell out from the infantry battalions owing to foot trouble & were brought into Camp by means of our own to Ambulances, six of which arrived yesterday evening. The Field Ambulance received rolls or men out, falling out. We are all bivouacked in a field. In view to the few in being received & sent to patients out of whom we have admitted. I have transferred six men probably Enteric Spinal meningitis to HAZEBROUCK and one probable Diphtheria to MERVILLE (No 7 Casualty Clearing Ff). Also four other Sick men cases to the latter Hospital.	
VIEUX BERQUIN	30	2 pm	Left above at 8 a.m. and marches here arriving at 10.10 am. Ambulance has opened for the reception of sick & wounded in his good room of the female school. The men and three officers are billeted in the school buildings. Treated a number of minor sick and transferred some to Casualty Clearing Hospital at MERVILLE	

J Elder
Lieut Col RAMC
O/c 6? Field Ambulance

Aug 1

62nd F.A.
Vol. 2

19/44
121

25th Missouri

Aug 15.

CONFIDENTIAL.

WAR DIARY

of

62ND FIELD AMBCE.

— VOL II —

from Aug 1/15 to Aug 30/15

Army Form C. 2118

WAR DIARY
or
INTELLIGENCE SUMMARY
(Erase heading not required.)

Instructions regarding War Diaries and Intelligence Summaries are contained in F.S. Regs., Part II. and the Staff Manual respectively. Title Pages will be prepared in manuscript.

Place	Date	Hour	Summary of Events and Information	Remarks and references to Appendices
Camp Berguin	August 1/VIII 15		This ambulance was inspected by Surg-Gen Macpherson.	
	2nd		This unit divided into its 3 sections. C section remaining at Sele behind Vieux Berquin & carried on as F.A. + Div. Rest Station. This unit (personnel) were fully employed in cleaning the buildings & in medical charge of unit until return of the other 2 sections on 10·VIII·15. A sec. marched today to 26th F.A. of Bac St Maur and were attached for instruction to that unit. B sec. proceeded to the 95th F.A. near Sailly & were similarly attached	
Vieux Berquin	10th		The 6.3rd F.A. rejoined here today, after having been instructed in F.A. work during trench warfare.	
	11th		B Sec. took over hospital duty. A+C Sec. loaded up in readiness to move off on receipt of orders. One admission - accident, practised clearch.	
	12th		B sec. continued duty. A+C during fatigues + lecture.	
	13th			
	14th			
	15th		B Sec. remained at Vieux Berquin. A+C sections proceeded to Nouveau Monde + Bts near Laventie Stn.	
	16th		All were medically inspected.	
Nouveau Monde	17th		A pet. formed a hospital in the school & recieved several slightly wounded cases. C sec. formed and advanced D.S. at Laventie collecting wounded from Regl HQ Posts in trenches. B sec. at Vieux Berquin.	
	19th		Sec. joined up today leaving 1 officer + officer at Laventie A.D.S. Lt. Townsend was handed over to 2/1st Regt	
	20th		B sec. remained at Vieux Berquin. Capt Phillipe Rowe joined from Royal Irish Regt + taken sheep The 2nd i/c. unit. C sec Rowe attached for instruction. A.D.M.S. VIII Div. Col. Dunn inspected the F.A.	
	24th			
	26th			
	27th		One left today. Some casualties from Laventie	
	29th		Laventie shelled wounding 10 5 wounded + civilian being treated here.	
	30		This Ambulance extended in to Quercnu re by Nouveau Monde Bridge. A+C Sec. both to new unit today	

Smear Phillip
CAPT. R.A.M.C.
for O/C 62nd FIELD AMBULANCE

62ws R.a.
Vol. 4

12/7909

20 [signature]

FL 162/1.

Dec 1915

War-Diary
of
62ⁿᵈ Field Ambulance
Vol IV

From Dec 1/15   To Dec 30/15

WAR DIARY
or
INTELLIGENCE SUMMARY.
(Erase heading not required.)

Army Form C. 2118

Place	Date	Hour	Summary of Events and Information	Remarks and references to Appendices
NOUVEAU MONDE	Dec. 2nd		Capt. Williams took over duties of M.O. 1/c X11 Kings Liverpool Regt.	
	6th		S. Sgt. Wellington from 1/1st 2A taken on strength of this unit. A.D.S. at SAILLY taken over by our sec. of this unit from 60th FA	
	8th		Capt. Thorne took over duties fm Capt Williams. Capt hulin took over duties of M.O. 1/c 90th Bde R.F.A. Capt Jepson proceeded on leave from 8th Inst. The funnell over it was found today.	
	11th		Lieut Roberts returned to FA today from clearing duty as M.O. 1/c 92nd Bde R.F.A. owing to Rhys using the cook house became flooded and had to be moved	
	12th		Father Gill gave a cinematograph display to patients in hospital wards this evening.	
	13th		A sec h went on route march this morning	
	14th		N.O.S. h transferred to Port & Clino fm FLEURBAIX, 61st FA taking over the A.D.S at SAILLY.	
	15th		Capt Pridham fm lieut Roberts in charge.	
	17th		Capt Pridham took over duties of M.O. 1/c 93rd Bde R.F.A. Capt. Arlins relieves Capt. Pridham at A.D.S. Capt. Williams + R.M.O's 12 hrs proceeded on leave	
	18th		Capt Calford evacuated sick to No. 2 Cas. hurlee	
	24th		leave granted to Capt. Arlins + 2 NCOs + 2 men from today until 1/5/16	

WAR DIARY
or
INTELLIGENCE SUMMARY.

Army Form C. 2118.

Place	Date	Hour	Summary of Events and Information	Remarks and references to Appendices
NOUVEAU MONDE	Dec 25		W/a returns men revert to all patients never quick. A cricket was given this evening	
			by surgical ward for patient men.	
	27		Lieut MILLER refuctastic arrival men attaches for duty to this unit	
	28.		Reinforcement of 10 men arrived today from 58th & 59th F.A.'s	
			Lieut MILLER transferred to 61st F.A. for duty	
	29.		'B' Sec. under Capt. Jepson made a route march Today	
	30.		A Sec. under Capt. Phillips " " " "	

Mac Phillips
CAPT. R.A.M.C.
for O/C 62nd FIELD AMBULANCE.

20th Div.
69no F.A.

F/16712

Jan 1916

— CONFIDENTIAL —

WAR DIARY

of

62ND FIELD AMBCE

from Jan 1/16 to Jan 31/16

WAR DIARY or INTELLIGENCE SUMMARY.

Army Form C. 2118.

Place	Date	Hour	Summary of Events and Information	Remarks and references to Appendices
NOUVEAU MONDE	1.7.16		Lieut. Robert proceeded to England on leave. C sect. on duty at A.D.S. Heurteux.	
	3.7.16		B sect. made a route march.	
	4.7.16		B sect. relieved C sect. at A.D.S. Bearer party (6th Fld. Amb) admitted wounded.	
	5.7.16		Capt. Collins took over duties of M.O. Wimp. (1.S.) who was struck off the strength of the unit.	
	10.7.16		C sect. marched to MORBECQUE CHATEAU & took over from 26th F.A. (vice Capt. Snow) "C" sect. 25th F.A. arrived & took over the F.A. from this unit. B sect. at A.D.S. was relieved by me sect. of 26 F.A. at Heurteux A.D.S.	
	11.7.16		Unit paraded 7.30 am marched to MORBECQUE & formed a Ambulance there relieving 25th F.A. Capt. Turner with wagons reached a newly flat & went sick.	
	12.7.15		Capt. Turner partly reported at Château on completion of his duties. The Trevor interpreter was attached from this unit today. Capt. Martyn took over duties at No.10 F. N.O.Y.C.I. today.	
	13.7.15		vice Lieut. Rader who proceeded to England.	
	15.7.15		Rev. Plummer Agar Bridge left unit vice Rev. W. & 11th Rifle N.Q.	
	17.7.15		Capt. Phillips proceeded to England on leave. Capt. Hunt took over duties of M.O. 1/c 7th D.C.L.I.	

Army Form C. 2118.

WAR DIARY
or
INTELLIGENCE SUMMARY.
(Erase heading not required.)

Instructions regarding War Diaries and Intelligence Summaries are contained in F. S. Regs., Part II. and the Staff Manual respectively. Title pages will be prepared in manuscript.

Place	Date	Hour	Summary of Events and Information	Remarks and references to Appendices
MORBECQUE	18.1.15.		Divisional training commenced, this unit were drilled made roll nominal Reveille. Robertii took over duties of No. 1/c XII D.S.S. Lieut Parker Stone reported.	
	19.		arrival to duty today. Ruth were of B crew.	
	19.1.15			
	22.1.15	10.45 A	XXIV Div took over from this ambulance this unit marched to ARNEKE + took over the beginning of a billet.	
ARNEKE	23rd		Infirmary cleared up and accommodation made for about 50 & 60 patients. All men employed on fatigue.	
	27th		Lt. Col. Gill proceeded on leave to Selford. Ruth were of 2nd crew. Capt. Muir took over duties of Sanitary Res. Inoculation with new T.A.B. vaccine commenced.	
	31st		Unit with bicycles went on a route march were inspected by the G.O.C. 1st Cavalry while on movement.	

Murer Phillips

62nd. J. Arnb.

Feb 1916

62nd 7a.
1016

Army Form C. 2118

62nd FIELD AMBULANCE

WAR DIARY
or
INTELLIGENCE SUMMARY
(Erase heading not required.)

Instructions regarding War Diaries and Intelligence Summaries are contained in F. S. Regs., Part II. and the Staff Manual respectively. Title Pages will be prepared in manuscript.

Place	Date	Hour	Summary of Events and Information	Remarks and references to Appendices
ARNEKE	1.2.16		Field Ambulance in bivouac here, collecting patients from 61st Cav. Artillery	
	2.2.16		Capt. Beau and detachment proceeded to WORMHOUT to take over from 2nd West Riding F.A.	
	3.2.16		The Ambulance marched to WORMHOUT and with detachment formed a F.A. there collecting from local artillery re 61st Inf. Bde. 1 Sec. & 2 officers left at ARNEKE to form a D.W.R. Rest Station. Quatermaster proceeded to return from leave to England dept.
WORMHOUT	5.2.16		Forces proceeded in this section here busy with medical work, lectures to the training was continued. The O.C. visited 61st Inf Bde. had his dis'n and inspected the Ambulance
	6.2.16		Lt Col Gill returned from leave today. A.D.M.S. 61st Div came over to camp about noon. Was with to Poperinghe. Lt Parker took over duties of A.D.M.S.C.I. Surg. Gen Porter D.M.S. II Army inspected the unit this afternoon.
	7.2.16		
	8.2.16		New site at Hilhoek to this F.A. was expected by the O.C. this afternoon.
	11.2.16		Capt. Turner and detachment proceeded to WATOU in rear of 61st Inf Bde. took over duties of 10th F.A. The unit moves on 13th inst.
	12.2.16		Capt. Rathbun proceeded on leave to England. Leave for 12th cancelled.
	13.2.16		Paraded at 8.30 am and marched via WATOU to HILHOEK about 4 miles
	14.2.16		S.W. of POPERINGHE and relieved the 2nd F.A. 14 D.W." Advanced dressing station formed on ELVERDINGHE - POPERINGHE
	15.2.16		road, collecting sick and wounded from Reserve Bde. (61st) & D.R.S. opened at HILHOEK. 3 huts reserved for Field Ambulance patients

WAR DIARY or INTELLIGENCE SUMMARY

Army Form C. 2118
Sheet II

Place	Date	Hour	Summary of Events and Information	Remarks and references to Appendices
HILA OEK	17/11/16		D.M.S. 2nd Army Surg-General Porter inspected the unit today - men all employed at hospital duty fatigues	
	19th		W.O. Staten with us section commenced Field Ambulance work. Wounded chief to C.C.S. also R.S. Post formed in W. Canal Bank	
	21st		Aeroplanes came over and dropped bombs - none however falling near this unit. Work continued in number.	
	24th		O.C. inspected dug outs on Canal Bank. 10 men M officers ideas to collect cases from Regt M.O's	
	28th		Lieut Burghle Rome attached to unit for instruction cyph. Gralleon granted extension of leave until noon Sa 16.	

L. Phillips
Capt Ronne
to 1/1/6 2nd FA

2A Div.

S/ March 7/9/16.
April 7/9/16.

No. 62 F. Amb.

COMMITTEE FOR THE
MEDICAL HISTORY OF THE WAR
Date 9 - JUN. 1915

62 Jaml
Vol 7

WAR DIARY
or
INTELLIGENCE SUMMARY.
(Erase heading not required.)

Army Form C. 2118.

Place	Date	Hour	Summary of Events and Information	Remarks and references to Appendices
HILHOEK for POPERINGHE	Mar 1st 1915		Lt. Broughton R.A.M.C. attached to this unit yesterday. Work continued on improving drainage &c. Our section at POPERINGHE - ELVERDINGHE. He was under Capt. Pridham.	
	Mar 5th		A.D.M.S. inspected the D.R.S. Work continued on roads &c. Section during F.A. work with an A.D.S. in the Canal Bank.	
	Mar 8th		Lieut Golding attached for duty with this unit. Capt Roberts took over duties of M.O. i/c KOYLI	
	" 11th		Reinforcement of four men arrived today. Work commenced in interchanging huts & repairing woodwork &c.	
	" 14		Lieut Broughton took over duties of M.O. i/c 7th KOYLI.	
	" 16		Capt Turner took over duties of M.O. i/c 7th Dec.ns	
	22		Capt Jepson had no duties of M.O. He & Capt. Roe R.F.A. Capt Turner returned to his unit & proceeded to leave with its men. Bno Archer continued at Dressing Station with Advanced Dressing Station on the Canal bank.	
	27th		All work delayed owing to rain	
	28th		All Men employed in fatigues & were making	
	30th		Surg Gen Pike and Surg Gen S. Anthony Bindly Inspected the D.R.S. Today.	

Phillips

Army Form C. 2118

WAR DIARY
or
INTELLIGENCE SUMMARY
(Erase heading not required.)

U 12 7 Ant Vol 5

Place	Date	Hour	Summary of Events and Information	Remarks and references to Appendices
HILL 60 EK.	1/4/16		2 sections forming D.R.S. here one section in ELVERDINGHE – POPERINGHE road forming aid Dressing Station. A party at CANAL BANK forming an A.D.S. Also collecting from two Reg's in that area. Capt.	
	6/4/16		Tunn took over duties of M.O. 1/6/7 Sgts.	
	8/4/16		Capt. Robt. returned this unit from being M.O. 1/6/7 K.O.Y.L.I. Section entered on duties work at D.R.S. in reserve trenches in CANAL BANK, repairing refurnishing dugouts, draining + sanitary work generally took on entire of M.O. (1/2 93rd Fd. RFA Capt. Parke + 4 men proceeded on leave down to indicated M.O. R.F. Tuckey	
	10/4/16		Each GM Witt Walsh Wormhoudt on 16th 7 A about 20 men to Calais + Welfs of DRS ETAPERINGHE N.D.S. looked over to 60/2 A	
	13/4/16		2nd Cpl. returned today. Capt. Parker took men across of M.O. 1/2 7. Sill Renvele Bank.	
	16/4/16		Brec. invalided from D.S. + evacuated at HOPOUTRE to RAPArs Today departed at 5 pm. Capt. Roling relieved which	
	17/4/16		Brit. orderly opened a Eng. There to give medical to remaining troops. Any Pole. Lieut. Rubenstein reported for duty.	
WORMHOUDT	19/4/16		DRs 12 now of F.A. moved to WORMHOUDT today. (in Artillery Divil Camp) in ideal after rest. Removed ovelain unhoulget.	
	20/4/16		Agent in field W.PMHOUT sely. men were employed abmy improving the camp has labors re built.	

WAR DIARY
or
INTELLIGENCE SUMMARY
(Erase heading not required.)

Army Form C. 2118

Place	Date	Hour	Summary of Events and Information	Remarks and references to Appendices
	25/4/16		Col. Sluie. D.D.M.S. XIV Corps inspected the rest[n] at WORMHOUT	
	26/4/16		Took over F.A. at HERZEELE from 60th F.A.	
	28/4/16		B.C.A. Gill M.B. reft. arrived from Calais Today. 'C' Sect. at HERZEELE & D.Rs. tents erected	
WORMHOUT	30/4/16		Capt Innes relieved Capt Don O.C. sanitary sect. today. Capt Roberts proceeded on leave. Capt Jebson relieves Capt Bird. No 16 F. now D.Rs. huts commenced today in field opposite school	

P. Phillips
Capt. R.A.M.C.
O/C 2ND FIELD AMBULANCE.

20th Div.

May 1916.

No. 62 F. Amb.

COMMITTEE FOR THE
MEDICAL HISTORY OF THE WAR
Date 26 JUN 1915

WAR DIARY
or
INTELLIGENCE SUMMARY
(Erase heading not required.)

Army Form C. 2118

Instructions regarding War Diaries and Intelligence Summaries are contained in F. S. Regs., Part II. and the Staff Manual respectively. Title Pages will be prepared in manuscript.

Place	Date	Hour	Summary of Events and Information	Remarks and references to Appendices
In the field	1/v/16		Field Ambulance D.R.S. at WORMHOUDT with a section at HERZEELE. All men engaged in construction of D.R.S.	
	3.v.16		Work on D.R.S. continued; hindered by weather. Stretchers & blankets &c. erected.	
	7.v.16		Marched at 1.30 p.m. today to WATOU. 'B' section joined at HERZEELE. Ambulance established at WATOU CONVENT. R. & O. Gill proceeded on leave	
	11.v.16		2 B.S.D.c of the unit marched in rear of Bdr. Reo where are carrying out a tactical exercise between VLAMERTINGE & CANAL BANK. Aid posts formed at BRIELEN & VLAMERTINGE. 3 casualties resulted which were returned Capt Adam R.A.M.C. joined the unit in lieu of Lt. Cox with 7 men taken in the strength from last date	
	16.v.16		C. section "closed to". Today ready [?] of at our hours notice.	
	16.v.16		Lieut Gill returned from leave. Quarter-master proceeded on leave today.	
	2.v.16		Marched from WATOU to CONVENT Rue de Bruges POPERINGHE when a Brltulance was formed.	
	2.v.16		Moved from CONVENT to Red Farm Dressing Stn, VLAMERTINGHE, taking over from N°4 FA. Aid posts at St JEAN & POTIJZE between was from gds Stn. Dressing station at ASYLUM & CANAL BANK Taken over by.	

Army Form C. 2118

WAR DIARY
or
INTELLIGENCE SUMMARY
(Erase heading not required.)

Instructions regarding War Diaries and Intelligence Summaries are contained in F.S. Regs., Part II. and the Staff Manual respectively. Title Pages will be prepared in manuscript.

Vol 9

Place	Date	Hour	Summary of Events and Information	Remarks and references to Appendices
In the Field	24.v.16		Lieut voote the A.D.M.S. went tonight to St Jean to inspect Regt aid Posts of 12th King's Liverpool Regt	
	26.v.16		Relieved 1/60 2A. at aid posts running station between path of this unit reported road connecting POTIZE with St JEAN & ambulance rendered it unfit for motor traffic.	
	28.v.16		POPERINGHE was shelled this afternoon but no casualties were brought in. 2A	

J. L. Lith.
LT. COL. R.A.M.G.
O.O. 89TH FIELD AMBULANCE.

1875 Wt. W593/826 1,000,000 4/15 J.B.C. & A. A.D.S.S./Forms/C. 2118.

Confidential

War Diary
of
Lieut-Colonel J.G. Gill.
Officer Commanding
62nd Field Ambulance R.A.M.C.
20th (Light) Division

1st July 1916 to 31st July 1916.

20/
62. F. Amb.
Vol II
July

COMMITTEE FOR THE
MEDICAL HISTORY OF THE WAR
Date 5 - SEP 16

Army Form C. 2118

WAR DIARY
or
INTELLIGENCE SUMMARY
(Erase heading not required.)

Instructions regarding War Diaries and Intelligence Summaries are contained in F.S. Regs., Part II. and the Staff Manual respectively. Title Pages will be prepared in manuscript.

Place	Date	Hour	Summary of Events and Information	Remarks and references to Appendices
Red House VLAMERTINGHE -POPERINGHE Road	1/7/16		H.Q. + 1 section above at Main D.S. taking sick & wounded from troops in vicinity 61st Bde via A.D.S. in trenches. One sect. at PROVEN taking sick from XIV CorpsHQ & troops in vicinity and from main D.S. One sect. at A.D.S. - Asylum YPRES with personnel wheeled stretchers at Regt. Aid Post of batteries at CANAL BANK, ST JEAN & POTIJZE. Collection from bearers being by M.A.W at night & wheeled stretchers by day.	
	2/7/16		The Prince of Wales inspected the Hospital Field Ambulance today	
	3/7/16		Work continued on improving Menin Dressing Station, having huts, huteing & repairing trenches.	
	5/7/16		Dispositions as before; 60th F.A. are relieving this sect. at A.D.S. Touvins tonight	
	6/7/16		Aid Post & A.D.S relieved by 60th F.A. this evening all personnel withdrawn from aid-posts & A.D.S	
	7/7/16		2 sections of F.A. now at Rest Farm, sick being collected from troops in vicinity by 61st Bde, one in D.W. Reserve. 1 officer & men at post in CONVENT, Rue Bruge, POPERINGHE	
	8/7/16		1 section at H.Q. sent to relieve 1 sect. at PROVEN	
	9/7/16		Major-General W.D. Smith inspected the ambulance this afternoon	
	10/7/16		2Bdes &61st Bde relieve 2 Bdes of 60 Bde, medical arrangements were made for him	
	11/7/16		1 sect. relieved 61st F.A. on A.D.S. in Prison, YPRES sent personnel to Aid Posts at POTIJZE, MENIN ROAD HILLS, & RAILWAY EMBKT. Rt. Ar. Group commenced	

WAR DIARY
or
INTELLIGENCE SUMMARY

Army Form C. 2118

(Erase heading not required.)

Place	Date	Hour	Summary of Events and Information	Remarks and references to Appendices
RED FARM	12.7.16		1 Oct. WTS at PROVEN, one at RED FARM & one at A.D.S. to YPRES. Sick runners being collected as usual. Post at POPERINGHE relieved today. POPERINGHE sheltered two casualties, brought to RED FARM.	
	13.7.16		POPERINGHE sheltered two casualties brought to RED FARM.	
	14.7.16		O.C. 62nd F.A. proceeded to WATOU to take over arrangements via O.C. 1/5 F.A.	
	15.7.16		POPERINGHE sheltered & relieved two casualties admitted	
	16.7.16		16th F.A. relieved 62nd F.A. A.D.S. and POS, all personnel of 62nd F.A. withdrawn from YPRES.	
WATOU	17.7.16		62nd F.A. relieved by 16th F.A. 62nd F.A. marched to WATOU, reclaim at PROVEN relieved also. Found main body on march. Ambulance stored at WATOU rides off 6th F.A. Bee moved troops & watter Unit carried in imping camp clearing up Ambulance.	
	18.7.16			
	19.7.16		Received orders to move to BAILLEUL area tomorrow, all weapon equipment packed up & patients evacuated.	
BAILLEUL	20.7.16		Transport left for BAILLEUL area 9 am. Main body proceeded motor lorries. Took over from 73rd F.A. Main D.S. established at DRANOUTRE, HQ. relieving at BAILLEUL. A.D.S. at WULVERGHEM - NEUVE EGLISE R⁰.	
	21.7.16		Sick wounded being collected from 61st Bde Moved troops. 73rd F.A. moved out & this unit occupied all huts vacated by them. About 60 sick were taken over.	
HONDINGHEM	22.7.16		Received orders to move to near HONDINGHEM in area of 60th Bde. Handed over to 50th F.A. and moved to Div area. Sick of new Bde Group collected.	
	23.7.16		Ambulance prepared to move to CASSEL to entrain.	
	24.7.16		Marched at 1 am to CASSEL, arriving at 3.30 am, entraining into 161 Coy. A.S.C. Proceeded to DOULENS by	

Army Form C. 2118

WAR DIARY
or
INTELLIGENCE SUMMARY
(Erase heading not required.)

Instructions regarding War Diaries and Intelligence Summaries are contained in F.S. Regs., Part II and the Staff Manual respectively. Title Pages will be prepared in manuscript.

Place	Date	Hour	Summary of Events and Information	Remarks and references to Appendices
HALLOY	24/7/16		Rain during detraining by 4 p.m. marched through DOULENS to WATS at HALLOY where an ambulance was established. Sick collected for 161st Bde. group.	
Bus les ARTOIS	26/7/16		Moved suddenly at 2 p.m. to Bus les Artois arriving there about 7 p.m. occupying old F.A. camp.	
	28/7/16		Received A.D.Sn. at COLINCAMPS relieving detachment of 139th F.A. Taking on all regimental aid posts ie now occupied by 61st I.Bde. Main D.S. Rele. Bu Bus.	
COUIN	28/7/16		Marched to COUIN & relieved 130th F.A. A.D.S. remained at COLINCAMPS sick collected from 61st Bde. M.D.S. placed at	
	29/7/16		A.D.Ms. inspected dressing stn. at COLIN CAMPS rather dressing almost this ambulance. 139th F.A. moved out	
	30/7/16		Work continued in cleaning up & improving camp	
	31/7/16		D.D.M.S. XIV Corps inspected Main Dressing Stn., work continued in camp surroundings	

P. Philip Capt.
LT COL R.A.M.C.
O.C. 62ND FIELD AMB.

Confidential

War Diary

of

O.C. 62nd Field Ambulance. R.A.M.C.

20th (Light) Division

1st August 1916 to 31st August 1916.

62nd F.A.

Aug 1916

WAR DIARY or INTELLIGENCE SUMMARY

Army Form C. 2118

(Erase heading not required.)

Place	Date	Hour	Summary of Events and Information	Remarks and references to Appendices
COUIN	August 1915		Main D.S. at COUIN with A.D.S at EUSTON + COT IN CAMPS + teams kept at the Sugar Factory Shelters & White City. Collecting sick & wounded from 61st Res. which are in the trenches	
	Aug 3rd		Work commenced on improving dugouts &c	
	"	4th	Surgeon General inchd inspected the Main D.S of this unit at COUIN this morning	
	"	5th	Work continued in find line by improving dugouts at COUIN, digging a new one at EUSTON, reinsecting the Sugar Factory to EUSTON by a trench	
	"	6th	77th Field Ambulance sent an advance party - preliminary to taking over - to the Sugar Factory & White City to study the workings of the line	
	"	7th	77th FA took over about Aid Party, ADS, we still return & return wounded over to O.E 61	
	"	8th	Personal Equipment returned from Cot in Camps, also 15 officer and S.O, OR left behind to continue work in dugout	
	"	9th	General Snow visited Shelter inspected the new frommey Shr. at COVIN this afternoon	
	"	10th	Work in dugouts continued	
	"	13th	12th	
	"	13th	61st Bde relieve Takentre through taking men from 6th Bde	

Wt. W593/826 1,000,000 4/15 J.B.C. & A. A.D.S.S./Forms/C. 2118.

WAR DIARY
or
INTELLIGENCE SUMMARY

(Erase heading not required.)

Army Form C. 2118

Place	Date	Hour	Summary of Events and Information	Remarks and references to Appendices
COIGN	13th		A.D.S. at COIGNCAMPS relieved A.D.S at EUSTON & RED COTTAGE taken over by 2nd 7A from 61st 7A during the day of hostile attack by H.M. Gas co before personnel did not hand off in relief until 14th	
"	14th		took entrances on dugouts on Central Avenue Beauchamp	
"	16th		Ambulance being relieved by No 4 7A; we move to DOULLENS area tomorrow. Ifld Gill made heavy R.D.M. Gas Dev.	
SARTON	17th		marched to SARTON today, where an entrance was opened in	
GEZAINCOURT	18th		marched via DOULLENS to GEZAINCOURT when Ambulance was opened	
"	19th		Transport marched with Bde Transport to VILLERS BOCAGE Ambulance remained at GEZAINCOURT and are moving by bus columns to ALBERT area	
"	20th		marched this morning to Entrained at CANDAS, travelled via AMIENS to MERICOURT where we detrained and marched to MERLANCOURT where we halted for the night opened a section of the 7A	
"HAPPY VALLEY"	21st		marched to "HAPPY VALLEY" near BRAY where we bivouaced for the night	
	22nd		2 Tents S·D· sent to DIVE COPSE to form Corps Main Dressing Stn, Bearer Div. sent to form Divisional Bearer Div. under Lt·Col Calburn at Bronfay Fm 1 Tent S·D· proceeded to CARNOY to form Dressing Stn Bde QM stores for medical Personnel equipment & under 1st Pln Kendale	

WAR DIARY
or
INTELLIGENCE SUMMARY

(Erase heading not required.)

Army Form C. 2118

Place	Date	Hour	Summary of Events and Information	Remarks and references to Appendices
CARNOY	22nd		Established at SAPPER CORNER	
"	23rd		Dressing Stn at CARNOY in dugout receiving cases from Left Beaver Post at Bernafay Wood, all local casualties sick	
"	25th		many casualties during the past two days, am having the D.S.	
"	26th		I k/left killed & seven wounded belonging to the Ambulance at BRIQUETERIE	
"	27th		A.D.M.S inspected R.A. Left Beaver Post; also communication by road very difficult owing to heavy rain. D.Lgt fld is expected to be evacuated to CARNOY.	
"	28th		Roads in very bad condition owing to rain, ambulances frequently getting bogged, received orders to attack on 30th. Preparation made for reception of cases & great stock of dressings to laid in: etc. Notice have directions boards placed in all roads	
"	29th		Rain very heavy indeed today, increasing the difficulties of evacuation owing to weather conditions attack is postponed	
"	30th		and sick admitted is very low owing to rain being round.	
"	31st		Weather improved roads drying up. Operation postponed.	

[signature] Capt RAMC
O.C 6 br⟨?⟩ F.A.

Confidential

War Diary

of the

Officer Commanding 62nd Field Ambulance

20th (Light) Division.

1st September 1916 to 30th September 1916

Army Form C. 2118.

WAR DIARY
or
INTELLIGENCE SUMMARY.
(Erase heading not required.)

Instructions regarding War Diaries and Intelligence Summaries are contained in F.S. Regs, Part II. and the Staff Manual respectively. Title pages will be prepared in manuscript.

Place	Date	Hour	Summary of Events and Information	Remarks and references to Appendices
CARNOY	1 Sep 1916		One tent S.D.N. (A) here, with QM at SAPPER CORNER and small detachment to supply stretchers, medical units & establishments of Div. Tent S.D. are treating all sick evacuated from head units three kuspt in from BERNAFAY WOOD. 2 TentsS-DivS (B+C) with Corps Main Dressing Stn at DIVE COPSE under Capt Board. The Bearer Div. is with Div 14th Bearer Section under Lt Col Osborn at BRONFAY FM collecting cases from RegtlAid Posts re BRIQUETERIE + BERNAFAY WOOD. D.A.D.M.S. XIV Corps inspected CARNOY recent to the above Bearer posts. A number of "gassed" cases admitted owing to lachrymator shells, which weather never improved today, where still coming in regu rat.	
"	2nd		Weather improved. Gases arising direct Considerable artillery activity. One nav killed in Bearer division.	
"	3rd		Attack on GUILLEMONT by 20th Div today. Three have been to be directed a continuous stream of wounded were treated and dispatched without travels from 9.0am today until 9.0am 4th. About 900 cases were treated. Including about 30 Germans.	

WAR DIARY
or
INTELLIGENCE SUMMARY.

Army Form C. 2118.

Place	Date	Hour	Summary of Events and Information	Remarks and references to Appendices
CARNOY	4th		Attack still continues but wounded coming in, in large numbers, weather fine. Capt. Prothero was wounded today at Bernafoy wood. 500 wounded rick panniers from Gun today by our 50 hundreds of wounded dressed but a good number of pick passed through.	
	5th		CARNOY St. man relieved tonight by 113 F.A. when SAPPER CORNER. Tent SD of A Div Recn. Sqn at Bernafoy farm.	
	6		The advn part of the field ambulance marched below SAND PITS, SA MÉAULTE Hyginerced these with the 61st Rde. Tent SD of FA remain with Captains at DIVES copse all the MT personnel wagons still attached what MAC	
MEAULTE	7		Ambulance remained with Bde in bivouacs and collected sick & wounded from whole group.	
"	8		Marched at 6.30 pm to MERICOURT L'ABBÉ passing through TREUX bivouacced at MERICOURT	
MERICOURT	9th		Ambulance formed her tents erected, collection of sick wounds from sub group. Ambulance proceeded tonight	

WAR DIARY
or
INTELLIGENCE SUMMARY

Place	Date	Hour	Summary of Events and Information	Remarks and references to Appendices
MERI-COURT	10		Capt Jepson took med duties of No/C 7th Hants. Lt Col Crowder attached to 1/4th after Church Parade of Bde. No morning after which the Brde Commander addressed the Bde. Sunny	
	11		One day equipment was checked & men marched in river	
SAND PITS	12		Equipment being made up. May/I MO to replace Capt Leaver & Gilbert marched at 4 pm. Today to SAND PITS near MEAUTE where Ambulance bivouaced for the night. Lt Garden joined his unit. Ambulance remained at SANDPITS. Capt Carris joined the unit & Lt	
	13		Garden transferred to 1/1 2A. Capt Gilbert took over duties M.O. 1/107th Sani. L.I. Capt Leaver duties 9/10/2 (6th or Bucks). Beavers morning of Thames Eply Wh	
YGRADET	14		marched to Citadel today. Bivouaced there pm. Rd.	
	15		Beavers sent Capt henched into Bde & BOIS TATUS near CAROY – in afternoon marched TWATERLOT Fm where the Bde was in reserve to XIV Corps	
	16		Marched 4.30 am Bde attacked with 9th Div along GIVCHY – LES BOEUFS Rd. Beavers D. JWs were retained at GIVCHY loading port with	

WAR DIARY or INTELLIGENCE SUMMARY

Army Form C. 2118.

Place	Date	Hour	Summary of Events and Information	Remarks and references to Appendices
"	16		9 guides & A Bearers, about 10 a.m. after the position had been reconnoitered Tent S.D. were taken up the GIVENCHY - NEUVE CHAPELLE Rd to near a pill box where an A.D.S. was found to take over. He worked his Reg'l S.B's. they were then carried by hand over the back Nof GIVENCHY to GIVENCHY Bombing Post where they were handed over to ambulance wagon. The bearers were employed until about 5 a.m. 17th and after the Bn had been relieved they returned to GUILLEMONT Dressing St. The Tent S.D's remained during these operations at the Château.	
CARNOY	17		Marched with Bde to CARNOY & were joined by Tent S.D Tent S.O of B under Capt [?] proceeded to GUILLEMONT D.S. Capt Main & Tent S.O of B proceeded to Bernafay wood D.S.	
CARNOY	18th		Capt Turner & bearers of 'A' Section went to GUILLEMONT Dressing St. to assist in removal of wounded which owing to the state of the roads was very difficult. Three ambulance wagons were also sent.	
"	19th		Capt Nolan & Tent S.D returned to CARNOY. Bde was to have moved to Citadel but this has been postponed. Capt Nolan & Tent 'A' leave GUILLEMONT D.S. Wellins Capt Turner 'A' leaves	

Army Form C. 2118.

WAR DIARY
or
INTELLIGENCE SUMMARY.

(Erase heading not required.)

Instructions regarding War Diaries and Intelligence Summaries are contained in F. S. Regs., Part II. and the Staff Manual respectively. Title pages will be prepared in manuscript.

Place	Date	Hour	Summary of Events and Information	Remarks and references to Appendices
"CITADEL"	20th		Marched to CITADEL this afternoon. Lt Col Gill rejoined took over command from Capt Philipps. Return yesterday Capt Evans & Adam with Two P.D. drivers attended Musketry Rele	
	21st		Moved to MEAULTE town	
MEAULTE	22nd		Moved to billet at MEAULTE this afternoon	
"	23rd		Lt Col Gill received 30 or so new LP men. New drafts & available men given foot drill. All equipment checked over deficiencies made up.	
"	24th		Bn church parade attended. G.O.C. presented medals town of Rele. All were employed in packing wagons cleaning billet	
"	25th		have sent Cattle and all personnel bathed. moved at 5pm today CITADEL when Lt Col Gill rejoined. Capt Adam was sent to MAY'E 12" Kings in place of Capt Colvin who was evacuated sick.	
DUBLIN POST Nr MONTAUBAN	26th		Marched to Dublin Post where H.Q of JA were established 14th JA relieved Capt Evans & 1 lieut LP with 18 S.D. under Lt J Ingram were sent Hem Apts at Guillemont & heaven men and horses at Talus Wood Rele [illegible] were sent by 2½ length [illegible]	

1577 Wt.W10791/1773 500,000 1/15 D.D.&L. A.D.S.S./Forms/C. 2118.

Army Form C. 2118.

WAR DIARY
or
INTELLIGENCE SUMMARY.
(Erase heading not required.)

Place	Date	Hour	Summary of Events and Information	Remarks and references to Appendices
DUBLIN POST	26		Lt Robertson returned proceeded sick	
"	27		Bde is being relieved by New Troops tonight; arrangements made to evacuate all British wounded thro' me A.D.S. to Bernes.	
"	28		Capt Evans that returned about 9.0 am after having been relieved by New Zeal. Bde proceeded CARNOY area remained in reserve	
"	29		61st Bde relieved 62nd Bde 21st Div in front of Guedecourt. Dressing Stn established at LONGUEVAL ROAD near BERNAFAY WOOD, sick & wounded of Bde being collected driver by hand carriage about 3½ miles from Regtl aid Post near Guedecourt. H.Q of F.A. relieved at Dublin Post.	
"	29 30		Very quiet in Bde front, only about 15 casualties in last 24 hours. Evacuation to A.D.S. with affair owing to length of carry	

S. Phillips
CAPT. R.A.M.C.
for O/C 62nd FIELD AMBULANCE

Confidential

War Diary
of
F.A. 62 Field Ambulance
20th Division

1st October 1916 to 31st October 1916

WAR DIARY or INTELLIGENCE SUMMARY

Place	Date	Hour	Summary of Events and Information	Remarks and references to Appendices
MONTAUBAN	Oct 1		H.Q. & 1 Tent S.D at Dublin Post, 1 Tent S.D at Bernafay Wood forming A.D.S. All bearers there except 32 attached to battalions. Collected Bearer Div. collecting from Adv. Bearer Pos. S. of GUEUDECOURT to where cases brought from Reg.l Aid Post by bearers attached to battalions. From A.B.P. cases are taken to Bernafay Wood D.S. by hand carriage. Horse Ambulances 1 Tent S.D. attached 2 Ambulances. Few details obtained W.M.E.P. & XIV Corps M.D.S. Arrears of work entailed as above. & Casualties from shelling. Evacuation	
	Oct 2		difficult owing to rain.	
	Oct 4		61st Fld relieved by 59th Fd. tonight. 60th FA relieved the Bearers of this unit. The Bearer M.T.S.D. returned to DUBLIN POST	
	Oct 5		Bearer Div. spent day resting (eating & checking equipment	
	Oct 6		Relieved 60th FA at Bernafay Wood D.S. resumed on collecting from 61st Rec. & as before.	
	Oct 7		Bosche made an attack today, which it was successful, many wounded, chiefly cases being much more numerous than usual. Col. 16th 9.A. Inspected the Reg.l Aid Posts with new bearing Trainer. Off bearers, including Brit. land carriage our 24 hr.	

WAR DIARY or INTELLIGENCE SUMMARY

Army Form C. 2118.

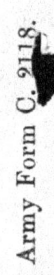

Place	Date	Hour	Summary of Events and Information	Remarks and references to Appendices
	Oct. 8		in removing wounded. Bearers of 60th F.A. employed as well. Many casualties still remaining who front area, owing to late date of the ground this was very difficult. (Lt. D.S. Beaven relieved 20th tonight)	
MEAULTE	Oct. 9th		Relief of 20th Div F.A. completed by 9.0 am today. All bearers were evacuated owing to the H.O. his entrance work in the area. H.Q. 2 Tent S.D's & Beaven Div. St. reached at 3.30 pm MEAULTE, many tobbed in the road transport did not arrive until 11 p.m.	
	Oct. 10		Remained at MEAULTE, day spent in cleaning up.	
	Oct. 12		Capt. Evans proceeded on 3 days leave to Paris. Equipment checked, cleaned.	
	Oct. 13th		Inspection of Bde. Group by XIV Corps Commander - Br. Gen Cavan, today.	
CORBIE	Oct. 15th		Marched to billets at CORBIE arriving at 4 p.m. Lieut. Gill Renwe took over duties of Adjt. during Col. Hayes absence on leave.	
	Oct. 16th		Capt. Evans rejoined the unit. Equipment transport cleaned, repaired.	
NEUVILLE	Oct. 18th		Marched via BUSSY to billets at ALLONVILLE.	
FREMONT	Oct. 19		Marched via CROISY VAUX FREMONT where F.A. was established. Lieut. Gill proceeded on leave to England.	

WAR DIARY
or
INTELLIGENCE SUMMARY.
(Erase heading not required.)

Army Form C. 2118.

Place	Date	Hour	Summary of Events and Information	Remarks and references to Appendices
FRANCE	Oct 24		Advd. arrived between F.A. Tabella billets in ST SAUVEUR. Billets arranged, holding party sent over.	
ST SAUVEUR	Oct 25rd		Moved at 9.0 am to ST SAUVEUR rui VAUX where very good billets were obtained for P.A. Cpl Hohman & three not arrived, hiding out.	
	Oct 25th		Horsing, details, checking equipment re provisional Divisional P/S commenced.	
	Oct 26th		All ranks undertook outlie except those at 2/12 training C.O.S. returning to the unit today.	
	Oct 26th		Until relieved for M.A. Ons. set. O.C.'s + took me covered of the unit.	
	Oct 27th		Training & P.O.L. outline during. Weather little cold to due.	
	Oct 30th		4 Lieut Gill proceeded on leave to Grenoble; other leave cancelled.	
	Oct 31st		Transport packed & everything made ready for move tomorrow to No. 3 Reserve Area.	

Ralph Capman
Lieut 6 m/T

Original.
Nov. 1916

S/

Secret.

14 of 862
Vol 15

War Diary.

of the

Officer Commanding 62 Field Ambulance, attached

20th (Light) Division

1st November 1916 to 30th November 1916

COMMITTEE FOR THE
MEDICAL HISTORY OF THE WAR
Date -3 JAN. 1917

WAR DIARY
or
INTELLIGENCE SUMMARY.

(Erase heading not required.)

Army Form C. 2118

Place	Date	Hour	Summary of Events and Information	Remarks and references to Appendices
St SAUVEUR	Nov. 1st 1916		Left St Sauveur about 10.0 a.m. Travelled via REQUIGNY & CAVILLON to billets	
MOLLIENS VIDAME	2nd		at MOLLIENS VIDAME. Field Ambulance found here. Col. Gill on leave. Billets thoroughly cleaned. Collection of sick from 61st Inf. Bde. Group arranged.	
"	3rd		Cases being evacuated to various M.R.S. near HANGEST.	
"	4th		Capt. Aden returned. Numerous unbooked entered in Hospital sheets.	
"	5th		Major Kendrick returned from leave.	
"	6th		Capt. Roberts proceeded on leave to England. Instructional drill for personnel of F.A. continued.	
"	9th		Colonel Gill returned from leave today. Drills in morning & later were employed training for Bde. Sports.	
"	10th		Fire drill carried out. All ranks drilled with smoke helmets &c. Indoor	
"	12th		61st Bde. had a steeplechase meeting. 3 rink of this unit ran.	
"	13th		Volunteer reported for duty. M.Green employed at 2/2 North C.C.S. was transferred to 61st Inf. Bde. Group.	
"	14th		G.O.C. 1st Army inspected the Ambulance intitbts Bde. Group travelled at 10.30 a.m. from MOLLIENS VIDAME to L'ARBRE a MOUFLERS	

Army Form C. 2118

WAR DIARY
or
INTELLIGENCE SUMMARY.
(Erase heading not required.)

Instructions regarding War Diaries and Intelligence Summaries are contained in F. S. Regs., Part II. and the Staff Manual respectively. Title pages will be prepared in manuscript.

Place	Date	Hour	Summary of Events and Information	Remarks and references to Appendices
L'ARBRE à MOUCHES 2/ARBINES	Nov. 1916 14th		near MARINET. Fair billets for all, but rather cramped. M.O. billeted at all units of Role group collected.	
	15th		Lt PRINGLE evened for duty. Company & Squad drill carried out. Four O.R. detailed for duty at XIV Corps Main Dressing Station.	
	18			
ALLERY			Coys L'ARBRE & MOUCHES at 1pm and marched via METIGNY to ALLERY. When field Ambulance was formed; Sick of all units of R.O. group Collected.	
			Hr Billets were dry & good.	
	19		Lt PRINGLE took over duties of MO to 91st Bde R.F.A. vice Capt WILLIAMS proceeding on leave. Capt TROWER attached to 2nd E. Kents. is struck off the strength of the unit.	
	20		Company and Squad Drill carried out. Lt COLMER taken over duties of MO to 7th K.S.Y.L.I. & is struck off the strength of the unit: Capt JEPSON returned to the unit & is taken on the strength.	
	21		Company & Squad Drill Continued	
	22		Capt EVANS. returned from leave.	
	23.		Capt PHILLIPS. proceeds on leave. Squad & Company Drill Continued.	

WAR DIARY
or
INTELLIGENCE SUMMARY.
(Erase heading not required.)

Army Form C. 2118

Instructions regarding War Diaries and Intelligence Summaries are contained in F. S. Regs., Part II. and the Staff Manual respectively. Title pages will be prepared in manuscript.

Place	Date	Hour	Summary of Events and Information	Remarks and references to Appendices
ALLERY	Nov 24 1916		Lt FARQUHARSON returned to Unit after relieving Lt WALKER who is on Tram Route march in the morning; All ranks paraded with Shrapnel helmets.	
YZEUX	Nov 25		Unit marched from ALLERY at 9 am & marched via SOUES, HANGEST and BOURDON to YZEUX. Field Ambulance found here and Collection of Sick from Bn Kept arranged. The billets were cramped & very dirty.	
	26		Fatigue parties cleaning billets all day. Lt COLMER returned to Unit being relieved by Lt FARQUHARSON of Heavy misalichap 17"KWYLI.	
	27		Cleaning of Billets area continued; Capt ROBERTS took over medical charge of 92 A.S.C.R.F.A. vice Capt MILLIGAN proceeded on leave. Field Ambulance Transport left ALLERY at 11.30, Capt ADAM in charge; for SAILLY-LE-SEC. They were told to go for the night of the 27th at MOLLIENS-au-BOIS.	
SAILLY-LE-SEC	28		Parade at 9.15; marched off at 9.30 for HANGEST entraining there for MERICOURT SAILLY-LE-SEC where we arrived at 4.35 PM; marched to SAILLY-LE-SEC arriving there at 5.30 PM. Field Ambulance found from 61st Bde Group arranged. Billets were very dirty; the French troops has been billeting here, in much of the space available for the men. The Transport arrived at 3 PM.	

WAR DIARY
or
~~INTELLIGENCE~~ SUMMARY.

(Erase heading not required.)

Army Form C. 2

Place	Date	Hour	Summary of Events and Information	Remarks and references to Appendices
SAILLY-LE-SEC	Nov 29 1916	30	Fatigue parties cleaning billets and areas occupied by troops all day. Cleaning process continued: Route march in the morning.	

J.R. Gill
Lt. Col. R.A.M.C.
O.C. 62nd FIELD AMBULANCE

"Original"
Dec 1916

140/903
Vol 16

20 Dec
Confidential.

War Diary.
of the
Officer Commanding 62nd Field Ambulance, R.A.M.C.
20th (Light) Division.

1st December 1916 to 31st December 1916.

COMMITTEE FOR THE
MEDICAL HISTORY OF THE WAR
Date 31 JAN. 1917

WAR DIARY
or:
INTELLIGENCE SUMMARY

(Erase heading not required.)

Army Form C. 2118

Place	Date	Hour	Summary of Events and Information	Remarks and references to Appendices
SAILLY-le-SEC	Dec. 1.		Inspection Parade 9 am, follows by Route march: At 2 P.m. Practice Fire Alarm	
BUSSY-les-DAOURS	2		Left SAILLY-le-SEC at 11 am and marched to BUSSY-les-DAOURS via VAUX-sur-SOMME, CORBIE & AUBIGNY, a clear cold day. Its men marched well arriving at BUSSY at 2 P.m. Collection party from two Battalions of 61st Bde in CORBIE, & the other two Battalions were in MEAULT and 60 Field Ambulance arranged for the disposal of their sick. Billets in BUSSY were Cramped, the village was very muddy.	
	3.		Inspection Parade 9 am. Followed by Squad & Company drill. Marching Order Parade at 2 P.m: Capt. Phillips returned from leave at night. A Re-	
	4		V Cullnes stunt of strength for returns having taken over temporarily, medical charge of 9th Reserve Park.	
	5		Inspection Parade, Squad & Company Drill in the morning. Inspection Parade + Stretcher Drill in the afternoon. Cleaning up	

Army Form C. 2118

WAR DIARY
or
INTELLIGENCE SUMMARY
(Erase heading not required.)

Instructions regarding War Diaries and Intelligence Summaries are contained in F.S. Regs., Part II. and the Staff Manual respectively. Title Pages will be prepared in manuscript.

Place	Date	Hour	Summary of Events and Information	Remarks and references to Appendices
BUSSY les-DAOURS	Dec 6.		Inspection Parade cancelled because of rain: Collection of Kit from Tun Rd taken in hand. CORBIE continued.	
	7.		Inspection Parade & Route march in the morning; weather very cold	
	8.		Inspection Parade August Company Drill in the morning; Remain began in the afternoon.	
VILLE-sous-CORBIE	9.		The Field Ambulance marched to VILLE-sous-CORBIE. via AUBIGNY, CORBIE, MERICOURT, L'ABBE & TREUX. very cold and raining heavily during the whole march. Billets very cramped in VILLE. Capt. E. PHILLIPS, Capt. ADAM and Bearer Division left, and became Capt. E. PHILLIPS in Command of Col HARVEY. O.C. XV Divisional Reserve. Tent Division	
CARNOY	10.		Lt Col GILL in Command marched to CORPS CARNOY. via MEAULT & MAMETZ to the XIV Corps Dressing Station there. Lt Col GILL Took over Command of M.D.S. at noon.	
	11.		Aeroplane bombs dropped near MDS during the night; very heavy revere is falling necessitating depth dug outs & shrapnel proofs at close the mens dug out.	

1875 Wt. W593/826 1,000,000 4/15 J.B.C. & A. A.D.S.S./Forms/C. 2118.

Army Form C. 2118

WAR DIARY
or
INTELLIGENCE SUMMARY
(Erase heading not required.)

Place	Date	Hour	Summary of Events and Information	Remarks and references to Appendices
CARNOY	11.		In the afternoon the G.S.Waggons were unpacked, & the equipment checked.	
	12		Cleaning the equipment all day. Lt. V. COLMER left for England at night.	
	13		All the equipment this contact. Began station side from the Camp at BRONFAY FARM + from Camp on CARNOY- MONTAUBAN Road. There were very few wounded, the sick an mostly cases of Trench Feet.	
	14		Began conducting standing for home of Fricourt this morning the standing taken Was very bad, mud very very deep; we an running the upper hay of mud and leaving a thick film. Rain's falling heavily Capt. ROBERTS returned to unit; he had been Detention No. 62 B12 R.F.A. who was away on leave. Construction of horse standings continuous and railway lining of M.D. pathways at M.D.S started upon.	
	16		Officer and 2nd. Division of 52 Field Ambulance reported at M.D.S. for duty.	
	17		Horse standings completed; some shells fell near M.D.S. during the night.	

WAR DIARY
or
INTELLIGENCE SUMMARY

Army Form C. 2118

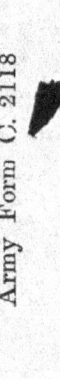

Place	Date	Hour	Summary of Events and Information	Remarks and references to Appendices
CARNOY	Dec 19		Very heavy rain all day; men working on drainage of the Camp; the collection of sick from New area is being continued; its working smoothly; the Construction of dugouts has to work for, work is heavy.	
	20		Head tent out in; Equipment of field Ambulance cleaned.	
	21		Heavy rain; it unyone hindered collection of sick continued.	
	23		A very heavy gale, two marquees were blown down and hay fatigue parties were necessary to make the others secure; no one hurt. Equipment checked collection of sick continued. Capt JEPSON left to take over medical charge of 7.Sm.L.I.s. Capt. CAIRNS on going on leave.	
	24		Heavy wind again; no tents blown down.	
	25		Rain is steady, fatigue parties employed cleaning the Drain Camp. M.D.S.	
	26		Two Horse Ambulance Wagons sent by A.D.M.S. 17th Division to assist	
	28		in collection of sick from Craw area.	
	29		A good deal of shelling during the night; 10 one free Wagons M.D.S.	

WAR DIARY
INTELLIGENCE SUMMARY

Army Form C. 2118.

Place	Date	Hour	Summary of Events and Information	Remarks and references to Appendices
CARNOY	Dec 29		began to build new incinerator in the afternoon.	
	30		Collection of sick continues. Infirmary Evening Rounds	
			made very difficult unfront.	
	31.		Fatigue parties clearing & scraping floors & trenches.	

H. Evans
CAPT. R.A.M.C.
O/C 62nd FIELD AMBULANCE

"Original"

Confidential.

War Diary

of the

Officer Commanding 62nd Field Ambulance, R.A.M.C.

20th (Light) Division

1st January 1917 to 31st January 1917.

COMMITTEE FOR THE
MEDICAL HISTORY OF THE WAR
Date 13 MAR. 1917

Army Form C. 2118.

WAR DIARY
or
INTELLIGENCE SUMMARY.
(Erase heading not required.)

Instructions regarding War Diaries and Intelligence Summaries are contained in F.S. Regs., Part II. and the Staff Manual respectively. Title pages will be prepared in manuscript.

Place	Date	Hour	Summary of Events and Information	Remarks and references to Appendices
CARNOY.	1917. January 1st		Lt Col G.H.L. RAMC. left the unit in the morning to be Acting ADMS 20th Division. Capt. S. PHILLIPS RAMC took over command of the 62 Field Ambulance, the H.Q. of which are at the XIV Corps Main Dressing Station.	
	3.		Lt J.V. DUFFY. RAMC. reported his arrival and was taken on the strength of the unit. Four Large fatigue parties were at work making arrangements for treatment of Trench Fest. Cases at the Main Dressing Station.	
	5		Capt W.B. JEPSON RAMC was ordered to report to DDMS HAVRE and was struck off the strength of the unit. Fatigue party cleaning & checking equipment of the Field Ambulance.	
	6		Continued cleaning Equipment.	
	11		N.Y.Sen L.I. Hon Medical Officer being on leave, Major S. PHILLIPS and Bearer Division of Field Ambulance returned to the H Quarters of the Unit. Large fatigue parties were put on cleaning & improving the drainage of the Main Dressing Station.	
	13.		Capt. S. PHILLIPS RAMC was ordered to take up the duties of DADMS 8th Division & relinquish his duties. Capt. H EVANS RAMC assumed Command	

Army Form C. 2118.

WAR DIARY
or
INTELLIGENCE SUMMARY.
(Erase heading not required.)

Instructions regarding War Diaries and Intelligence Summaries are contained in F. S. Regs., Part II. and the Staff Manual respectively. Title pages will be prepared in manuscript.

Place	Date	Hour	Summary of Events and Information	Remarks and references to Appendices
CARNOY	January 16.		of the unit. Lt. B.G. CONNOLLY & Lt. J. COPLANS reported has arrived and were taken on the strength of the unit.	
	17.		Heavy snow fell and all were in action ; large fatigue parties necessary to clear the snow.	
	19.		Still freezing : the number of sick on much . Divine worship and there is a great increase in the number of cases of Trench Feet since the frost started.	
	20.		The Welsh Division takes place and from the Corps in the area around here are very few wounded in this part of the line at present.	
	22.		Capt. T.V. DUFFY R.A.M.C returned to the unit	
	23.		Fatigue party took in a Pack Store at the Main Dressing Station, the use of being troubles there. Morning owing to the number of patients.	
	24.		There was a fire at the Main Dressing Station. burning of marquees.	
	25.		Lt. J.COPLANS took over medical charge of the 7th K.O.Y.L.I. the medical officer going on leave. The 62 Field Ambulance left the XIV Corps Main Dressing Station at Suzanne	

1577 Wt.W10791/1773 500,000 1/15 D. D. & L. A.D.S.S./Forms/C. 2118.

Army Form C. 2118.

WAR DIARY
or
INTELLIGENCE SUMMARY.
(Erase heading not required.)

Instructions regarding War Diaries and Intelligence Summaries are contained in F. S. Regs., Part II. and the Staff Manual respectively. Title pages will be prepared in manuscript.

Place	Date	Hour	Summary of Events and Information	Remarks and references to Appendices
CARNOY	Jan 25.		They marched via MAMETZ & FRICOURT to MEAULTE when they were billeted. It was cold & wintry. The billets at MEAULTE were a little cramped.	
MEAULTE	26		Marched from MEAULTE at 8.45 am. for CORBIE via MERICOURT & HEILLY. Weather very trying to the men marching. Arriving at CORBIE. Hospital opens in the Chateau at CORBIE where the field Ambulance was also billeted. Sick were evacuated from his Battalion Aid Post Buyer at COISY & CARDONNETTE.	
CORBIE	27.		Battn. marched from CORBIE at 8.45 am to CARDONNETTE via PONT NOYELLE, QUERRIEU & ALLONVILLE. Weather crisp & cold. Arrives at CARDONNETTE at noon. Hospital opens there and collection of sick from B.M. Buyer's front arranged. The billets were very good.	
CARDONNETTE	28.		Cleaning billets and area carried on all day.	
	29.		Inspection of men. Squad & Company drill 9.30 – noon. Wagons cleaned in afternoon.	
	30.		Inspection Parade at 9 am. Route march 9.30 – 11.30. Checking arms	

Army Form C. 2118.

WAR DIARY
or
INTELLIGENCE SUMMARY.

(Erase heading not required.)

Place	Date	Hour	Summary of Events and Information	Remarks and references to Appendices
CARDONNETTE.	Jan. 31.		Cleaning equipment in the afternoon. Collected from 61st Brigade front Casualties. Agnes & company order. Checking & cleaning Equipment Continued. noon. 9.30 —	

Evans Capt R.A.M.C.
O.C. 62nd FIELD AMBULANCE.

OFFICER COMMDG
8 JAN 1917
62ND FIELD AMBULANCE

Confidential.

War Diary

of the

Officer Commanding No. 3 Ambulance, Rear

20th (Light) Division

1st February 1917 to 28th February 1917

COMMITTEE FOR THE
MEDICAL HISTORY OF THE WAR
Date 4 — APR. 1917

Army Form C. 2118.

WAR DIARY
or
INTELLIGENCE SUMMARY.

I. 62 Field Ambulance

(Erase heading not required.)

Place	Date	Hour	Summary of Events and Information	Remarks and references to Appendices
CARDONNETTE	Feb 1-1917		Lt-Col J.G.GILL returned to the unit and assumed command. Inspected horse at 9 am. follows by a Route march; checking & cleaning A. Section Equipment in the afternoon; hard frost prevailing.	
	2.		Squad and Company Drill in the morning. B Section Equipment checked and cleaned. The collection of sick from the Brigade front is being carried out.	
	3.		A Route march in the morning. C Section Equipment checked & cleaned as also the wagons. Lt-Col GILL left the Unit to take up the Duties of ADMS 38th Division. Capt H. EVANS took over command temporarily. Route march in the morning; inspection of Iron Rations & smoke helmets in the afternoon. Received orders to return to CARNOY MAIN DRESSING STATION on the 7th & 8th. The Battalion of the B.De. are returning by train on the 7th & 8th.	
	6th		Lt-Qm KENSHOLE returned from leave having been wanted two weeks extension on medical grounds. Squad & Company Drill in the morning; Packing wagons in the afternoon.	

Army Form C. 2118.

2. 62 Field Ambulance.

WAR DIARY
or
INTELLIGENCE SUMMARY.

(Erase heading not required.)

Place	Date	Hour	Summary of Events and Information	Remarks and references to Appendices
CARDONNETTE	Feb. 7		Marched from CARDONNETTE to MEAULTE at 8.45 am via ALLONVILLE, QUERRIEU, CORBIE, MERICOURT L'ABBÉ, & TREUX. Mules fresh and the distance was 19 miles. Arrangements were made for this to be taken at a halt near CORBIE. We arrived at MEAULTE	
MEAULTE.	7.	3.30 pm	Unpacked & the men were curried in a motor lorry.	
CARNOY.	8.		Left for CARNOY at 9 am and arrived at MAIN DRESSING STATION here at 11 am. at 2 p.m. Capt- ADAM. & 60 Bearers left for Bearer Camp at GUILLEMONT to come under Command of A.D. HARVEY O.C. 20th Divisional Reserves. Capt. T.V. DUFFY took over medical charge of the 11th D.L.I. The 4th Division Major Butler at the M.D.Sstn. a turkle inch shell fell near the Horse lines yesterday; 1 casualty; cleaning & oiling wagons all day.	
	9.		Began to thaw.	
	11.			
	12.		Major E.F. L'ESTRANGE arrived and took over Command of the Unit. Capt. T.E. ROBERTS returned from leave.	

Army Form C. 2118.

3. 62 Field Ambulance.

WAR DIARY
or
INTELLIGENCE SUMMARY.
(Erase heading not required.)

Place	Date	Hour	Summary of Events and Information	Remarks and references to Appendices
CARNOY	13th February		Assumed Command of 62 Field Ambulance yesterday 12.2.17. Inspected Transport Lines, horses and Mules. Also mess shed - Inspected Ambulance wagons and G.S. waggons, all clean and in good order. Freezing hard. Checks Inspected. "Armed Balance" - A, B, & C checks. Harness and Saddles being cleaned.	S.L.2
	14th February		No 63364 Pte GROSVENOR J.E. R.A.M.C. proceeds to C.C.S. Captain J.V. DUFFY R.A.M.C. proceeds to medical charge of 11th Battalion. D.L.I. (Pioneers, slight flu) Have lecture in Inspection of N.C.Os and men. 1st Division. Collecting sick from Brigade in rest and Camps in vicinity.	S.R.8
	15th Febry		Had post during the night. Cleaning Arrangements and G.S. waggon carried out. Lieut. G. CONNOLLY R.A.M.C. to report to O.C. Bearer Division for temporary duty. No 34851 Pte OSBORNE. E. R.A.M.C. attached to 61 Field Ambulance. Collecting Sick from CARNOY Camps continuing.	S.L.9
	16th Febry		Captain T. E. ROBERTS R.A.M.C. posted as temporary medical officer to 7th D.G.L.S. Inspected harness and transport lines - slight frost.	S.L.9

Army Form C. 2118.

WAR DIARY
or
INTELLIGENCE SUMMARY.
(Erase heading not required.)

4. 62 Field Ambulance.

Place	Date	Hour	Summary of Events and Information	Remarks and references to Appendices
CARNOY	17.2.17		Heavy frost last night. usual fatigues cleaning camp - Inspection of Motor Ambulances and personnel A.S.C. M.T. No 101672 Pte GARBUTT. A. R.A.M.C. No 74053 Pte PARSONS. W.J. No 101672 Pte GARBUTT.A.R.A.M.C. No 52809 Pte PASQUILL.R. rejoined from leave.	R.P.
	18.2.17.		Captain O.J. GREENIDGE. R.A.M.C. and Lieut A. LEITCH R.A.M.C. reported for duty with 62 Field Ambulance from A.D.M.S. 20th DIVISION. Lieut W. FARQUHARSON R.A.M.C. M.O.i/c. No 24/F. 352 (A.M.D.1) pronounced by a Medical Board unfit for general service is struck off the strength. Captain T.E. ROBERTS R.A.M.C. posted as R.M.O. 7.D.C.L.I.	P.L.P
	19.2.17		Captain O.J. GREENIDGE R.A.M.C. admitted to Hospital and transferred to 3/2 London Casualty Clearing Station is struck off the strength. No 32950 Pte Mc WHANNEL R.A.M.C. and No 39699 Pte SIDE R.A.M.C. attached to 33 Sanitary Section for duty. No M/04637. Pte TASKER.A. A.S.C. M.T. attached to J. Corps Supply Column. No 3749 Pte G.E. MCILROY R.A.M.C. transferred to 62 Field Ambulance from 57 Field Ambulance authority D.D.M.S. XIV Corps. No T.F. 2362 Pte STRETTON. E. R.A.M.C. transferred to XIV Corps Rest Station.	S.W.P

Army Form C. 2118.

WAR DIARY
or
INTELLIGENCE SUMMARY.
(Erase heading not required.)

5   62 Field Ambulance

Place	Date	Hour	Summary of Events and Information	Remarks and references to Appendices
CARNOY	20-2-17		Lieut. G CONNOLLY. RAMC posted as R.M.O. 7th D.C.L.I. Captain G.M. ADAM. RAMC reporting 62 Field Ambulance from the Beaver Camp. Checked Equipment of A. Section 62 Field Ambulance R.E.	R.E.
	21.2.17		Lieut. J COPLANS RAMC. Evacuated sick to Corps Rest Station - he is struck off the Strength. Lieut. A. LEITCH. RAMC posted as R.M.O. to 7th K.O.Y.L.I. Thaw precautions orders. Inspected H.P. helmets.	R.P.
	22-2-17		Inspected Transport lines. Present if ASC personnel - ADMS. 20th Division inspects C.M.D.S.	S.R.9.
	23-2-17		No 34714 Pte A.W BAXTER. and No 33857 Pte G. OLIVER transferred to Transportation Depôt. BOULOGNE. authority D.A.G. Base. AB/20 X ADMS 20th Division L103 A/2 22-2-17. No 2362 Pte. E. STRETTON RAMC reported unit from 1/2 LONDON C.C.S. No 12569 Sgt. J. POWELL.A.S.C. transferred to 161 Company A.S.C. No T/2 015992 Sgt. P.J AMES. ASC.161.Co. is taken on the strength.	S.R.9.
	24.2.17		Inspection of Horse transport, Ambulance waggons and G.S. waggons Reports condition of roads at Corps Main Dressing Station to D.D.M.S. XIV Corps. recommend for road metalling.	R.P.
	26-2-17		Captain G.M. ADAM. RAMC. posted for Temporary duty to 20th Divisional Workshops in addition to his duties with 62 Field Ambulance R MC. posted as M.O. to 20 Divisional Workshops in addition to his duties with 62 Field Ambulance. From L.J. Captain T.E. ROBERTS	S.R.9

1577 Wt. W10791/1773 500,000 1/15 D. D. & L. A.D.S.S./Forms/C. 2118.

WAR DIARY
INTELLIGENCE SUMMARY

Army Form C. 2118.

62 Field Ambulance

Place	Date	Hour	Summary of Events and Information	Remarks and references to Appendices
CARNOY	27.2.17		No 34186 Pte W. McKEOWN R.A.M.C. transferred to Transportation Depot BOULOGNE and is struck off the strength - authority A.D.M.S. 20th Division. L.108 dated 24.2.17. No 35016 Pte T. FARRELL. No 76571. Pte A. CHISLETT and No 38629 Pte T. DIXON. R.A.M.C. attached to 2/2 London Casualty Clearing Station for temporary duty. No 42071 Pte T. EVANS R.A.M.C. and No T4/040031 Driver T. MARTIN were evacuated to C.C.S. and are struck off the strength. Captain G.M. ADAM. R.A.M.C. and No 63233 Pte W. WHITE R.A.M.C. attached as R.M.O. and orderly respectively to 7th Som. L.I. Inspection of R.H. Helmets of personnel R.A.M.C. and A.S.C.	R22
	28.2.17		No 53291 Pte J. CLARKE and No 33260 Pte H. TILLBURY R.A.M.C. attached to 61 Field Ambulance for temporary duty. 1 N.C.O. and 5 O.Rs posted 16 Bearer Camp TRONES WOOD for temporary duty. 8 O.Rs. Ranks posted to A.D.S TRONES WOOD.	R29

S.R. Evans Lieut-Col. R.A.M.C.

"Originals"
May 1917

"Confidential"

WO 19
140/2042

War Diary

of the

Officer Commanding 62nd Field Ambulance, RAMC.
20th (Light) Division

1st March 1917 to 31st March 1917

COMMITTEE FOR THE
MEDICAL HISTORY OF THE WAR
Date 11 MAY. 1917

WAR DIARY
INTELLIGENCE SUMMARY

Army Form C. 2118.

7. 62 Field Ambulance –

Place	Date	Hour	Summary of Events and Information	Remarks and references to Appendices
CARNOY	1st March 1917		Visited Bearer Camp at TRONES WOOD. Also Advanced Dressing Station at GUINCHY. Dug outs for stretcher cases complete. No 3 & 8 L/Cpl. S.E. OPENSHAW. Raine, transferred to transportation Depot, BOULOGNE. 8 orderlies Trench Division 62 Field Ambulance posted for temporary duty as Wagon orderlies to 60 Field Ambulance. Dressing Station TRONES WOOD – Splenic use of Fox Reynolds to personnel Raine and R.S.C.	SAE
	2.3.17		Collection of sick from CARNOY Camps continues – Suspected hel¾ air balance to field Ambulance. Received notification from D.D.M.S. XIV Corps that Captain J. COPLANS. Raine. have been evacuated to the Base – (sick) –	Opl.
	3.3.17		A.D.M.S. 20th DIVISION visited No 3 & 8 Dep. S.E. OPENSHAW Raine transferred to transportation Depot – BOULOGNE and is struck off the strength – sleeper equipment A. Section. Slight rain. Prophylactic treatment for trench feet to be carried out for 13 Battery pns at GUILLEMONT.	Opl.
	4.3.17		CAPTAIN. R.M. FARRER. Raine. reported for duty with 62 Field Ambulance. for Respirators arrived. Notifies XIV Corps Gas Officer.	SAE
	5.3.17		Has box Respirators fitted and tested by N.C.O. sent by Gas Expert. Officers and O.R. tested at CARNOY sparayed – tear gas used as a test. Slight frost. N.E. wind. cold –	SAE

WAR DIARY
or
INTELLIGENCE SUMMARY

(Erase heading not required.)

Army Form C. 2118

8. 62 Field Ambulance —

Place	Date	Hour	Summary of Events and Information	Remarks and references to Appendices
CATNOY	6-3-17		CAPTAIN CHANDLER. F.C. R.a.m.c. reported for duty with Field Ambulance authority- A.D.M.S. 20th DIVISION- Freezing, but up in all the extra accommodation- Inspected pack Saddlery-	P.R.8.
	7-3-17		9 OTHER Ranks reported for duty from R.a.m.c. details ROUEN. Reinforcement- Freezing hard. First N.E. wind very cold- A.D.M.S. visits- Inspected transport E.R.E. Gives orders regarding shoes of motor Ambulances. Reduces to 10 miles an hour. authority A.D.M.S. 20th DIVISION-	
	8-3-17		No. 34187 Pte MUIRHEAD R. No. 49288 Pte JONES S. No 55987 Pte GREENHALGH. No. 63399 Pte STOW P. R.A.M.C. appointed acting 2Cpls without pay from 5-3-17. Inspected P.H. Helmets- Carried out experiments with improvised pack saddles for carrying equipment, stores, water and dressings in accordance with A.D.M.S instructions-	E.R.E.
	9-3-17		No T3/024049 Driver H. FISHER. H/T. transferred to A.S.C. Base Depot. HAVRE- authority A.D.M.S. 20th DIVISION. L.125- did- 9-3-17- Inspected G.S. waggons and G.S. Limbered waggons-	E.K.8.
	10-3-17		Bra Resphatal drill- A.D.M.S. 20th DIVISION visits Corps main Dressing Station XIV Corps- Paid R.A.M.C. and A.S.C. personnel 62 field Ambulance- Invalids A.D.S. GINCHY- Brig out for wounded completed. No T3/027155 Driver R. HALL.A.S.C. H.T. awarded 10 days F.P.No.2. misconduct to the prejudice of good order and military discipline- "Using improper language to a Superior in language of (No T4/104180 Driver W. ROOKE. A.S.C. H.T. absent from Ambulance. fined 5 days pay-	P.R.8.
	11-3-17		Inspected motor Ambulances. 62 field Ambulances. New station benches for patients put in at XIV Corps. M.D.S. R.H. Kelmel- drill- Prophylactic measures for trench feet continued at C.M.D.S-	P.R.8.
	12-3-17		Captain T.L.P. BENNETT. R.a.m.c. and Lieut. J.D. WALKER. R.a.m.c. reports to 62 field Ambulance for duty. No T3/024249 Dr H. FISHER. A.S.C. H.T. is struck off the strength-	P.R.8.

WAR DIARY or INTELLIGENCE SUMMARY

Army Form C. 2118

9. 62 Field Ambulance

Place	Date	Hour	Summary of Events and Information	Remarks and references to Appendices
CARNOY	13.3.17		No T/1.3712 Master GRIFFITHS, J. A.S.C. M.T. reports for duty. Four driv cars out. Continued building bath house for patients and personnel R.A.M.C. Separate compartments and framework with carnpeted iron sides and roof.	S.K.2
	16.3.17		No 4.0639 Pte MORRIS W. appointed acting L/Cpl with pay from 2.3.17 inclusive authority D.G.M.S. No B.1540 dated 11.3.17. Lieut. WALKER J.D. R.A.M.C. and No 345540 Pte MITTON H. R.A.M.C. attached to 61 Field Ambulance and are struck off the strength of this unit for rations M 34693 Pte JOYCE J. R.A.M.C. proceeds to transportation depot Rouen for casualties from No 14 Camp Carnoy carried by bearers – 10 deaths.	Ak.l.
	18.3.17		No 34186 acting Cpl McKEOWN W. R.A.M.C. confirmed in the rank of Corporal from 1.2.17 authority R.A.M.C. Corps orders No S. 1.2.17. Captain TUTT. M.R. R.A.M.C. reports his arrival for duty. Captain FARRER R.H. R.A.M.C. assumed duties of M.O./c 7th K.O.Y.L.I on 16.3.17. Captain CHANDLER T.C. R.A.M.C. assumed duties of M.O./c 7th S.L.I on 16.3.17. Captain TUTT. W.R. R.A.M.C. took over the duties of M.O./c 9.2nd Brigade R.F.A. on 16.3.17. Captain ADAM. G.M. R.A.M.C. returns to 62 Field Ambulance and is taken on the strength from 16.3.17. Completed bath house for personnel and patients. LIEUT. LEITCH. returned to K.O.Y.L.I and is taken on the strength for rations from 16.3.17.	SK.2
	20.3.17		The Ranks of 62 Field Ambulance returned from 61 Field Ambulance. No 67412 Pte HAMPSON. H.W. R.A.M.C. transferred to 4th Army Aircraft Park for duty and is struck off the strength – No 39433 Pte HAMILTON R.C. R.A.M.C. Returns for duty and is taken on the strength. Inspected Box Respirators (personnel) P.H. Shelter drill.	SK2
	21.3.17		Captain ADAM R.A.M.C. and No 63238 Pte WHITE. W. R.A.M.C. attached to 61 Field Ambulance for duty with Bearer Division. LIEUT. LEITCH. A. R.A.M.C. 10th took over duties of M. O.O/c School of Instruction No 73640 Pte WILLIAMS B. R.A.M.C. proceeds to duty at School of Instruction in N.Welly M.O.	SK2
	23.3.17		CAPTAIN FARRER. R.A. R.A.M.C. proceeds on M.O.O/c 7th K.O.Y.L.I. CAPTAIN CHANDLER. F.C. R.A.M.C. proceeds on M.O.O/c 7th S.L.I. LIEUT. WALKER. J.D. R.A.M.C. returns from 61 Field Ambulance on Brawl Division.	AL.2

Army Form C. 2118

WAR DIARY
or
INTELLIGENCE SUMMARY

(Erase heading not required.)

Army Form C. 2118 — 10. 62 Field Ambulance

Place	Date	Hour	Summary of Events and Information	Remarks and references to Appendices
CARNOY.	25.3.17		No. 21087 Pte. LACEY. H. R.A.M.C. reported from Detention Camp. 20 Division - No. 5108 Pte. FLEMING.J R.A.M.C. granted good conduct badge under article 1080 Ryl. Returned Pack Stores Panniers to Reserve Park. Box Respirators issued to personnel Raml and A.S.C. ranks to accommodate 150 patients Kits.	D.R.[?] MT
	27.3.17		9 Other Ranks reported for duty from A.D.M.S. 20th Division. Received instructions from D.D.M.S. XIV Corps to hand over surplus medical and surgical Equipment to 134 C.C.S. Supplies to C.R.S. GROVETOWN. A.D.M.S. 2nd Division. instructions regarding ammunition to C.M.D.S. CARNOY. Carried out 62nd Field Ambulance to be in XV Corps.	M.T.
	29.3.17		No. 3 9910 Sgt FISHER. F. and No. 74896 Pte HANDY. G. R.A.M.C. transferred to Transportation Depot. BOULOGNE on 25.3.17. authority A.D.M.S. 20th Division. Reports to BRIGADIER GENERAL BOULOGNE. 61 Infantry Brigade for instructions regarding medical arrangements at BUS - 1 G.S. Limber Waggon - 1 water Cart. 1 G.S. Waggon. sent to C. 61 Field Amb and with personnel authority A.D.M.S. 20th Division. to O.C. 61 field Ambulance. CAPTAIN BENNET R.A.M.C. and 30 Other Ranks. report for duty with Reserve Division.	D.R.[?]
	30.3.17		3 Horse Ambulance Waggons sent to O.C. 61 Field Ambulance to C. 61 field ambulance returning (to O.C. 61 Field Ambulance with personnel 2 Horse Ambulance attacks to CMDS returning to O.C. 61 Field Ambulance ce— No M/S. 2727 acting Sergeant MASON. G.F. A.S.C. MT. promoted to the Rank of Sergeant authority M.G. Section P.3/1177). No 34599 a/Cpl. RISELEY.T.G. R.A.M.C. promoted to Pte Rank of Acting Sergeant with pay from 18.3.17 inclusive - authority D.G.M.S. No B.1450/626 dates 24.3.17. LIEUT. WALKER. R.G. Ramc. posts as M.O.Y.C. 7 D.C.L.I.	D.R.[?]
	31.3.17		Lieut. CONNOLLY. R.G. Ramc. Lieut. CONNELLY. R.G. Ramc. joins 62 field Ambulance in relief of checked Equipment and Stores Ammunition, Inspected Harness and Saddlery.	D.R.

E.F. La Fauve, Lieut. Col. R.A.M.C.

140/7086

COMMITTEE FOR THE
MEDICAL HISTORY OF THE WAR
Date −6 JUN. 1917

20th Div.

62nd F.A.

Army Form C. 2118

WAR DIARY
or
INTELLIGENCE SUMMARY
(*Erase heading not required.*)

CONFIDENTIAL

WAR DIARY

OF

62nd FIELD AMBULANCE

FROM 1st April 1917 TO 30th April 1917

WAR DIARY
or
INTELLIGENCE SUMMARY
(Erase heading not required.)

Army Form C. 2118

62 Field Ambulance

Place	Date	Hour	Summary of Events and Information	Remarks and references to Appendices
CARNOY	1.4.17		3 O/R's Ranks R.A.M.C. & 7 Other Ranks A.S.C.(H.T) with 8 mules and 4 heavy draught horses, 3 horse ambulances attached to 61 Field Ambulance for work in the forward area evacuating sick and wounded. It drives as O.C. M.T. and Lieut. Watley Dental areas reported to O.C. 61 Field Ambulance for duty. Packed all equipment, medical stores, supplies etc. in G.S. waggons, and limbers waggons. C Section transport and personnel to remain at CARNOY. A Section with modified transport to move to ROCQUIGNY. B Section to move to COMBLES. 62 Field Ambulance to carry out Reserve Area work. Evacuation. No M/2/10.4963. Driver LISTER ASC (M.T.) fined 3 days pay. Preparing to report Ambulance unfit for the road.	SM2.
	2.4.17		Captain BENNETT F.L. Rank. 2 O.R. Rank. 11 O.R. ASC(HT) 4 heavy draught horses. 12 mules. and 2 Motor Cars attached to 61 Field Ambulance for duty. A O/R's ASC (M.T) attached to 61 Field Ambulance for duty Night Relay Posts. At O.31.A.8.5 and U.2.C.6.8. and loading post at O.27.d. with 2 Motor Buses. An arrange with O.C. 61 Field Ambulance regarding Evacuation of Reserve Area. ROCQUIGNY to O.M.D.S. at MARICOURT. Map Reference Sheet 57.c. 1. edition Trenches Box Respirators & personal Kneel. Bag & ASC 62 Fld Ambulance - Captain ADAM Rank granted 10 days leave to U.K. [??????] Central - Leave commenced [????]. Holland Officers and 3 O.R. In CARNOY. COMBLES and ROCQUIGNY	SM2.
	3.4.17		O.R's all ranks to carry one Haversack Ration. C. B of A. 100 withdrawn respectively parade at 8am W 4.17 Marching in back M/O 2 - 8. 15 am.	VR2.

WAR DIARY or INTELLIGENCE SUMMARY

Army Form C. 2118

12. 62 Field Ambulance

Place	Date	Hour	Summary of Events and Information	Remarks and references to Appendices
ROGBIGNY	4.4.17		A Section and Headquarters. left CARNOY at 9 a.m. B Section left at 8.30 a.m. 2 G.S. Waggons 2 G.S. limber waggons and two water carts accompanied sections. A section arrived at ROGBIGNY at 1.30 p.m. Heavy snowstorm - preparations for heating sick and wounded completed at 4 p.m. made use of existing building. Sections commenced arriving at 5 p.m. receiving from 40 Cas. 61 Field Ambulance at LECHELLE and BUS Neryeslives. Several walking cases sent to 2nd Relay Post by wheeled stretcher. Thus bring cases and sitting up cases unable to walk sent to Horse Ambulance to Motor Ambulance at 2nd Relay Post. BAPAUME ROCOIGNY Road at U.2.C.3.9. Sheet 57.C. Walking cases sent to 1st Relay Post. Severe cases sent by trolly on DECAUVILLE Railway from 1st Relay Post to COMBLES.	P.S.
	5.4.17		Weather arnus in fours condiller half drunks and A.T.S. given at ROCOIGNY before departure to COMBLES. about 130 wounded passed through from 7am to 4.45 from 5.a.m. to 6.a.m. 57.4.17 to COMBLES at 10am. Time Motor Ambulance Car (Motor) to Renecogne at 1-2m. Relay post. at U.2.C. 4.5. Sheet. 57.C. Total wounded passed through to 8p.m. 207. Captain P. BENNETT Royal /c at Dressing Station COMBLES. Captain J. ADAM. R.A.M.C. proceeded on leave in Kinnoation of contract in days 6.4.17 & 20.4.17. No65562 Pte. BAUCOTT H. R.A.M.C. was evacuated to No 3 C.C.S. 10.day-	P.S.
	6.4.17		Two Motor Ambulance Cars collecting from 1st Relay Post 0.31 & 6.5 Sheet 57C. Moved to have 2 motor ambulances at 1st Relay Post. The time taken by Horse Ambulance from ROCOIGNY to FREICOURT U.19.A Sents. and relieving a Cause of Considerable delay in evacuating wounded- the DECAUVILLE Railway could be made more use of trucks fitted for lying and sitting cases would be a great convenience. Main ROAD was in bad condition for motor transport between ROCOIGNY and FREICOURT. was under repair. Captain T. BENNETT R.A.M.C. 91 R. Ramf. 11 O.R. A.S.C. (H.T) 4 D.R. A.S.C. (M.T) with 4 heavy draught horses. 12 mules and 2 cobs attached to 62 Field Ambulance from 61 Field Ambulance.	P.S.

WAR DIARY
or
INTELLIGENCE SUMMARY

Army Form C. 2118

13 62 Field Ambulance

Place	Date	Hour	Summary of Events and Information	Remarks and references to Appendices
ROCQUIGNY	7.4.17		Captain J.D. WALKER. Rank. Posted to 7th D.C.L.I. permanently as his O/C. Very few wounds passed through Bearer Relay Station during previous 24 hours. Inspected Box Respirators of Bearers. also P.H. helmets - arranged for shellac for personal respirators. Box Respirators completion.	Ok2
"	8.4.17		No M/2/022237 Pte HERRING A.J. A.S.C. (M.T.) is attached to 60 Field Ambulance temporarily and is giving the duty of rations from 7.4.17. Captain J.A. GRAY Rank and Captain E.G. WALSH Rank reported to 2 Field Ambulance for duty.	Sh2
LECHELLE	9.4.17		4 & O.R. Bearers detailed for duty with Battalions 9.61st Brigade to relieve 60 Field Ambulance - 4 N.C.Os and 28 men took over Relay Post at N.4.b.2.0 and P.32.d.2.9 respectively Sheet 57e. NO 34126 Pte HUMPHRIES R. and NO 61726 Pte GRAVES R. Rank proceeds to ABBEVILLE to report to Railway Signal Officer, authority A.D.M.S. 20 Division - Captain C.O. WALSH Rank posted as W.O.I/C 1st Kings Liverpool Regiment (temporary). A Section and Headquarters 62 Field Ambulance moved to LECHELLE and took over Bearer Platoon from 60 Field Ambulance - 2 O.R. Rank and 2 O.R. A.S.C. with 16 heavy draught horses are attached to this unit from 60 Field Ambulance.	Sh2
"	11.4.17		Captain J.C. CHANDLER Rank. took over duties of M.O./C. 7 Somerset Light Infantry permanently on 8.4.17 was struck off the strength of this unit - No 35016 Pte FARRELL T Rank and No M/2/133896 Pte JORDAN Q/C. (M.T.) rejoined from A.D.M.S. 20 Division - No T/3/022518 Dr L.A. BAGGOTT A.S.C. (HT) evacuated to 2/2 Lon. C.C.S. No 368 23 Pte FIELD J Rank admitted to hospital and transferred to X Corps M.D.S. on 9.4.17, No 39642 Pte H.C. PRESCOTT Rank was wounded on the 8.4.17 and returned to duty after being dressed.	Ok2
"	13.4.17		13.O.R. 61 Field Ambulance attached to this unit and are taken on the strength for rations - Clerks Greyhead A.R.C. declared. Parade with Box Respirators for personal Rank and A.S.C. H.T. and M.T.	Ok2

WAR DIARY
or
INTELLIGENCE SUMMARY

Army Form C. 2118

62 Field Ambulance

Place	Date	Hour	Summary of Events and Information	Remarks and references to Appendices
LECHELLE	14.4.17		No. M/2/105/045 Pte THUMPSTON C. ASC (M.T.) granted leave to ENGLAND from 13.4.17 to 23.4.17 with 14 days ration allowance — No M/2/105/87 Pte COOK. S. ASC (M.T.) included to 62 Field Ambulance and is taken on the strength for rations — ADMS visits Ambulance. Arranged for an ADS at NEUVILLE P.22 b 9.4 — Working party sent to prepare ground & spread (with 2 NCOs and 12 men) the necessary stretchers, blankets and Chloroform of Ammonia at ADS. Officer i/c 8th Battalion 6/M3/West in charge. All bearers as former base posts and today going forward. Evacuation will be from METZ and will be at PT P.9.4. Final S.P.E. Primarily by wheeled stretchers to NEUVILLE. Road is bad condition from METZ to NEUVILLE. Paid Personal Army aux Lift.	Dist.
"	15.4.17		No M/2/153794 Pte LAWSON. P ASC (M.T.). No 30624 Pte BRIGHT J. RAMC. with one bearer Ambulance reports for duty from 62 Field Ambulance — New Regimental Numbers have been allotted to the following personnel RAMC in accordance with Army Council Instruction 380. 1917. Remarks. NAME. RANK. Former No. New No. ROCKEY.J.T. Pte 1877 457145 3/1 WESSEX Field Ambulance. FLEMING T.J. " 568 459007 3/2 " " JOSE. S. " 2392 459467 3/2 " " FRASER. J. " 2352 461535. 3/3 " " " 26th Field Ambulance.	S.A.P.
"	16.4.17		No 040287 Pte WARDLOW T. RAMC Proceeds to C.C.S from C.R.S. on 4.3.17. No M/2/104983 Pte LISTER J.M. No M/2/153794 Pte LAWSON P. ASC (M.T.) and No 30824 Pte BRIGHT J. RAMC attached to 20th Division A.S.C. Workshops, and are struck off the Strength of this unit for rations. A.D.M.S. 20th Division visits Ambulance — Captain P. BENNETT RAMC details for duty at A.D.S. NEUVILLE.	S.A.P.
"	17.4.17		Paid with Rex Regimental personnel RAMC SAE MT projectile transport and Saddlery. No 64081 Pte Mc.CORMACK.T. RAMC transferred to 62 Field Ambulance from 61 Field Ambulance.	S.A.P.

Army Form C. 2118

15
62 Field Ambulance

WAR DIARY
or
INTELLIGENCE SUMMARY
(Erase heading not required.)

Place	Date	Hour	Summary of Events and Information	Remarks and references to Appendices
LEOMELLE	16.4.17		Captain. P.J. CONNOLLY. R.A.M.C. posts for duty at A.D.S. NEUVILLE. Visited R.A.P's at S 20 & 4.8. METZ- and P.18 C.9.4. (Sheet) C. M.O.'s in charge of dressing shelters/posts. Arrangements for bathing of personnel. Recce. M.C./62 Field Ambulance. Bearers to be relieved on opportunity occurs. Clean clothing stores from 33 Stationary Section BUS. A/Tus 20 DIVISION visits Ambulance.	R.2
	19.4.17		A/Tus 20 DIVISION issued instructions regarding disposal of surplus Equipment and Motor rifle face pieces. Bearer party working at NEUVILLE making standings for motor ambulances and road to field for parking transport. Pees and orders regarding saluting. Provisional Orders - No 56,29 Pte J. HARRIS R.A.M.C. transferred to transportation Depart 14.4.17. and is struck off the strength of this unit from 15.4.17. Captain. J.G. RAY. R.A.M.C. posted for duty at A.D.S.	R.1
	20.4.17		No 30024 Pte J. BRIGHT. R.A.M.C. and No. M/2/163394 Pte. LAWSON. P. A.S.C. M.T. returns from Workshops on 18.4.17 and are taken on the strength of this unit. for rations. 2 O.R's with 2 heavy draught horses referred to 60 Field Ambulance. and are struck off the Strength of this unit for rations 20.4.17. A.D.M.S. 20 DIVISION visits Ambulance.	P.4
	21.4.17		No 34187 Pte MUIRHEAD.B. and No 63399 Pte S/W.P. R.A.M.C. are appointed Lance Corporals both pay from 20.4.17. authority- A.D.M.S. No N/182/38/17. dated 20.4.17. No 50799 Pte SMITH. W. R.A.M.C. and No 9/4/060799 Driver REES.D. Reported for duty from 61 Field Ambulance with the heavy draught horses and one Ambulance Wagon. Casualty wightdrawn and instructions to be issued for Prevention of disease head out- break for personnel R.A.M.C. and A.S.C.	S.R.9

1875 Wt. W 593/826 1,000,000 4/15 J.B.C. & A. A.D.S.S./Forms/C. 2118.

WAR DIARY or INTELLIGENCE SUMMARY

Army Form C. 2118

16 **62 Field Ambulance**

Place	Date	Hour	Summary of Events and Information	Remarks and references to Appendices
LECHELLE	22.4.17		No. M/2/104983 Pte LISTER J.W. A/c (MT) returned from workshops on 19.4.17 and is taken on the strength of this unit. No. 528 09 Pte PASSVILLE A. Paws is struck off strength from 20.4.17 to 30.4.17 with ration allowance. Pte STRETTON. E. joined Regimental No. 2362 has now been allotted a new Regimental No. 4/9199.2.N. reporting Field Ambulance. Received orders from A.D.M.S. 20 Division to prepare for evacuation of wounded. 59th and 60th Brigade carrying out operations. Line to be advanced and TRESCAULT occupied. Captain P.BENNETT Reui- and Captain J.ADAM R.A.M.C to accompany bearers. Relay posts to be formed, also Loading post and Rear posts. Extra Stretcher Blankets, Shell dressing and medical comforts to the centre R.A.P.'s. Four Squads Bearer bearers to be attached to each Battalion under instruction of N.O. of Battalion, the following arrangements have all Bearers post Field Ambulance with two Medical Officers kept in front.	A.9
			Attack commenced at 5pm. 16 wounded arrived at 10pm. Horse Ambulances returned at P18.c.7.2 also Ford Ambulance. One Ambulance Platoon at Loading Post @20.b.4.8 wounded carried by bearers or wheeled stretchers from @14.d.0.8 and @15.c.2.9. to ambulances and Ford ambulance. Spare stretchers and Blankets sent by bearers to R.A.P's. wounded given hot drinks and returned if necessary at L.A.D.S. @20.A.02. 28 wounded passed through A.D.S. at NEUVILLE. from 10p.m. 22.4.17. to 12 noon 23.4.17.-	S/18.
"	23. " 17		Two wounded arrived from A.D.S. METZ at 8.30am. Bearer Officer with all the First aid Field Ambulance reported to A.D.M.S. 20th Division, Shapcotts at R.A.P. METZ. also loading post formed. Relay posts and R.A.P's at METZ and K.6.S.L.T.@ 13 & Central.	
			Good casual passes granted to the following under a field 1050 Reg.l warrant. No. 457145 Pte ROCKEY No 72.16. No. 20195 Pte ROXBOROUGH C.2.4.17. No. 2034 Pte SMITH E.12.16. No. M/2/079019 Pte JONES. C.4. 20.4.17. No.M/2/046737 Pte TASKER.A. T.W.D. No.M/2/23560. Pte JORDAN. Pte A.G returning from holidays.	

WAR DIARY
or
INTELLIGENCE SUMMARY 1/6 Field Ambulance

Army Form C. 2118

(Erase heading not required.)

Place	Date	Hour	Summary of Events and Information	Remarks and references to Appendices
LECHELLE	24.4.17		Opened an Advanced Dressing Station at NEVILLE on the 22.4.17, occupied dismantled house on a road at PREVOST. Transport in wood store by - Reserve M.O. personnel in huts behind dressing station. Tarpaulins used to make shelter for reception of wounded & sick and wounded. No change in disposition of bearing posts Relay posts or RAPs	S.A.P
	25.4.17		Orders received from A.D.M.S. to prepare for Casualties from 6th Brigade in right sector of line - have to take place tonight. Have to be utilized later. BILHEM. to be occupied. 12 KRR's and 13 RBs attacking from our trenches and trunks in reserve. One Bearer Post Division 3/4 U/S reported for duty - as reserve. Bearers - Captain HAWKINS, Reeve 1/6 Bearers. Cold wire received at 7.30pm. Commenced Zero Hour of attack. Four motor ambulance and 4 j.h. light - and - zero wheeled stretchers used from RAPs. Extra stretchers, blankets and Shell Dressings sent to Relay posts and RAPs up to being wounded arrived at 1.30 a.m. 35 wounded carried out satisfactorily. No delay occurred at 26.4.17. Evacuation was carried on touring posts. Relay posts on touring posts.	O.K.P
	26.4.17		No T/S/1293 Sgt Smith HORSBURGH G. granted a good conduct badge from 14.11.16 Unit added 1060 R.W. No35170. Pte DAWSON G. Reeve. Q. Proceeded to transportation OAT Depot BOULOGNE 25.4.17 notified. A.D.C No 1874 5/21/B23) A. fatigues in camp. Dw. Drur. Pack Store stationary being brought -	O.K.T
	27.4.17		Weather fine clear, Allowed bearers from RAPs - arrange for bathing and clean clothing of men -	Ok.T
	28.4.17		No 53291 Pte CLARK J. Reeve. proceeded on leave 10 days to United Kingdom. 27.4.17 to 7.5.17. No 50265 Pte GALLIMORE. H. Reeve reported. Unit 27.4.17. Latrines routine. Bln. Units and Shapenin Cartfld. Athers 2nd Division Mental Recruitment	S.A.P

1875 Wt. W593/826 1,000,000 4/15 J.B.C. & A. A.D.S.S./Forms/C. 2118.

WAR DIARY or INTELLIGENCE SUMMARY

Army Form C. 2118

18 62 Field Ambulance

Place	Date	Hour	Summary of Events and Information	Remarks and references to Appendices
NEUVILLE	29.4.17		A.D.M.S. 20th DIVISION visited Ambulance. D.D.M.S. XV Corps visited ambulance on 28.4.17. Fine weather continues - alteration in disposition of R.A.P. and Relay post as follows: R.S.L.I. R.A.P. left B.13 a central. R.B's R.A.P. central B.14 d.10.5.6" Orifice of trench R.A.P. N.W. B.15.d.4.5. K.R.R's R.A.P. Remains B.18 d.0.8 - Arrange that an horse ambulance remains at 6.20 A.M. to collect cases from forward area. NEUVILLE village was shelled 10 p.m. to 12 midnight. Weather fine.	S.L.
	30.4.17		Tents for Hospital huttus. in hollow below Dressing Station. P.22.c.6.5. Sheet 62 F. Inspected Transport - arranged for motor ambulance to be no horse ambulance - Portion following Posted 6.20 A.M. taken over by TOWN MAJOR METZ as a billet.	R.7

S.L.L. Grainger
Lt. W. Raune

COMMITTEE FOR THE
MEDICAL HISTORY OF THE WAR
Date 10 JUL. 1917

20th Divn.

No 62. F.A.

Army Form C. 2118.

WAR DIARY
or
INTELLIGENCE SUMMARY.

(Erase heading not required.)

Instructions regarding War Diaries and Intelligence Summaries are contained in F. S. Regs., Part II. and the Staff Manual respectively. Title pages will be prepared in manuscript.

WO 21

CONFIDENTIAL

WAR DIARY

OF

62nd Field Ambulance

FROM 1st May 1917 TO 31st May 1917

WAR DIARY or INTELLIGENCE SUMMARY

Army Form C. 2118

19. 62nd Field Ambulance

Place	Date	Hour	Summary of Events and Information	Remarks and references to Appendices
NEUVILLE	1st May 1917		No M2/10296 Cpl TOMLIN. H.S. A.S.C.(M.T.) was transferred to C.M.D.S. XV Corps 29.4.17. 3 Maj Ranks 61st Fd Ambulance returns to their Unit and are struck off the Strength. Lt Rahm - visited aid posts of Battalions 60th Infantry Brigade - HAVRINCOURT WOOD - Shed 57.C Ravine personnel in dug outs well protected - sufficient room for men sheltering easy, at a time - ample blankets and shell dressings, dressings to clean, one Thomas splint to each R.A.P, 1st instructed J.Q.S.W. Task with practice - R. by wheeled stretcher can be used from two R.A.P's through HAVRINCOURT WOOD to dressing post at P.18.c.7.2. also at Q.20.B.58. METZ side of shrine where horse ambulances are halted. Shed 57.C. anti-Enteric inoculation of Ravine & 2nd personnel commenced.	HAVRINCOURT R.9.
	2.5.17		No. 34545 Cpl GLANCY. T. R A.M.C. is appointed acting Sergeant with pay from 22.4.17. vice authority D.G.M.S. 14501608/admin 29.4.17. Parade of personnel Field amb No 62. with Rev Reginald Gillivrass Wesleyan Medical Officer to Infantry Brigade - describes probable methods of requesting presence of Certain ambulance in that Battalion. Demonstrates probable methods of providing him area a life shed 57.C. Enemy shelled during the morning.	Sh.9.
	3.5.17		Head Quarters 62 Field Ambulance moves to NEUVILLE. No. M/S/2727 Sgt G.F. MASON A.S.C. awarded Reprimand absenting himself from Camp from 3.30pm to 5.30pm without permission. No 38629 Pte DIXON J. R A.M.C. forfeits 3 days pay & G.C. Badge approving late on guard. 1/2 hour.	P.9.
	6.5.17		No M2/10221b Cpl TOMLIN. H. A.S.C. M.T. was evacuated to 46 Casualty Clearing Station and is struck off the Strength. Captain J.A. GRAY R A.M.C. took over temporary duty as medical Officer 1/c 232 Army Troops Coy RE No 45658 Pte A. FENNELL R A.M.C. grants leave from 6-5-17 to 18-5-17 with 10 days ration allowance.	Sh.2.
	9.5.17		No 33738 Pte C.H. BALMENT. grants leave from 9-5-17 to 19-5-17 with 10 days ration allowance. Visited Relay posts and Regimental aid posts - Relay posts at Q.15.c.2.9. P.18.d.8.6. RAP's at Q.7.d.8.6. Q.14.d.v.8. & Q.15.c.4.8. Shed 57.c.S.E.	Sh.9.

WAR DIARY
or
INTELLIGENCE SUMMARY 20. 62 Field Ambulance

(Erase heading not required.)

Army Form C. 2118

Place	Date	Hour	Summary of Events and Information	Remarks and references to Appendices
NEUVILLE	10.5.17		No.19199 Pte STRETTOR. E. RAMC. appointed Acting Lance Corporal without pay — Per Respiration drill for personnel RAMC and A.S.C.	Sht.
	12.5.17		Captain J.A. GRAY. RAMC. posted to 60th Field Ambulance authority A.D.M.S. 20th Division. LIEUT. B.G. CONNOLLY. posted to Medical charge of 91st Brigade R.F.A. from 7.5.17. The 20th DIVISIONAL front is being extended to its right on the nights 12/13th and 13/14 May. on completion it will be held by 3 Brigades in the line viz. — Right Sector 60th Infy Bde Centre Sector 59th Infy Bde Left Sector 61st Infy Bde — 59 Brigade Operation order no 36 — Reference Map. 57 c. S.E. 1/20,000.— Medical arrangements for centre sector will be as follows. Right & Centre Battalions 62 Field Ambulance (A.D.S.† NEUVILLE) Left and Reserve Battalions 61 Field Ambulance (A.D.S. RUYAULCOURT) Rifle Brigade Boundaries will be as follows:— (a) Rear (through) Q.12 Central — Q.17.b.3.0 — Q.17.c.1.0.— Q.22 Central — Road Junction Q.27.a.0.4. P.35.a.7.3. (b) Stream running through Q.9.c.6.8. (inclusive to Centre Sector) — Q.4.c.0.0.— Q.9 Central — Q.14. Central — Cross roads. Q.19.b.2.4.— NEUVILLE CHURCH inclusive to Centre Sector.) 20th DIVISION Rifle Operation Order no 54 — by Col. E.W. SLAYTER. C.M.G. A.D.M.S. XV Corps is being temporarily re-organized and 20th Division will lose 3 Brigades in the line from night May 12th/13th. 60 Infantry Brigade will relieve 120th Infantry Brigade between R.7.d.5.9. and the Paper belt right on night May 12th/13th Continued —	S/A8. S/A9. M.9

WAR DIARY
or
INTELLIGENCE SUMMARY

Army Form C. 2118.

21. 62nd Field Ambulance.

Place	Date	Hour	Summary of Events and Information	Remarks and references to Appendices
NEUVILLE	May 12th/13th	5.17	May 12th/13th. 59 Infantry Brigade will extend to the right on night MAY 13th/14th to about Q.4.2. Central, taking over from 60th Infantry Brigade. 61st Infantry Brigade will extend to their right on night May 13th/14th to about Q.4.c.5.8. taking over from 59th Infantry Brigade. 60th Infantry Brigade reverts to command of 20th DIVISION at 18.am. MAY/14th. etc. DIVISIONAL front will extend from R.14.d.0.1. to present left. MEDICAL. 62nd FIELD AMBULANCE will be responsible from 6.p.m. on 12th for evacuation of sick and wounded from the Centre and right Battalions only of the 59th Infantry Brigade and in addition, from 6.p.m. yesterday, Brigade front extending to R.7. d.8-9.60 (Right) Brigade front to R.14. d.8-9 Sheet 57.C.1.50.000. from the night of 13th and 14th with the exception D.60 (Right) Brigade will evacuate any casualties responsibility of 62nd Field Ambulance will include any casualties that may be billeted to the centre and right battalions of the Central Brigade (5-9th).	S.R.9.
1A	5.17		Casualty sick and wounded from 5 Battalion front. Represented as Posts as follows. 5 F.P.A. Centre Battalion (Centre Brigade) Q.15.d.4.8. 6 R.A.P. Right Battalion Centre (Brigade) Q.15.d.0.10. R.A.P. No 7 Left Battalion right (Brigade) Q.13 b.2.4. R.A.P. No 8 Centre Battalion right Brigade. 15 "RAVINE. R.19 (a.9.2.) R.A.P. no 9. Right Battalion R.20 (a.1.9.) R.A.P. no 9. evacuation from Centre and right Battalions to Brigade in to ADVANCED DRESSING STATION METZ Q.20.9.2.2. From all 3 Battalions of Right Brigade to Loud Inspect at QUEENS CROSS- Q.28.7.7. Thence by motor ambulance and Lorries carriage along METZ-FINS ADVANCED DRESSING STATION METZ and evacuation Dressing Station.	S.R.9
16	5.17		62nd Field Ambulance will be relieved by/on on the night 1/22nd undated at 6/pm. by an au Ireland of 42nd DIVISION. Field Ambulances Relieved to be prepared to continue.	

Army Form C. 2118.

WAR DIARY
or
INTELLIGENCE SUMMARY.

No. 22.
62nd Field Ambulance

Place	Date	Hour	Summary of Events and Information	Remarks and references to Appendices
NEUVILLE	continued 16-5-17		To march off with the Brigade at present in front of YPRES on morning of that day relieved - Unit will control the 62nd Field Ambulance being attached to the 60th Brigade Group. Until arrival in new AREA when change over will take place. 20th DIVISION will be relieved in the line by 42nd DIVISION (less 1 HOWITZER BATTERY)	A.9.
	17/5/17		Commencing on MAY 19th (?) On relief 20th DIVISION will move to FIFTH ARMY AREA and will be transferred to I ANZAC CORPS. Field Ambulances will be relieved under orders of A.D.M.S as follows:- 61st Field Ambulance by 1/2 2nd Lancs Field Ambulance on May 19th. 60th Field Ambulance by 1/1 East Lancs Field Ambulance on May 21st. 62nd Field Ambulance by 1/3 East Lancs Field Ambulance on May 22nd. Relief to be complete on each day by 6 p.m. at which hour Field Ambulances come under orders of Brigadier for Purposes of march into new area. The Division will move with I ANZAC. Corps AREA, in accordance with Table "A". B wills will be allotted by AREA COMMANDANT: "A" AREA. That (BAPAUME) - C on arrival in new AREA. Troops of 20th DIVISION come under orders of G.O.C. I ANZAC. Corps (Lt Gen GREVILLIERS) Command of that unit pass to G.O.C. 42nd DIVISION at 10 a.m. MAY 23rd at which hour DIVISIONAL HEADQUARTERS will close at LITTLE WOOD and re-open at The MONUMENT nr. BAPAUME MISC. that 57. C. MEDICAL. In accordance with Para 3 (a) and conforming with Table "A". (1) 61st Field Ambulance on relief by 1/2 East Lancs Field Ambulance Unit will march with Infantry Brigade under orders of 13.g.c 61st Infantry Brigade on MAY 20th. (2) 60th Field Ambulance on relief by 1/1 East Lancs Field Ambulance will join up and move under orders of 13.g.C. with 59th Infantry Brigade Group on MAY 22nd. (3) 62nd Field Ambulance on relief by 1/3 East Lancs Field Ambulance will move under orders of B.G.C. 60th Infantry Brigade Group on MAY 23rd. Details of unit's Conveyances by R.G.C. that the unit will be opposed between	A.9.

Army Form C. 2118.

WAR DIARY
or
INTELLIGENCE SUMMARY.
(Erase heading not required.)

23. 62nd Field Ambulance.

Place	Date	Hour	Summary of Events and Information	Remarks and references to Appendices
NEUVILLE	17.5.17	continued	Rearrangements of 61st and 62nd field ambulances to their correct affiliated Brigade Groups will take place after arrival in new AREA, on receipt of orders from this Office. 3 details of Brigades move to New AREA will be arranged by 62nd field ambulances with H.Q. of Brigades. Surplus stores will be taken over by relieving Units. Receipts will be forwarded to A.D.M.S. where applicable. These receipts will be pro forma as published in 20th Division. R.20/5137/14 of 8/1/17 and stores be forwarded as early as possible. Table "A". MOVE of 20th DIVISION to FIFTH ARMY. (ANZAC CORPS AREA)	A.P.
			FORMATION. FROM. TIME ROUTE. TO REMARKS.	
	MAY 20th		61st Infantry Bde Group. YTRES (AREA) To be clear of North and East area through LECHELLE by 5 p.m.	Under orders of B.g.C. 61st Infantry Brigade.
	MAY 22nd.		59th Inf Bde Group. do. No restriction. Army and all roads may be used. Except the following ROYAUL-LECHELLE before 12 noon.	Under orders of 13.9.E. 59th Infantry Brigade.
	MAY 23rd.		60th Inf Bde Group. do. Nos 1+2 Cross Roads Route through LECHELLE before 12 noon. 2 pm. To be clear of N & S line LECHELLE by 2pm. COURT- BERTIN- COURT- BERTIN- COURT- HAPLIN- COURT- BERTIN- COURT- BARASTRE-	Under orders of B.g.C. 60th Inf.Bde
			DIVISIONAL H.Qrs. LITTLE WOOD. BEAULENCOURT MONUMENT HIS C	Under orders of Camp Commandant No.1 BAPAUME

WAR DIARY
INTELLIGENCE SUMMARY

24. Field Ambulance –
62nd Field Ambulance

Army Form C. 2118.

Place	Date	Hour	Summary of Events and Information	Remarks and references to Appendices
NEUVILLE	19-5-17		1/20 DIVISION RAMC. OPERATION ORDER No 86. Reference MAP 57c. 1/40.000. (a) 61st Field Ambulance will move with 61st Infantry Brigade on MAY 20 in accordance with same. O.O. No 65. (b) Under orders of D.D.M.S. 1st ANZAC Corps 61st Field Ambulance will take over the WARKING WOUNDED DRESSING STATION – H.12.b.6.4. from 14th Australian Field Ambulance. Relief to be completed by 8 p.m. 21st instant. C. By arrangement with A.D.M.S. 5th Australian Division H.12.b.6.4. by 10 a.m. 21st inst. in order that they may be shewn the line during the day. Army Corps of WALKING WOUNDED (MAIN DRESSING Station) Should commence at the same hour. d. A. DECAUVILLE DETRAINING POST at H.26.d.0.3. will be taken over by 4 p.m. 21st instant. (Relieving 3rd Australian Field Ambulance) members of Detachment will be one Non-Commissioned Officer. (2)(a) 62nd Field Ambulance will move from V.24.a.3.0. with 59th Infantry Brigade on 22nd inst in accordance with Reduc. O.O. No 65. (b) O.C. 62nd Field Ambulance will take over MAIN DRESSING STATION (LYING CASES) at H.16.d.8.5. from 8th Australian Field Ambulance – Relief to be completed by 8 p.m. 23rd instant. c. By arrangement with A.D.M.S. 5th Australian Division Bearer Division of 62nd Field Ambulance will reach H.16.d.8.5. by 10 a.m. 23rd instant. Taking over of MAIN DRESSING STATION (LYING Cases) (Mules) commence at the same hour. (3)(a) 62nd Field Ambulance will move with 60th Infantry Brigade in accordance with Reduc. O.O. No 65. (b) The BEARER DIVISION 62nd Field Ambulance will report to O.C. MAIN DRESSING Station (LYING CASES) H.16.d.8.5. by 10 a.m. 24th inst. (c) Orders as to disposal of H.A.M. and TENT DIVISION 62nd Field Ambulance after march to BEAULENCOURT on 23rd inst. will be issued later.	S.A.D.

WAR DIARY

Army Form C. 2118.

Unit: 61 Field Ambulance.

Place	Date	Hour	Summary of Events and Information	Remarks and references to Appendices
NEUVILLE	20.5.17		Medical Arrangements. 1(a) The new front will be held by two Brigades in the line -- RIGHT SECTOR 59th Infantry Brigade (taking over night 24/25th) LEFT SECTOR 60th Infantry Brigade 23-4/26th (b) 61st Infantry Brigade will be grouped in RESERVE AREA - in VRAUCOURT - BEUGNY - YTRES LINE - FAVREUIL. (c) The front held runs approximately U.23 a.6.2 - U.29 b.6.10 - U.29 b.7.5 - U.29 b.10.5 - U.29 b.0.8 - 1 Straight to C.6 c.5.0 - Straight to D.14 a.0.0 - B5 D.20 a.7.7 - (d) LEFT DIVISIONAL BOUNDARY - U.23 a.6.2 Burnt wharf Railway cuts C.4 a and C.5 - Straight to C.13 central Chapel to B.24 c.3.5 - (e) INTER BRIGADE BOUNDARY - C.6.C.5.0 - C.16 Central back to VAUX - 2 POSITION OF MEDICAL UNITS. (a) LEFT BRIGADE SECTOR. REGIMENTAL AID POSTS. C.5 b.7.8 - C.5 d.6.3. RELAY POST. C.11 a.5.2. - BEARER AND RELAY POST (COLLECTING POST). C.10.5.7.7 (b) RIGHT HORSED AMBULANCE. LOADING POST (night) C.9 d.5.5. (day) C.14 Central. BRIGADE SECTOR - REGIMENTAL AID POSTS - C.23 b.6.9 - C.24 d.8.5 - C.30 a.8.5. RELAY POST. C.29 c.5.9. HORSED AMBULANCE. LOADING POST C.22 d.6.3. ADVANCED DRESSING STATION (one light ambulance loading hut) C.20 d.2.5. MAIN DRESSING STATION (one H.Q.N. F.Amb.) H.16 c.7.6.4. (2) In laying wounded H.16 d.8.5 - R) RESERVE BEARER CAMP H.16 d.8.5. (f) H.Q.N. F.Amb. IN RESERVE - H.16 d.8.5 - (g) DECAUVILLE ENTRAINING POINT - I.7 d.3.0.5. DECAUVILLE DETRAINING POINT - H.26 A.S.4 - (h) DIVISIONAL REST STATION (in process of erection in Cuybaury use of 48th and 29th Division) NIC - EVACUATION. (i) WOUNDED. Cases are evacuated by the Regimental Stretcher Bearers to the Regimental aid Post. From Regimental aid Post of LEFT SECTOR - by Relays of Field Ambulance Stretcher Bearers (via) (BEARER and) RELAY POST - C.10 c.7.7.6 (three Ambulance) LOADING POSTS to ADVANCED DRESSING STATION - (C.20 d.2.8.) from where cases are evacuated by motor ambulance. FROM REGIMENTAL AID POSTS OF RIGHT SECTOR - by Relays of Field Ambulance Bearers via RELAY POST at C.29 c.5.9 - to HORSED Amb. (one Amb.) LOADING POST - at C.22 d.6.3 - to ADVANCED DRESSING STATION - C.20 d.2.9 - *Continued*	1/A/1.

WAR DIARY

2/6 6th Field Ambulance

Army Form C. 2118.

INTELLIGENCE SUMMARY

Place	Date	Hour	Summary of Events and Information	Remarks and references to Appendices
NEUVILLE	20.5.17		(continued)— C.2.O. d.2.8: FROM ADVANCED DRESSING STATION. Cases are evacuated by M.T. ambulance to MAIN DRESSING STATION for walking wounded or MAIN DRESSING STATION for LYING WOUNDED as required. FROM MAIN DRESSING STATION for WALKING WOUNDED (H.2) cases are taken by MOTOR LORRY and DECAUVILLE RAILWAY to respective destinations FROM MAIN DRESSING STATION FOR LYING CASES (H.16) patients are conveyed by MOTOR AMBULANCE CONVOY CARS 6/ their Respective destinations.— from DETRAINING POINT for WALKING WOUNDED (H.26 d.51.4) cases are taken by motor ambulance to Casualty Clearing Station— (4) EVACUATION OF SICK— Slightly sick from forward area follow the same route as wounded to MAIN DRESSING STATIONS from where they are evacuated by car and DECAUVILLE Railway via and inland POST a. H.26 d.30. to Britannic circle at POTIJERS. LYING SICK by same route as wounded to Casualty Clearing Station at BREVILLERS.—	118.
	21.5.17		Captain G. ADAM RAMC. took over Medical Charge of 12" King's Liverpool Regiment. Inspection of the Respirators of personnel of Raul Aux. Hospitalier channel Raul. Watch on inter Companies as Louising equipment on gel Brigade houses over A.D.S. and R.A.P.'s centre and reports 3 addition. Receipts for respirators 1/3 and 1/1 East Lancs as his field ambulance respectively. Equipment Reserve— Arrangement for evacuating from new front will be for the present as follows— ADDENDUM to Raul of MDS. Order no. 86 dates 19.5.17 (1) O.C. 6⁰ FIELD AMBULANCE. will be the O.C. Beaur Division— (2) O.C. 6⁰ FIELD AMBULANCE. will be the O.C. Beaur Division— (Y) ADVANCED DRESSING D.C. 6.15⁰ Field Australian STATION and MAIN DRESSING STATION (LYING. WOUNDED)— (r) (C) 6⁰ and will be in Command of MAIN DRESSING STATION (WALKING WOUNDED) (cars and 6⁰ Field Ambulances will each provide a Bearer division of officers and 50 other ranks for working the front line RIGHT SECTOR of front line will be 40 Bearer in the Cine (abs 40 in Reserve)	927.

WAR DIARY

62 Field Ambulance

Army Form C. 2118.

Place	Date	Hour	Summary of Events and Information	Remarks and references to Appendices
NEUVILLE	21-5-17		Reserve - Front Line will be relieved every 2 (two days) LEFT SECTOR - will be worked by 2 Bearer Divisions (1 to Reserve) of whom 1 Bearer Division (80 men) will be in the line and 1 Heavy Division (a mix) in Reserve (a) the prototype will be as follows - Bearer Division - Field Ambulance relieving Left Sector will do 2 days in the line and 2 days Resting followed by 4 days duty in Right Sector (all Reserve) relieved by 61 Field Ambulance Bearer Division. Time to commence at 10am 5 am on 23rd instant (b) 60 Field Ambulance Bearer Division takes over Right Sector at 5am on the 23rd. This unit will be relieved by Bearer Division of 62 Field Ambulance at 5am on the 25th instant. At 5am on the 27th instant 62 Field Ambulance Bearer Division takes over Right Sector and 61 Field Ambulance Bearer Division relieves 62 Field Ambulance in left Sector. Bearer Division will be accordingly necessary in manning the MAIN DRESSING 60 Field Ambulance will be so available and advanced Dressing Station 1 & 2 more Bearer Station (LYING WOUNDED) and Receiving (90-50) and advance by the left Sector and 10 men from Bn Division in Reserve to carry from the Bearer Division in Reserve in the Right Left will form a working party of 40 men to continue the salvaging of the A.D.S.	W.L.
	22-5-17		Camp left transport over to 1/3 and 1/1 East Lanc Combd Field Ambulance.	Col.
	23-5-17		Packed at Dewtrieul - Continued march to BIHUCOURT via TRES. BUS. ROQUIGNY. at 4.15pm arrived at - 13AV4ENC9R. at 7.30pm.	P.R.
BEAULENCOURT	24-5-17		Halted for 10 minutes Ambulance on the line of march - Camp allotted to G for Report inspected W 11 d Sheet 57 D. 1/40 000. Remained at Camp B. infant J 23rd March'd out from Camp at 6.30pm for FAVREUIL H16 - to Camp at H16 c.4.6- Sheet 57 E. 1/40,000. Took through RANCOURT and cross country routes - on arrival of 6th infantry Brigade at FAVREUIL to be by Field Ambulance they became attached to the 6th infantry Brigade and the 6/M Field Ambulance at 10.00 RAN Brisbane to ascertain Brigade Ambulance will be used by A of this 2nd Division 62nd Infantry Brigade Orders with us will arrived at Camp H16 C.4.6 at 8.30pm	C.R.

Army Form C. 2118.

WAR DIARY
or
INTELLIGENCE SUMMARY.

(Erase heading not required.)

28 62nd Field Ambulance.

Place	Date	Hour	Summary of Events and Information	Remarks and references to Appendices
FAVREUIL	26-5-17		CAPTAIN. P. BENNET RAMC and CAPTAIN. R. WALSH. RAMC. W/K & OR's Rearm Division joined 62nd Field Ambulance at 10 am on receiving instructions "ret" instant for duty in LEFT SECTOR of FRONT LINE. CAPTAIN J.A. PRIDHAM. RAMC joined the Amb' ulance for duty. ADMS 2nd DIVISION VIDE Camp?	S.R.?
	28-5-17		CAPTAIN H. EVANS RAMC granted leave to ENGLAND from 28-5-17 to 7-6-1917. MOVED TRANSPORT Lines to side of wood at FAVREUIL. H&b C.4.B. made flooring to horses parked haragen underneath trees. Personnel RAMC and ASC in tents. New steering section for sick of 61st Infantry Brigade. ADMS 2nd DIVISION VIDE Camp?	S.R.?
	30-5-17		The Rank proceed to duty to St Nheris Hospital WARLOY. (47. C.C.S.). Nurs O.R'o proceeded to duty to 4th Corps School on 29-5-17. CAPTAIN. C. WALSH RAMC proceeded to ENGLAND on BOULOGNE in accordance of Enclosed authority ADMS 2nd DIVISION NO M.20/2050 dated. 29-5-17.	R.R.
	31-5-17		Received orders from AD'MS 20th Division to take over GAS CENTRE. at AVESNES. les BAPAUME. H2b.B.4.4. on 18th June 1917. Taking over to be completed by 12 noon 1-6-17. Advanced party to leave FAVREUIL by 10 am on 1-6-17.	R.R.
			S.F.H. Cohango Lt Col RAMC	

140/2230

COMMITTEE FOR THE
MEDICAL HISTORY OF THE WAR
Date -7 AUG. 1917

No. 62. 7. A.

June 1917.

Army Form C. 2118

WAR DIARY
or
INTELLIGENCE SUMMARY

(Erase heading not required.)

Vol 2.2

Confidential

War Diary

of

62nd Field Ambulance BAMC

From 1st June 1917
To 30th June 1917

Army Form C. 2118.

WAR DIARY
or
INTELLIGENCE SUMMARY.

(Erase heading not required.)

29 62 Field Ambulance

Instructions regarding War Diaries and Intelligence Summaries are contained in F. S. Regs., Part II. and the Staff Manual respectively. Title pages will be prepared in manuscript.

Place	Date	Hour	Summary of Events and Information	Remarks and references to Appendices
FAVREUIL	1 June 1917		62 Field Ambulance moves to AVESNES LES BAPAUME. H266 C.S. Sheet 57E and relieves No XIV AUSTRALIAN FIELD AMBULANCE at GAS CENTRE. LIEUT. P. CONNOLLY RAMC and No 34540 Pte H. MITTER RAMC returned duty from 910 Brigade RFA on 31.5.17 Hosp. tents and stores taken over receipts given.	N.A
AVESNES LES BAPAUME	3.6.17		LIEUT. A. EMERSON RAMC reported for duty with unit. Bath House latrines and ablution Room erected. One inebriate, making room for motor Ambulance.	N.A.
			CAPTAIN P. BENNETT RAMC. and No 34277 PTE J WAR(I)NG RAMC attached to 60 Field Ambulance for duty with Bearer Division by 62 Field Ambulance No 13394 PTE McLEAN W. RAMC granted leave from 3-6-17 to 13-6-17.	
	6.6.17		LIEUT R.G. CONNOLLY RAMC took over duties of Sn. O./C. 92nd Bde. RFA No 34540 PTE MITTON H RAMC attached to 92 13gde RFA for duty. No 34167 Sgt B. MUIRHEAD B. RAMC is promoted to the rank of acting Corporal with pay from 9-5-17 authority D.G.M.S. 13/453/1916- M/24-5-17.-	N.A.
	8.6.17		No 76284 Pte FELIX D RAMC reports for duty.- Inspection of Small Box Respirators and Pth Helmets - No 45831 Pte BIRKIN J.T. reint on return after acting left with pay from 7-6-17 inclusive. No T/3/024096. LIEUT MILLBOURN A.S.C.(M.T.) granted leave from 8-6-17 to 18-6-17	SJ
	9-6-17		Box Respirator drill for personnel RAMC attd A.S.C. No 45831 PTE J.P. BIRKIN attached Acting left with pay for Captain ROBERTS J.E. RAMC assumed duties as M.O./C. 92nd Brigade RFA. LIEUT 1st CONNOLLY RAMC reverted from 92 Bgde RFA	C.R
	12- 6-17		LIEUT B CONNOLLY RAMC. proceeds to A.D.M.S. for temporary duty, and DADMS	C.R
	16- 6-17		Captain J FERGUSON RAMC reports for duty from 48th Division	C.R
	20 6.17		LIEUT. A EMERSON RAMC Attd(A) to 62 Field Ambulance	C.R

WAR DIARY or INTELLIGENCE SUMMARY

Army Form C. 2118.

30. 62 Field Ambulance

Place	Date	Hour	Summary of Events and Information	Remarks and references to Appendices
AVESNES LES BAPAUME	21/6/17		D.M.S. III.ª ARMY inspected 62 Field Amb whilst on 20.6.17 proceeded on leave to U.K. Period 22.6.17 to 2.7.17 handed over charge to Captain T.A. PRIDHAM. Revd. Lt T.A. EMERSON returned from 6 O.F.Amb.	S/4
	22/6/17		Capt T.E. ROBERTS R.A.M.C. returned from 92 Bde R.F.A. Lt CONNOLLY returned from IV Divl. H.B.	Ap.12
	23/6/17		17 O.R. returned from duty at MARLOY O'town Hospital and Lt EMERSON & 1 Tent sub division (20 O.R.) proceeded to No. 3 CCS for duty.	Ap.12
	24/6/17		40 O.R. proceeded to III Army Rest Camp at VALERY sur SOMME Capt EVANS & 5 O.R. & 1 motor car proceeded to LE MEILLARD near DOULLENS XXIX Divl Bo admin huts & report to O.C. No. 6 F. Amb.	Ap.12
	26/6/17		Began subdivision (70 O.R.) returned from duty with 60 F. Amb.	Ap.12
	27/6/17		Handed our En Centre and all Camp to No 5 Aust admin F Amb. Sent small advance party to G.17 a central sh.t 57c to new camp at BIHUCOURT.	
BIHUCOURT	28/6/17		Zeppelin Proceeded at 10am to new camp at G.18 c central Camb under orders of S.O.C. 61st I.D. at 9 am. Tent sub division and Lieut EMERSON returned from duty with No 3 CCS	Ap.12
	30/6/17		All Tx transport less one motor car left 7.30am to join column of 61st ENF BDE barrefast. The transport proceeded to ACHEUX Ret. Mar. LENS road, 0-00	Ap.12

COMMITTEE FOR THE
MEDICAL HISTORY OF THE WAR
Date 10 SEP. 1917

140/298

No. 62. 7.O.

July 17

Army Form C. 2118.

WAR DIARY
or
INTELLIGENCE SUMMARY.
(Erase heading not required.)

Vol 23

Confidential
War Diary
of
62nd Field Ambulance R.A.M.C.

From 1st July 1917
To 31st July 1917

Army Form C. 2118.

WAR DIARY
or
INTELLIGENCE SUMMARY.

62 Field Ambulance

(Erase heading not required.)

Place	Date	Hour	Summary of Events and Information	Remarks and references to Appendices
BIHUCOURT	1/7/17		62ⁿᵈ Field Ambulance Gen Transport entrained ACHIET LE GRAND 9 a.m. & detrained CANDAS EXCHANGE 11 a.m. Then marched to LE MEILLARD where it went into billets. On water cart proceed to FAVREUIL to report to reinforcement camp, where it proceed 5 a.m. next morning LENS	M.
LE MEILLARD	2/7/17		On water cart proceed Ambulance train covering work.	M.
	3/4/17		Sent Court Mart papers forward to Divd H.Q. re a Sanitary officer.	P.R.
	4/7/17		Took over charge of 62 Field Ambulance from Captain A. PRIDHAM RAMC. G.O.C. 20ᵗʰ DIVISION inspected Personnel and Transport of 62 Field Ambulance (A.D.M.S. 20ᵗʰ DIVISION accompanied G.O.C. Programme of weekly Training of Field Ambulance completed. Particular attention given to Lectures on Sanitation. Gas and anti-gas measures.	P.R.
	6.7.17		Inspected all billets. Sunday arrangements. Schofuching. Teaching stretcher parade. Inspection of NCOs No 35925 Pte/Sgt WELLINGTON Reward in Grant's leave from 5.7.17 to 15.7.17. Company drill. Box Respirator drill.	P.R.
	8.7.17		Inspection of Horse Transport and harness. Route march. Completed bathing arrangements of personnel and patients. Arranges for clean clothing for billets. Practical instruction in Bearer exercises. Training. Stretcher Bearer & Road Bearers	Ph.R.
	10.7.17		Practical instruction in Field Sanitation. Field kitchen etc. Road march. Anti bacteric inoculation of Unit Completed. A.D.M.S. visits Ambulance	Ph.R.
	14.7.17		Inspected billets. Kit-inspection. Stretcher drill. Lecture forward Cleanliness and Economy of food. A.D.M.S. visits Ambulance	Ph.R.
	16.7.17		Divl Bearers reform their Battalions on completion of course A.D.M.S visits Ambulance Graund Enclosures.	Ph.R.

WAR DIARY
INTELLIGENCE SUMMARY

Army Form C. 2118.

32 62 Field Ambulance

Place	Date	Hour	Summary of Events and Information	Remarks and references to Appendices
LE MEILLARD	15.7.17		Captain J. FERGUSON RAMC took over medical charge of 12th Kings Liverpool Regiment. Captain G. ADAM rejoined unit - Kit inspection. Checks Equipment, medical.	S.R.
	16.7.17		Rapido Billet. Route march - Checks conduit of pannier. Initial. Commences packing of transport, G.S. limbers, waggons. A.D.m.S. visits Ambulance. Orders to prepare to move on 21/7 to new area map 27. E Central. PROVEN Area. Pt. Captain R. EVANS & 6 Other Ranks proceeds as advance party, to new area.	S.R.
	20.7.17		Continues packing waggons. Captain P. BENNETT RAMC assumes/temporary medical charge of 7 Somerset Light Infantry. Captain A. CHANDLER RAMC proceeded on leave. Lieut P. CONNOLLY RAMC and 2 Other Ranks Joined Ambulance - march out from LE MEILLARD at 9. am 21.7.17. to entrain at DOULENS north. to arrive there at 12 noon. Commence entraining train due to leave at 15.19. pm.	S.R.
	21.7.17		Batteries at DOULENS north at 1 pm. Train No 22 left at 15.20 pm. MOTOR Ambulance proceeds by Road. ST. POL. LILLERS. HAZEBROUCK. STEENVOORDE. PROVEN. then arrives at 3.30 am. personnel and transport arrives at P.4. AREA. PROVEN. E.12 Central map 27.C at 6. am.	S.R.
PROVEN AREA HANDEKOT	22.7.17		62 Field Ambulance occupies camp at HANDEKOT. E.4. N.4.9. Sector. Inspection of Box Respirators. Checks Equipment. Commences taking in sick & butchery Regiment.	S.R.
	24.7.17		LIEUT EMERSON RAMC - proceeds to XIV Corps Reinforcement Depot for temporary duty.	S.R.
	26.7.19		Orders from A.D.M.S. 20 Division to send Ted Division to MOYSON FARM to form Collecting Post. Arrangement to meet by 8 Buses 114 Corps Reserve Division to relieve with 61 Infantry Brigade also its Transport.	S.R.

WAR DIARY or INTELLIGENCE SUMMARY

Army Form C. 2118.

33 6 Field Ambulance

Place	Date	Hour	Summary of Events and Information	Remarks and references to Appendices
HANDEKOT	26-7-17		Captain BENNETT Returns from temporary duty with 7 Som Lt Infantry. Reported to DDMS XIV Corps at Corps HQ. W.C.P. include most out-of-the ordinary equipment and had conference with C.R.A. MOSTON FARM. Arrange for taking party from Beaver Division to clean up and prepare Posts and huts for accommodation of wounded & sick.	R.R.
	30-7-17		Orders to move up and complete arrangements for Corps. W. C. Post. Tent Division turned off at 6pm for Officer for duty. Beaver and Ten Officer & Servants with 60 infantry Begins. Heavy Barrage commences at 3.50 am 31-7-17. Buses for emergency wounded to C.C.S. at MENINGHEM (PROVEN) arrive at 6 a.m. First wounded arrive at 5.45 am. Slight Cases.	R.R.
	31/7/17		Wounded continues to arrive in large numbers walking and by Lorries between 6 am and 10 am. Arrangements for treating wounded satisfactory. 200 wounded evacuated by 3 pm. Shell which 2010 were evacuated by hand and 20 am tons sergeants train in truck. Slight shelling of FARM and in Pill Box. Slightly shaken by shell striking dugout in which they were working. 1000 wounded passed through Corps W. Wounded Collecting Post by 4pm. Evacuation proceeding satisfactorily. A. Tom. Guard Division Relief 38 Division and takes 20th Division under MOSTON FARM.	R.R.

S.A.H. Brown Lt Col
RAMC

B.E.F.

SUMMARY OF MEDICAL WAR DIARIES FOR

62nd F.A., 20th Divn. 14th Corps, 5th Army.
from 21.7.17.

WESTERN FRONT, July-Sept. 1917.

O.C. Lt. Col. E.F. L'Estrange.

SUMMARISED UNDER THE FOLLOWING HEADINGS.

Phase "D" 1. Passchendaele Operations July- Nov. 1917.

(a) Operations commencing 1st July 1917.

B.E.F.

62nd F.A., 20th Divn. 14th Corps, 5th Army. WESTERN FRONT.
O.C. Lt. Col. E.F. L'Estrange.   July-Aug. '1

Phase "D" 1. Passchendaele Operations July- Nov. 1917.
(a) Operations commencing July 1st 1917.

1917.	Headquarters. At E.5.a.4.9.(27)
July 21st.	Moves and Transfer. Unit transferred with 20th Divn. from 4th Corps, 4th Army to 14th Corps, 5th Army and arrived at E.5.a.4.9. (27).
26th.	Medical Arrangements: Tent Divn. took over C.W.W. Coll Post at Mouton Farm B.14.a.2.9. (28.)
31st.	Operations: Offensive commenced at 3.50 a.m. Casualties: Evacuation: First wounded arrived 5.45 a.m. and continued to arrive in large numbers by lorries and walking. 900 wounded evacuated by 3. p.m., 200 by special train in trucks to C.C.S. Mendinghem. Remainder by buses. 1000 wounded passed through by 4 p.m.

B.E.F.   1.

62nd F.A., 20th Divn. 14th Corps, 5th Army. WESTERN FRONT.
O.C. Lt. Col. E.F. L'Estrange.   July-Aug. '17

Phase "D" 1. Passchendaele Operations July- Nov. 1917.
(a) Operations commencing July 1st 1917.

1917.   Headquarters. At E.5.a.4.9.(27)

July 21st.   Moves and Transfer. Unit transferred with 20th Divn.
                from 4th Corps, 4th Army to 14th Corps, 5th Army and
                arrived at E.5.a.4.9. (27).

26th.   Medical Arrangements: Tent Divn. took over C.W.W. Coll
                Post at Mouton Farm B.14.a.2.9. (28.)

31st.   Operations: Offensive commenced at 3.50 a.m.
                Casualties: Evacuation: First wounded arrived 5.45 a.m.
                and continued to arrive in large numbers by lorries
                and walking 900 wounded evacuated by 3. p.m., 200 by
                special train in trucks to C.C.S. Mendinghem. Remainder
                by buses. 1000 wounded passed through by 4 p.m.

B.E.F.

SUMMARY OF MEDICAL WAR DIARIES FOR

62nd F.A., 20th Divn. 14th Corps, 5th Army.

from 21.7.17.

WESTERN FRONT, July-Sept. 1917.

O.C. Lt. Col. E.F. L'Estrange.

SUMMARISED UNDER THE FOLLOWING HEADINGS.

Phase "D" 1. Passchendaele Operations July- Nov. 1917.

(a) Operations commencing 1st July 1917.

Aug. 1st.	Evacuation: Casualties:	Wounded continued to arrive by lorries, also large number of sick, many of the latter had no tally or sick report. 18 and 628 passed through by 4 p.m.
3rd.	Operations Enemy.	Shelling of batteries west of Mouton Farm. Some gas shells fell 200 yards N.
4th.	Operations Enemy.	1 outhouse demolished by direct hit.
5th.	" "	Mouton Farm bombed. O and 2 R.A.M.C. wounded.
8th.	Operations Enemy.	Elverdinghe shelled at intervals during the day.

B.E.F.

62nd F.A., 20th Divn. 14th Corps, 5th Army.   WESTERN FRON
O.C. Lt. Col. E.F. L'Estrange.   Aug. Sept.

Phase "D" 1(a) (Cont.)

1917.

Aug. 10th.	<u>Operations Enemy.</u> Heavy bombing of area.
15th.	<u>Operations.</u> Heavy bombardment commenced at 2 a.m.
16th.	<u>Casualties: Evacuation:</u> First wounded arrived about 6.3 Evacuation proceeding smoothly. 18 and 841 passed through by 6 p.m. Germans 6 and 57.
17th.	<u>Medical Arrangements:</u> Bearer and other personnel in front line return to original units.
18th.	<u>Moves Detachment:</u> 2 and 98 to Proven.
20th-23rd.	<u>Operations Enemy.</u> Considerable air activity.
24th.	<u>Moves:</u> To Panama Camp E.18.6.2.8. (27)
27th.	<u>Operations: Evacuation:</u> No details. Evacuation delayed by enemy barrage and machine gun fire.
28th.	<u>Medical Arrangements:</u> Wounded commenced to arrive about 6.30 a.m. all wet through, thoroughly exhausted and covered with mud. Evacuation completed smoothly.
30th.	<u>Decorations.</u> Pte. Carter R.A.M.C. awarded M.M.
31st.	<u>Operations Enemy.</u> Vicinity of Mouton Farm shelled.

Aug. 1st.	Evacuation: Casualties:	Wounded continued to arrive by lorries, also large number of sick, many of the latter had no tally or sick report. 18 and 628 passed through by 4 p.m.
3rd.	Operations Enemy.	Shelling of batteries west of Mouton Farm. Some gas shells fell 200 yards N.
4th.	Operations Enemy.	1 outhouse demolished by direct hit.
5th.	" "	Mouton Farm bombed. O and 2 R.A.M.C. wounded.
8th.	Operations Enemy.	Elverdinghe shelled at intervals during the day.

B.E.F.

62nd F.A., 20th Divn. 14th Corps, 5th Army.   WESTERN FRON[T]
O.C. Lt. Col. E.F. L'Estrange.   Aug. Sept. '[17]

Phase "D"1(a) (Cont.)

1917.
Aug. 10th.   Operations Enemy. Heavy bombing of area.
15th.   Operations. Heavy bombardment commenced at 2 a.m.
16th.   Casualties: Evacuation: First wounded arrived about 6.3[0 a.m.] Evacuation proceeding smoothly. 18 and 841 passed through by 6 p.m. Germans 6 and 57.
17th.   Medical Arrangements: Bearer and other personnel in front line return to original units.
18th.   Moves Detachment: 2 and 98 to Proven.
20th-23rd.   Operations Enemy. Considerable air activity.
24th.   Moves: To Panama Camp E.18.6.2.8. (27)
27th.   Operations: Evacuation: No details. Evacuation delayed by enemy barrage and machine gun fire.
28th.   Medical Arrangements: Wounded commenced to arrive about 6.30 a.m. all wet through, thoroughly exhausted and covered with mud Evacuation completed smoothly.
30th.   Decorations. Pte. Carter R.A.M.C. awarded M.M.
31st.   Operations Enemy. Vicinity of Mouton Farm shelled.

Army Form C. 2118.

WAR DIARY
or
INTELLIGENCE SUMMARY.

(Erase heading not required.)

Vol 24

Confidential

War Diary

of

62nd Field Ambulance R.A.M.C.

From 1st August 1917   To 31st August 1917

No. 62. 7.a.

COMMITTEE FOR THE
MEDICAL HISTORY OF THE WAR
Date -1 OCT. 1917

Army Form C. 2118.

WAR DIARY
or
INTELLIGENCE SUMMARY.

34   62 Field Ambulance

(Erase heading not required.)

Place	Date	Hour	Summary of Events and Information	Remarks and references to Appendices
MOOTON FARM B.14.a 3.8 SHEET 28 N.W. ELVERDINGHE	1st August 1917		Walking wounded continue to arrive by lorries. Large number of sick arrived between 6 a.m. and 6 p.m. Many of these sick had no tally or sick report, mostly from MORD a&b FARM. 38th Division walking wounded collecting post. The arrangements for clerical work of quick intake and rechecking of wounded works satisfactorily. Two days work being one. Reception and Evacuation. Received at Ambulance Camp, all particulars taken by clerks in A.M. Cars also received AF W3200. Serial Slip. Cases on A.M. Card to hint Serial Slip. Cases on the orderly officer for orderly officer if wounded. All patients (except through Reception hut) Clerical duties carried out by admin and recept through to Clerks working and A&D Books for Divisions. Evacuations that were made by factory, wounded where tea lemonade, bread butter jam and Palms were served —
Captain G.M. ADAM RAMC transferred to XIV Corps Rest Station at WORMHOUDT. On 31.7.17. Two trains of which holding 200 wounded each was for Evacuation Total passed through XIV Corps W.W.C.R. from 4 p.m. - 3 p.m. 18 Officers 826 other ranks. All sick sent to walk sent to sick collecting Post, went CANADA FARM. D.M.S. VIII ARMY visited.
Post. D.D.s in 20th and 38th Division visited, also Staff officer of Farm.	348
	2.8.17		D. Dir. XIV Corps visited MOOTOY FARM. Issued instructions to close down by 12 noon, all A&D Books to be completed. Divisional clerks to report sick wounded, field ambulances, Lorries to ascertain collected BLEUET FARM and MORD a&b FARM. Walking wounded from Further area not accessible between WHITE HOPE No 4. M.A.C. to Collect. MORD a&b FARM party cut up. CORNER and MORD a&b FARM party cut up.	B.14.03.8 Sheet 28 N.W. Sheet 28 N.W.

Army Form C. 2118.

35 / 62 Field Ambulance

WAR DIARY
or
INTELLIGENCE SUMMARY.
(Erase heading not required.)

Place	Date	Hour	Summary of Events and Information	Remarks and references to Appendices
MOUTON FARM. ELVERDINGHE	3.8.17		Slight shelling of PENELOPE West of MOUTON FARM by enemy between 12 midnight and 4 am. A few gas shells fell about 200 yards west of FARM. ELVERDINGHE heavily shelled at 2 am. A few sick & wounded from unit to hospital. Orders from A/DMS 20th DIVISION to send Bearer Divisn up to Field Amb^ce to report to D.C. 61 Field Amb^ce by 5 pm in approach park. Proceeded with 2 NCO's and 20 men to report at CANADA FARM 5 pm. Heavy wind - remainder of MOUTON FARM 100 yards N of A.D.S. by 4.2 H.V. gun. One ruined demolished by a direct hit. Heavy rain. Shelled by 4.2 H.V. gun.	S.R.
	4.8.17		2 Officers and 80 O.R. Bearer Division to hosp (detached in Rear) open to C. Bearer Divisn at PELISIER FARM B.2 a 3.0. Shelled 5 a.m. and 28 N.W. A.D. and 20th E. Officers to report at SUSSEX A.D.S. B/19. C.2.4. Shell 28 NW. A.D. and 20th Division visit MOUTON FARM. Forwarded a report to D.D.M.S XIV Corps at work done at XIV Corps walking wounded. Collecting road. From ZERO to 2nd August 1917. Cyclist to BENNET and LIEUT R. CONNOLLY. Read & Report with Bearer Divisn 62 Field Ambulance. MOUTON FARM shelled by 4.2 H.V. guns. Shells dropped about 150 yards to north. Heavy rain.	S.R.
	5.8.17		Aeros 20 D Division visited 62 Field Ambulance at MOUTON FARM B.14.a.2.8. Shell 28 NW. Warmer cleaning. Thick haze in the morning. 3 B.H.B. Shelled 28 NW to ..... put at COPPER MOLLE CABARET. FARM B.14.a.26 Shells few that Krupp 9 o'clock Matting at 1 pm 3 Bombs dropped in yard. Sgt MAIRE Rayne 340517 Pie HALL WM Raine wounded. 5 shells in the vicinity of MOUTON FARM	S.R.
	6.8.17		A few shells fell in the vicinity of MOUTON FARM. 4 sent to Field Ambulance damaged. 2 hours instruction Pte L KEEBLE 120 Bedorm Battalion large Game (totally) sent to CMDS in advance with volunteer from ADMS 20 DIVISION	S.R.

Army Form C. 2118.

WAR DIARY
or
INTELLIGENCE SUMMARY.

(Erase heading not required.)

36
62 Field Ambulance

Place	Date	Hour	Summary of Events and Information	Remarks and references to Appendices
MOOTON FARM. B.14.a.2.8 Sheet 28 N.W.	7.8.16.		A.D.M.S. 20th Division visited MOOTON FARM (62 Field Ambulance). Repairing huts. Walking Indian mailed A.D.S. SUSSEX FARM. Weather fine. No. 47691 Pte JSON: Ramc wounded gun shot evacuated to C.M.D.S. from A.D.S. SUSSEX FARM. E.19.c.2.4 Sheet 28 N.W.	S.2
	8.8.16.		Four other ranks RAMC also proceed on leave pivos. 9-8-16. 1-19-8-16 midday. A.D.M.S. 20th Division visited this heavy bombardment last night 10 pm. ELVERDINGHE Shelled at intervals during the day. Captain T.E. ROBERTS. RAMC posted for temporary duty as M.O/C 11th D.L.I. without A.D.M.S. 20th Division.	S/1
	9.8.17		Heavy showers during the night a few shells fell in vicinity of MOOTON FARM. Lieut. B.G. CONNOLLY joined us as M.O/C. J. KOYLI. (temporary). Pte. McILROY Ramc evacuated to C.M.D. S. XIV Corps. Ky.D.N. M/205134 Qd. McLOCKIE T. Ame MT. rejoined unit from C.C.S. DOULENS.	S.9
	10.8.17		D.D.M.S. XIV Corps visited Corps Walking wounded Collecting Post at MOOTON FARM. (B.14.a.2.8 Sheet 28 N.W.) arranged about running of Runs to Divisions Walking Wounded Collecting posts also evacuated by this H.C.S. Captain J. ADAM. RAMC rejoined 62 Field Ambulance from XV Corps Rest Station WORMHOUDT discharged from Hospital on the 10.8.17. MOOTON FARM to be relieved as Corps W.W. C.P. Shelling in vicinity of farm. Heavy bombing Raid between 11pm and 2am. Enemy aeroplane appeared to drop large numbers of heavy bombs in the direction of POPERINGHE and HAZEBROUCK. 2 Horse Ambulances 8 heavy draught horses, one G.S. limber waggon, 6 a.e. ORs and 2 Ramc ORs also left for 1 Beaver Division. Report to O.C. Beaver Division. POLISSIER. (Camp - B.21.a.3.1 Sheet 28 N.W.)	Ch.9

WAR DIARY
or
INTELLIGENCE SUMMARY.

Army Form C. 2118.

37. 62 Field Ambulance.

Place	Date	Hour	Summary of Events and Information	Remarks and references to Appendices
MOUTON FARM B.14.c.2.8 Sheet 28 N.W.	11.8.17		Showers during the night, cloudy & cool. One Wolseley Ambulance reported for duty from the Divisional Supply Column - repairs completed. Captain G. ADAM R.A.M.C. on Baltnear and 6 O.Rs. RAMC Bearer Division to 10th Bearer Camp. B.21.a.3.0.1 Sheet 28 N.W.	S/69
	12.8.17		Sean how during the night. 2 other Ranks reported from leave and and to B1 Field Ambulance for duty with Bearer Division. CAPTAIN ROBERTS Ram returns from Pretrial Leave. 1st Lieutenant KAME R.A.M.C. Mustard Reserve Corps U.S.A. reported for duty in accordance with ADMS 26th Division instructions. Raining during the night. Slight shelling in vicinity of MOUTON FARM. 3 O.R's reinforcements Rame reported product. Horse Ambulance Waggon Sent to Bearer Camp at PELISSIER FARM. B.21.A.3.1 Sheet/28	P.28.
	13.8.17		Showers. 6 men for Reserves, 4 horses and one personnel 200 B.U.okey km acted as O.C. Bearer Division. Operation Date from A.D.M.S. XIV Corps. XIV Corps walking wounded Collecting Post to remain at MOUTON FARM. Received order via A.D.M.S. for collection and evacuation of wounded. 15 Persons allotted to him to un-and fill the ground circuit via he was from MOUTON FARM just ELVERDINGHE -- WHITE HOPE CORNER -- F 15 d 6.5 & me (where Col. was pick up walking wounded from LEFT DIVISION) via WAALKRANTZ FARM (where they will but up walking wounded from RIGHT DIVISION) via MAP Sheetkey B.12.d.34) -- CHEARSIDE -- DAWSONS CORNER 11 Strength Septhya post to ELVERDINGHE -- ELVERDINGHE to MOUTON FARM the Rear hand vacuation line be from MOUTON FARM to the C.C.S's attending Em-following the Motor Ambulance Route via DROMORE CORNER of WIPRE CABARET etc. An officer of the Field Van belong men near the Corner W. and R. will Carried He touch at the 7th Attacks so that his Angestra 5th DIVISIONAL	P.28

Army Form C. 2118.

WAR DIARY
or
INTELLIGENCE SUMMARY.
(Erase heading not required.)

38 62 Field Ambulance

Place	Date	Hour	Summary of Events and Information	Remarks and references to Appendices
ELVERDINGHE MOUTON FARM.	14-8-17		Weather fine -: Completed fresh intake of evacuation huts. Re-arranged seating accommodation in Reception tent. Arrived roadway into MOUTON FARM. A.D.M.S. 20th DIVISION visited XIV Corps. W.W.C.P. Bell on Railway after MOUTON FARM attack by Pierce aeroplane about 3.30 pm, slight damage on planes. No persons escaped by rail chutes. Hospital in tents were arranged.	S.A.
	15-8-17		Heavy rain during the night. Copy of Section III (C) practical arrangements XIV Corps M.O. duties M 7/4 of the 6 duties from Ground 29th and 35th Divisions to report to the C.O. Field Ambulances MOUTON FARM 6.30 pm on 15th instant for duty at Corps walking wounded Collecting Post. The party from 29th Division will keep the A.D.M.S. of that Division fully Indirects fully trained touching Corps. From 35th Division will keep those "D" Formations and Corps Troops" respectively. Corps Troops will be included in the daily state and Corps Wing of 3rd Division, and Other Formations in those of Guards Division. Purple from 20 of 2nd Division Order No 254. A.Form NoS287 received 6 other vehicles Sick at XIV Corps W.W.C.P. from 29th, 36th and Guards Division. Heavy shelling in vicinity of ELVERDINGHE and MOUTON FARM. Station ELVERDINGHE and camp in vicinity of ELVERDINGHE Chateau-Railway. Heavy Bombardment commenced at 2 am. Continuous shelling by the enemy.	P.S.
	16-8-17		Braces for walking wounded arrived at 5 am. At two 29th Division vehicles MOUTON FARM first wounded arrived at 6.30 am. Tea has been arranged before the attack commenced. Lorries arrived back from Durrant WW Cap at 7.30 am Lin Lorries for hackney Plant. CCS MENDINGHEN did not arrive until 8.30 am. Evacuation proceeding satisfactorily to Cars waiting for loading at 9 am. Lorries has not returned from Cars to Lorries took 20 wounded in each dispatched between 7.15 and 9.30 am. Ambulance have received text from Divisional 5th Army neutral XIV Corps 16 to C.P. MOUTON FARM B 14 a 3.9 Sheet 28 N.W. DMS A.D.M.S. 29th DIVISION HQ Continued-	E.K.L.

WAR DIARY or INTELLIGENCE SUMMARY

Army Form C. 2118.

39 1/62 Field Ambulance

Place	Date	Hour	Summary of Events and Information	Remarks and references to Appendices
MOUTON FARM. ELVERDINGHE B.14.Q.3.8. Sh.28 N.W.	16.8.17	continued	Wounds arriving in large numbers. Ambulance cars, motor & supply lorries - Cars taken by lorries working forward circuit to Divisional W.W.C.Pôs at BOESINGHE and CHEAPSIDE - the hour and a half - Roads in fair condition. Some congestion of traffic on return journey. Relieved DAWS[?] & RIVER and ELVERDINGHE-ZR - walking wounded awaiting evacuation at 11 a.m. Lorries not available. Train loads[?] at 11.5 a.m. Train arrived at ELVERDINGHE at 11.20. 190 walking wounded entrained. Train departed at 11.35 a.m. - loaded to CCS MENDINGHEM number of walking wounded in train - 11 Officers 457 Other Ranks, 4 Other Germans and 140 R's. Genera runs through XIV Corps Walking Wounded Collecting Post up to 12 noon. Total passed through from 6 a.m. 16-8-17 to 6. a.m. 17.8.17 16 Officers British total 822 - 541 Other Ranks British. 6 German Officers and 57 Other Ranks prisoners.	Sh.1 Sh.2
	17.8.17		Vicinity of MOUTON FARM heavily shelled between 11 p.m. and 12 midnight - H.V. gun. Lorry returning empty from 20th Divisional W.W.C.P. at CHEAPSIDE (B.17.b.9.2 Sh.28 N.W.) reports no cases remaining at 6 o'clock. Driver ordered to return to XIV Corps W.W.C.P. MOOTON FARM. D.D.M.S. XIV Corps issued instructions at 8 p.m. that Lorries not to be used in forward area. Ambulance cars of 20th and 29th Divisions to evacuate walking wounded from Divisional W.W.C.Pôs. 10 Bombs returning to Corps troops supply column reporting to 8th Siege XIV Corps en route. Full lorries retained at MOOTON FARM and sent in to CCS MENDINGHEM - D's M.S. XIV Corps to arrange system to be closed - XIV Corps W.W.C.P. to be closed at 5 p.m. the remaining lorries to return to XIV Corps Troops Supply Column. A new 20th Div Siege ordered to return to MOUTON FARM. Issued instructions for all Bearer Division and transport bretren to P's Camp Area on 19th inst, only one Car and 3rd Division to remain at Camps 5 PROVEN AREA. 100 heaven to remain at ELVERDINGHE at 1.30 p.m. on 19th inst	Sh.9

WAR DIARY
INTELLIGENCE SUMMARY

Army Form C. 2118.

40 62 Field Ambulance

Place	Date	Hour	Summary of Events and Information	Remarks and references to Appendices
ELVERDINGHE MOTON FARM B14 a 2.5 Sheet 28 NW	18.8.17		Report of work done at XIV Corps W.W.C.P. during 16.8.17 sent in. 8.11 Four dies 15 O.R. and XIV Corps. Captain H. EVANS RAMC. LIEUT. BRUNSKI, KERSTOLE RAMC mentioned for good work also LT. W.O. S. PHILSON RAMC. During aeroplane dropped bombs near huts in ELVERDINGHE WOOD, bomb fell in direction of POPERINGHE, aeroplane continued and dropped two trip om Captain P. BENNETT RAMC and Captain ADAM Reginld 62 Field Ambulance from Reserve Division. A this 20 Division visited MOOTON FARM. Captain PRIDHAM RAMC to be in charge of Bearer Division and Establishing	BhI
	19.8.17		Captain P. BENNETT RAMC, Captain ADAM RAMC and LT. Col. PACK RAMC relieved by LT. COL. FREDING MC at 1.30 pm in PROVEN. Captain T. ROBERTS from ASD to PROVEN, from COPPERNOLLE with transport to 62 Field Ambulance. CAPTAIN PRIDHAM with 23 other ranks proceeded by bus to Area P.S. PROVEN.	B9
	20.8.17		Enemy aeroplane came over 1/2 mile South MOOTON FARM at 9.85 pm and in direction of POPERINGHE and PROVEN. Actual ant out dropped by Bush aircraft fire and brightend fires at 9.30 pm. Large volumes of smoke dispped in direction of POPERINGHE. Aeroplanes believed aeroplane passed our Railway line 400 yards East of MOOTON FARM. General Burial in group in natures line which was 3m up to the down. McKinnell and McKANE U.S. M.E.R.C. or LR.O. or from 24 Field Ambulance. 8 DIVISION Authority R.R.S. 14th Army No. P.721.299 DTD 16.8.17 LIEUT KAYS left for A. Full "KW" Corps at 16.30 am Captain "R WALLACE T.O. MC Church Parade, daily to 62 Field Ambulance Captain R ROBERTS arrived artillary 0400 on 0/15 7 ROYL. R (Inf Party) Captain R WALLACE R.T.O. Infantry Commanding proceeding in post 192 "A" Bigade RFA in place of Captain A MILLIGAN RAMC proceeding in leave of	B9

Army Form C. 2118.

WAR DIARY
or
INTELLIGENCE SUMMARY.   41. 62 Field Amb. in Base.

(Erase heading not required.)

Place	Date	Hour	Summary of Events and Information	Remarks and references to Appendices
ELVERDINGHE MOUTON FARM B.14.a.3.8. Sheet 28 NW.	21.8.17		Captain M.A. ZORKHAM A.S.R. reports for duty from 24th Field Ambulance. Enemy aeroplanes crossed South of MOUTON FARM, large number of Bombs dropped at ELVERDINGHE. Inspection of 61st Brigade with 62 Field Ambulance by Commander in Chief. Transport not to parade - Parade cancelled authority A.D.M.S. 20th Division. Men Carrallia were dining at XIV Corps walking wounded Collecting Post. The usually	R.I.
	22.8.17		Enemy dropped by Enemy aeroplane between DAWSON CORNER and ELVERDINGHE (ELVERDINGHE). Heavy firing commenced at 4:30 a.m. B.22.c.8.b suggested South of ELVERDINGHE continued between 4:35 a.m. to 6 a.m. Inspection of Base hospitals performed there and arc. follows by half an hour. Shelling of Battalions during the night. a few shells fell close to road, 100 yards just	R.I.
	23.8.17		MOUTON FARM. Enemy aeroplanes flew over MOUTON FARM at 9.30 p.m. Two bombs dropped near FARM. Forwarded A.F.3124 in duplicate Pte 37445 L/Cpl. Rollo Reinr. 323 & Pte G. CARTER Reinr. and 39457 Pte. W. OWERS Reinr. reconnaissance for Returns in connection with working during advance at LANGEMARCK - on 16/17 August 1917. Sick 4 1/2 Heavy Artillery Group to allow at MOUTON FARM, also List of Employment in Labour Companies South African Railway Construction Company, 19 WELSH REGIMENT Support Battalion. 62 Field Ambulance moves to P's AREA. (PROVEN). Two Medical Officers remaining at MOUTON FARM.	CW.E
PANAMA CAMP. E.16.b.2.8. Sheet 27 PROVEN AREA.	24.8.17		Heavy rain during the night. Inspection of Road Range & Ride. Inspection of G.S. Wagons. Stretcher bearers of Battalions 61st Infantry Brigade. Re-parking of lorries. 1st 32 Fd Battalion arrived with 61st infantry Brigade. August Report - 9.6.12 am Until - Visits MOUTON FARM, arranged to open up XIV Corps W.W.C.P. on 25th - Buses & killed walking wounded from Divisional walking W.CP. at CHEAPSIDE - walking wounded to be despatched in buses to CCS. MENDINGHEM.	Pat

Army Form C. 2118.

WAR DIARY
or
INTELLIGENCE SUMMARY.

42
62 Field Ambulance

(Erase heading not required.)

Place	Date	Hour	Summary of Events and Information	Remarks and references to Appendices
PAPAMA CAMP. E18 b 2.8. Sht 27 PROVEN AREA	25-8-17		CAPTAIN PRIDHAM RAW- to proceed to MOUTON FARM, with remaining personnel of 1 T. Det) DIVISION. XIV Corps walking wounded Collecting Post the pieces ready for wounded by 8 am 26-8-17. Road March Heavy. Division Sent extra Ambulance wagon received to replace Ambulance bus for evacuation of the Fast.	S.P.E.
	26.8.17		Two Motor Bicycles connected 10th Buse (French workers) - O.C. O.I.C. turned to 13 Ace for Replacement - Shelters Reaver of 13 Bulance from Brigade undergoing instruction in Stretcher Drill and 1st Aid - Checked Equipment learned vertical.	
	27.8.17		All preparations complete at MOUTON FARM. B.H.Q. 28 Shee 28 NW. Held Horses to the notified by 2 D.M.S. XIV Corps. 8 Lorries reported for duty at 6. a.m. Instructed N.C.O. S. Lorries as to Road lines Stopping places for each Lorry & working to includes from DIVISIONAL Walking Wounded Collecting Post of XIV Corps W.W.C.P Road in L-d Candidar Lories not to go through BOESINGHE take Mizon to & bitter beyond (WHITE HOPE CORNER) to DIVISIONAL W.W.C.P. near CHEAPSIDE- 1317 B32 Sheet call at DIVISIONAL at 9.30 p.m. (J.B.) Messenger from DIVISIONAL W.W.C.P. reported that first Wounds arrived at 9.30 p.m. (J.B.) O.C. DIVISIONAL W.W.C.P. Placed any wounded men able to sit down owing to heavy Enemy Barrage. that The Wounded had not been in lorry at daylight returned he did not expect large num bers, until daylight returned CHEAPSIDE for emergencies no further wounded arrived until 6.30 am.	25.10.0000 PR49
	28.8.17		Wounded commenced to arrive at 6.30 am- between 6.30 am. and 9 am. Lorries arrived at intervals of 2 hours, wounded not thoroughly and Pakauste . Thickly coated with mud, when taken in Shell Holes they were unable to get to A.D.S emptied ground hamager and Machine gun fire. To Officers and 63 other Ranks passed Through XIV corps W.W.C.P. by 1.30 pm. N.O. W. C. P. reported all patients clear at 9 pm. XIV Corps W.C.P. closed at 10 pm. A.D Battles Cleaves Evacuated Chats Returned to Units	S.R.E.

Army Form C. 2118.

WAR DIARY
or
INTELLIGENCE SUMMARY.
(Erase heading not required.)

62 Field Ambulance   43

Place	Date	Hour	Summary of Events and Information	Remarks and references to Appendices
PANAMA CAMP. D/E18 b 2.8. PROVEN AREA	29.8.17		Lorries working at XIV Corps w. to C.P. returned to unit - 10 Bearers and surplus men of 2nd Field Division 62 Field Ambulance reported at quarters from MOUTON FARM. B.14.a.2.5. Proven NW. Training of personnel of Shelter Bearers continued. Bearers & Field Ambulance clearing roads and making a path through camp - heavy showers at intervals, horse lines in a very bad state - many to heavy rain. Subsequent. The Area OPPOSITE AND ABOUT PROVEN AREA was shelled for some hours & casualties MOUTON FARM issued material during the night - no cas. 62 Fd.	S.1.?
	30.8.17		Rain at intervals during the day. Vicinity of MOUTON FARM shelled between 6 am and 10 am. Several crated to Bengal - to XIII Class C.P. for treatment. Two killed. Route moved to bearer Division. Was fully occupied clearing roads and vicinity of camp. Regained - Fd. sickness bearers continuing duty and during hrs. 18 and - NO.7293, Pte. 9. CARTER. Enrol. Eng no 39/47, Pte. W. OWERS granted leave privilege metal by XIV Corps Commands for leave observation fewest duty Reserved 4/6-8/9. — TO Corps No 28/14/68/22-8-17.	S.R.?
	31.8.17		Afternoon light rain during the night. Inspection of Transport and personnel and H.T. & Fd Ambulance - Continued Shelter Build. For repairs of bearers - Inspection of Cattle A.B.C. Pictures vicinity of MOUTON FARM Shells between 11 am and 1.30 pm. Sketch map of XIV Corps working to have Collecting Post attached.	S.R.?

P.T.L Crossing Lieut Col Comm

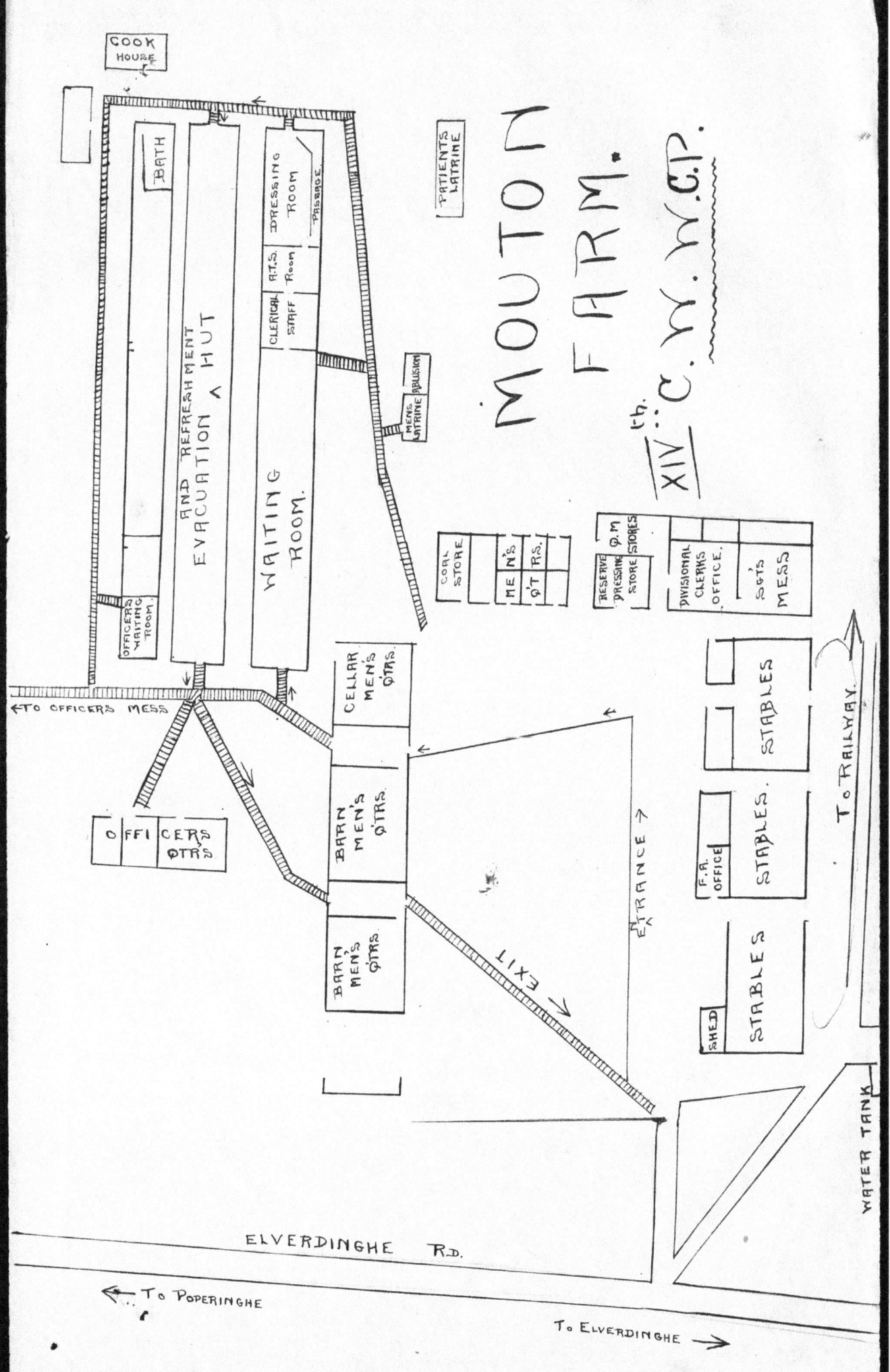

14/24/38

COMMITTEE FOR THE
MEDICAL HISTORY OF THE WAR
Date -5 NOV. 1917

No. 62. 7. a.

Sept. 1st.	<u>Decorations.</u>	Sgt. Rolls R.A.M.C. awarded M.M.
3rd.	<u>Operations Enemy.</u>	Aeroplanes dropped bombs in Proven area.
8th.	<u>Decorations:</u>	Capt. G. Adam awarded M.C.
9th.	<u>Moves:</u>	To 19/x 30.c. central.

62nd F.A., 20th Divn. 14th Corps, 5th Army. WESTERN FRONT
O.C. Lt. Col. E.F. L'Estrange. Sept. 1917.

Phase "D" 1. (a) (Cont.)

1917.

Sept. 9th. (Cont.)
Moves Detachment: O and 91 to 60th Field Ambulance for duty at Pelissier Farm.

Operations Enemy. Heavy shelling at Mouton Farm, portion receiving hut damaged by direct hit. No casualties.

12th. Operations Enemy. Mouton Farm bombed.

18th. Moves: To " " 28/ B.14.a.2.8.

20th. Operations: No details.

Evacuation: Casualties: Wounded commenced to arrive 7.30 a.m. 3 and 114 passed through up to 5 p.m.

21st. Evacuation: Casualties: Wounded still arriving. O and 52 passed through at 5 p.m.

Operations Enemy. Elverdinghe bombed. O and 3 killed O and 10 wounded.

28th. Moves: To Panama Camp E.18.6.2.8. (28).

Sept. 1st.	<u>Decorations.</u>	Sgt. Rolls R.A.M.C. awarded M.M.
3rd.	<u>Operations Enemy.</u>	Aeroplanes dropped bombs in Proven area.
6th.	<u>Decorations:</u>	Capt. G. Adam awarded M.C.
9th.	<u>Moves:</u>	To 19/x 30.c. central.

62nd F.A., 20th Divn. 14th Corps, 5th Army.   WESTERN FRONT
O.C. Lt. Col. E.F. L'Estrange.   Sept. 1917.

Phase "D" 1. (a) (Cont.)

1917.

Sept. 9th. (Cont.)
Moves Detachment: O and 91 to 60th Field Ambulance for duty at Pelissier Farm.

Operations Enemy. Heavy shelling at Mouton Farm, portion receiving hut damaged by direct hit. No casualties.

12th. Operations Enemy. Mouton Farm bombed.

18th. Moves: To   "   "   28/ B.14.a.2.8.

20th. Operations: No. details.

Evacuation: Casualties: Wounded commenced to arrive 7.30 a.m. 3 and 114 passed through up to 5 p.m.

21st. Evacuation: Casualties: Wounded still arriving. O and 52 passed through at 5 p.m.

Operations Enemy. Elverdinghe bombed. O and 3 killed O and 10 wounded.

28th. Moves: To Panama Camp E.18.6.2.8. (28).

Army Form C. 2118

WAR DIARY
or
INTELLIGENCE SUMMARY
(Erase heading not required.)

CONFIDENTIAL

WAR DIARY

OF

62ⁿᵈ Field Ambulance R.A.M.C.

FROM 1ˢᵗ September 1917 TO 30ᵗʰ September 1917.

Army Form C. 2118.

WAR DIARY
or
INTELLIGENCE SUMMARY.

(Erase heading not required.)

44
62 Field Amb'ul'ance

Place	Date	Hour	Summary of Events and Information	Remarks and references to Appendices
PARAMA CAMP E.18.c.2.8 Sheet 9	1st Sept		1917. Raining at intervals during the night. Strong breeze. Checks dispensed to Panama hutted and Surgical lines to field 200 yards West of Panama Camp. Area Commandant PROVEN AREA authorizes the new previous site. Ground cut up. ROUTE march for Stretcher Bearers. New hours put fut in to clear dump - 1st Lieut G. KINKEAD U.S.A. M.C. posts temporarily to medical charge 0-294 H.Q. in relief of Captain A. McKIM USA. Reserve, proceeding to Canada. D.O. 3794 Brigadier L. ROLLAND Grants the building hutted decoration of pavillions in the field by XVIII Corps Commander. Church Parade 9.30 am. Captain R.B. WALLACE DSO M.C. to relief by Captain H.J. MILLIGAN M.C. has been ordered to report to A.D.M.S. 2nd Division for leave to U.K. Captain T.E. S/Major S.C. PHILSON R.amc returns from leave. Duty J.K.OY L.D. Relieved by Captain R. CONNOLLY R.amc.	Ch.8
	2.9.17		ROBERTS, R.amc reports for duty, Joins J.K.OY L.D. R.amc.	R.9.
	3.9.17		Enemy aeroplanes dropped bombs in PROVEN AREA. between 10 pm and 2 am. No M.3/27=7 Cpl MASON G.F. A.S.C.(M.T.) Causalities to No 2 CANADIAN C.C.S. Dn. 2.9.17. Bvn Respirator Inspectors and DNW with 13 Respirators.	R.9.
	4.9.17		Route March for R.amc Personnel. Stretcher Bearers of Battalion 6yr. Bugler continuing Drill - Inspection of Equipment Surgical and medical.	Ch.9
	5.9.17		Captain ROBERTS S.I. R.amc returns from temporary duty with J.K.OY L.D. War S/le eyelets Trancepoch - 40 O.Rs P.B. reports for duty, Replace Battalion A.S.C. (M.T).	R.9.
	6.9.17		CAPTAIN ADAM Rame awards the military Cross. Authority delegated by HIS MAJESTY the KING, to the Cin C (Commander in Chief). No 34131 Pte Mc DONALD J.T. Rame was wounded on the 4.9.17. Returns to duty.	R.9.
	8.9.17		Captain R. WALLACE DSO M.C. Rame, Regains from 92nd Brigade RFA and proceeds to A.D.M.S 21st Division to report for duty.	R.9.

WAR DIARY
INTELLIGENCE SUMMARY

Army Form C. 2118.

Unit: 62 Field Ambulance
Page: 45

Place	Date	Hour	Summary of Events and Information	Remarks and references to Appendices
X 30 Central	9-9-17		Headquarters 62 Field Ambulance and transport moved to 19/X 30 C. Central. 83 Bearers O.R's. 5 A.C., H.T. rigs, 3 A.G.S. M.T. reported to O.C. 62 Field Ambulance for duty at PELISSIER FARM. Heavy thunderstorm during night, 2 Marl Auckland Wagons, 1 G.S. Wagons, and one water cart- Heavy shelling of MOUTON FARM. Portion of Receiving hut damaged by direct hit with S-7 H.V. shell. No casualties.	R.R.
XIV Corps 19-*Corps Sector Ambulance Centre*	10-9-17		Captain L.G. JACOB R.A.M.C. reported for duty in relief of Captain H. EVANS (Sr) RAMC. Captain P. BENNET. R.A.M.C. assumed temporary medical charge of 17 H.A.G. at PARROY FARM. B.16 d 2·7 Sheet 28 N.W.	R.T.
	11-9-17		Captain H. EVANS R.A.M.C. proceeded to H.Q. L. of C. to report to A.D.M.S. A.T. authority Genl. Ines. L.of C. No. M1/1457/17, dated 2-9-17. Captain L.G. JACOB R.A.M.C. detailed for duty, with Bearer Division 62 Field Ambulance at PELISSIER FARM. B.21 a 2·1 Sheet 28 N.W.	R.R.
	12-9-17		CAPTAIN P. BENNETT R.A.M.C. took over temporary medical charge of HAG. at PARROY FARM. Sheet 28 N.W. B.16 d 2·6 - Enemy aeroplanes dropped several bombs in vicinity of MOUTON FARM. B.14 a 2·8 Sheet 28 N.W. Several casualties in Camps. North of MOUTON FARM.	R.T.
			Commanded	
	14-9-17		Captain G. ADAM R.A.M.C. to proceed to England to report to in Reserve Training Bn. Dept BLACKPOOL for duty in INDIA & MESOPOTAMIA authority A.D.M.S. 20th DIVISION No N 534/17 dated 14-9-17. Lieut. A.N. ZINKHAN. U.S.R. reported for duty with 20th Division.	R.R.
	15-9-17		Lieut. A.N. ZINKHAN. U.S.R. proceeded to Bearer Camp for duty with Bearer Division - Building Shelters and dug-out at MOUTON FARM- Captain G. ADAM. M.C. R.A.M.C. left for ENGLAND - A Thus 20th Division reliefs.	R.R.
	16-9-17		also MOUTON FARM. Instructions from A.D.M.S. 20th Division to take over A.D. plans Collecting Post at CHEAPSIDE - B.17 d 9·0 Sheet No 62 field Ambulance to take over Divisional Walking Wounded Collecting Post 2 S.IX.W.	V.L.

WAR DIARY
or
INTELLIGENCE SUMMARY

Army Form C. 2118.

46 62 Field Ambulance

Place	Date	Hour	Summary of Events and Information	Remarks and references to Appendices
X30 E Central Sheet 19 E.S.D.6.	17.9.17		Under us instructions from A.D.M.S. 20th Division. H.Q. 62 Field Ambulance and transport till move to MOUTON FARM. XIV Corps. W.W.C.P. B14.a.2.8. Sheet 19 NW. 1st Lieut. A.M. ZINKHAN, U.S.M.R. required unit from Becca Camp -	Ch.8
MOUTON FARM XIV Corps W.W.C.P. 29/B14.a.2.8	18.9.17		Hdqs Bunches 62 Field Ambulance and the Field Detachment arrived at MOUTON FARM. at 10.30 am. the Field Detachment of 62 Field Ambulance left for Divisional Walking Wounded Collecting Post at CHEAPSIDE. 28/B13/A.15. Transport of 62 Field Ambulance at CANADA FARM. C.M.D.S. 28/A18.a.27. M.O.T/19.I.S.A. Acting Staff. Deputy Major G. ROSTRON RAMC HT provide to keep war diary duration of war. Signed Major B. Stuff (J. Paine) Major 2nd May 1917. authority a/c Section Ref SL72/180 dated 14.9.17	3X8
	19.9.17		CAPTAIN T. ROBERTS RAMC(T.C) Posted to 17 HQ in medical charge of active CAPTAIN R. BENNETT RAMC(SR). CAPTAIN P. BENNETT RAMC(SR) posted to Field Ambulance as Reserve Officer. 1st LIEUT H. GAUSS. U.S.M.R.E. joins 62 Field Ambulance for duty. Captain L.J. JACOB RAMC(T.C) rejoins 62 Field Ambulance from Benies Surrey on Field Ambulance A.D.H.S. 20th Division vacated 62 Field Ambulance	9C.9
	20.9.17		XIV Corps walking wounded Collecting Post opened - 10 Stores reported at MOUTEN FARM. to be used by Evacuation of Walking Wounded from advanced W.W.C.P. at CHEAPNIDE and Evacuation of Walking Wounded to arrival at 7.30 am. CC.Co.S. NE MENIN HEIGHT. (Journey commenced arrival 9.15 am. CAPTAIN T. ROBERTS RAMC(T.C) returns from CHEAPSIDE at 9.15 am. 1st Lieut A. ZINKHAN joins for duty at 62 Field Ambulance for duty. W Lieut XIV C.W.W.C.P. at MOUTON Divisional Walking Wounded Collecting Post CHEAPSIDE (28/B13/-) at 9.10 -3 Officers and 114 Other Ranks passed through XIV C.P. at MOUTON FARM between 6am and 5pm - Rev. D. Pain ELVERDINGHE - BOESINGHE Road to CHEAPSIDE - 1st half staff Spikan -	PhP

WAR DIARY
INTELLIGENCE SUMMARY

Army Form C. 2118.

62 Field Ambulance

Place	Date	Hour	Summary of Events and Information	Remarks and references to Appendices
MOUTON FARM 28/B.11.a.2.6.	21.9.17		Lorries continued evacuation during the night. 4 lorries working the forward circuit viz:- CHEAPSIDE to MOUTON FARM and 6 lorries working the backward circuit:- from MOUTON FARM to C.C.S. at MENSINGHEM. PROVEN- Rate taken to forward circuit- approximately 1 hour and a half. Time taken by lorries to backward circuit approximately 3 hours. Arrangements for walking wounded from ELVERDINGHE STATION to PROVEN. R.A.D. a train for walking cases (Arrived)- number of walking wounded been unable to entrain by trucks (arrived)- number of walking wounded also to R.O.D. Officer Int. INTERNATIONAL CORNER by telephone who notifies B.C. C.C.S. car send at MENSINGHEM. Number of walking wounded passed through Corps W. W.C.P. between 5pm 20-9-17 and 6am 21.9.17 7 Officers and 157 Other Ranks (British). 1 German Officer and 3 Officers and frightful names. Between 6 am. to 5pm. the 21st Officers and 52 German Officer Ranks kid. O.R.s. 5- Enemy Aeroplanes dropped bombs at ELVERDINGHE. 3 killed and 13. O.R. wounded were brought to C. to C.P.	D.H.
	22.9.17		EVACUATION by lorries during the night. Roads in fair condition. Number passed through between 5pm 21.9 and 6 am 22.9.17 Army through lectures. 5 Officers Brit. not German n.4. O.R's British 33. O.R's German 5- The Infantry Chaplain 62. L.Co. Ambulance bathed by O.E. Behar Division. (1) Bearers 62 L.Co Pte F.T. McCARTHY Pound Killed 4. O.R's wounded- 10 follows (No-32643) Pte J.WATSON Penn No 99330 Pte J. WELLS Penn No 53291 Pte J. CLARKE Penn No 63391 Pte H. WOOD Penn. Number passed through between 6 am. 22.9 and 5pm 22.9 52 O.R's British, 1 Officer British and 4 O.R's passed through helmets 5pm, 22 and and 12 midnight 22/23 ind. Corps walking wounded collected, patched and close. midnight 22/23 ind. A+D. Books completed and closed-	S.H.

WAR DIARY or INTELLIGENCE SUMMARY

Army Form C. 2118.

48. 62 Field Amb ulance

Place	Date	Hour	Summary of Events and Information	Remarks and references to Appendices
MOUTON FARM. C.W.W.C.P. B14 a 2.8 Sheet 28 NW	23.9.17		DDMS XIV Corps No. M.623. dated 22nd.10 Jan MOUTON FARM. Closes as Corps W.W.C.P. After shells fell in vicinity of MOUTON FARM. between 10 pm and 2 a.m. 14 Y Gun Probably moved 5.9. 10 lorries deliveries to 51 Amm Park Company Evacuation of walking wounded carried out by Motor Ambulance Cars 15 C.M.D.S. Instructions from ADMS 20th Division to close 20th Divisional Walking wounded Collecting Post at CHEAPSIDE 28/13.17 29.9.15. CAPTAIN L. JACOB RAMC is 14 F.R. RAMC returned to MOUTON FARM from CRS Dep at CHEAPSIDE on a holding party. 1st LIEUT ZINKHAN U.S.M.R. posted for temporary duty in medical charge of 20th A.C. ADMS 20th Division orders received notifying that later orders ADMS 28th & 29th Division No S 460. 26th Division will be relieved between 20th Division who will then hold the entire front by another Army on September 30th.	W.W.C.P. Sh 9. Sh 9.
	24.9.17		20th Division will commence to move to another Army on September 30th.	Sh 9.
	26.9.17		Operation Order No.3. 25th Division Read 25 September 1917. F Relief will take place as follows following 12th 28th September 59 Infantry Brigade Group from Reserve area to P Area taking over from 11th Infantry Brigade. (II). 61st Infantry Brigade Group from line to Support Area taking over from 12th Infantry Brigade (in case of 11 Battalion from 86 Infantry Brigade - 29 Division (IV). 29 September - 61st Infantry Brigade Group from Support Area to P's Area taking over from 10th Infantry Brigade. 2 (5). Moves to P Areas will be by Rail. Motors orders for which with will be issued by A.A of M.G. G. ENTRAINMENT will take place at ELVERDINGHE DETRAINMENT of PROVEN or LATE RYNTONAL CORNER-	Sh 9.

WAR DIARY
or
INTELLIGENCE SUMMARY.   49. 62 Field Ambulance

Army Form C. 2118.

Place	Date	Hour	Summary of Events and Information	Remarks and references to Appendices
MIDDAY FARM	26.9.17		MEDICAL arrangements of 20th DIVISIONAL Field Ambulances will take place as follows:- (I) Divisional Collecting Post (walking wounded) CHEAPSIDE B.17.b.9.2 and BEAUREVOIR including Post SOLFERINO FARM B.22.c.8.3 will be handed over by holding parties by 9 am on the 28". 62 Field Ambulance at Corps Walking Wounded Collecting Post will be relieved by noon on the 28" by 71st Division 11th Field Ambulance less (Bearer Divisions) will proceed to ELVERDINGHE. (b) AN RELIEF (III) 62 Field Ambulance less (Bearer Division) will proceed to 28" Field Ambulance DIS in P5 Area. Dr. RELLY (Bearer Division will carry on advance to Field Ambulance hut in P5 Area. (c) Woolley Parties will be sent in advance to Field Ambulance sites in P51, and P5 Area respectively to Field Ambulance sites in P51 and P5 Area. Between O.i.C. huts Ardennes. (d) All details of relief will be arranged direct between O.i.C. huts.	S.P.A.
Field Ambs Al 2.8 Sheet 28 N13	27.9.17		Major Park lent to report to O.C. 10th Field Ambulance at PANAMA CAMP. Major PROVEN. Captain J. PRIDHAM King proceed to PANAMA CAMP. P5 Area PROVEN. Captain J. PRIDHAM King proceed to PANAMA CAMP. to make arrangements for relieving of 62 Field Ambulance Staffing over personnel of Collecting Post at CHEAPSIDE B.17.b.9.2 (walking wounded) Corps Walking complete (5) handing over XIV Corps walking wounded Collecting Post at MOOTEN FARM B.14.a.2.8 to O.C. 11 Field Ambulance moves to PANAMA CAMP P5 AREA PROVEN. Balanes at ELVERDINGHE	S.P.A.
PANAMA CAMP PROVEN P5 AREA	28.9.17		62 Feb Ambulance moves to PANAMA CAMP P5 AREA PROVEN. Platoon at 4.30pm. delivered at PROVEN STATION at 5.30 pm. 20(ILLEGT) DIVISION warning order:- ADMS No S.476. The Division (less artillery) relieved by DIVISIONAL Infantry Column will be transferred from FIFTH ARMY (XIV Corps) to THIRD ARMY (II bt Corps) and temporarily detached to IV Corps. The DIVISION (less artillery) will move at an early date with IIII Corps AREA, from IV Corps AREA and will then relieve 40th DIVISION (less artillery) in the line. Continued	Sh.R.

Army Form C. 2118.

50 62 Field Ambulance

WAR DIARY
or
INTELLIGENCE SUMMARY.

(Erase heading not required.)

Instructions regarding War Diaries and Intelligence Summaries are contained in F. S. Regs., Part II. and the Staff Manual respectively. Title pages will be prepared in manuscript.

Place	Date	Hour	Summary of Events and Information	Remarks and references to Appendices
PANAMA CAMP PROVEN P.S. AREA 27/J18.b.2.8.	28-9-17 (Continued)		Line 3. The DIVISIONAL SUPPLY COLUMN will move by road. Remaining Troops including in para 1 will be moved by rail on 30th September. The 1st and 2nd batches then will entrain at PROVEN and HOPOUTRE and detrain at BAPAUME and MIRAUMONT and will be accomodated in BARASTRE AREA. Orders for these moves and train arrangements will be issued later from this Office. 4. A.A. & Q.M.G.	Ack
	29-9-17		Inspection of Equipment and clean clothing of Field Amb. Personnel. Unsuccessful for [?] and clean clothing for 200 ORs. Rand and A.S.C. Orders by Col. R.W. SLAYTER, CMG. A.D.M.S. Unit Comnding. Issued Order 20 Divis. O.11252. Motor Ambulances will move by Road tomorrow 29.9.17 via HAZEBROUCK, LILLERS, ST POL. ARRAS. BAPAUME. Column to clear HAZEBROUCK 12noon - 2 cars will rendezvous at Road Junction COOTHAVE - CORNER near PROVEN POPERINGHE Road at 8am 27/J21.a.2.6. 3. O.C. 61th Field Ambulance will detail an Officer to act as O/C. H/Q. The following Large Cars will be attached - 60 Field Ambulance. Two, 61th Field Ambulance two, 62 Field Ambulance One - 7. Staff Car Large Car from 62 Field Ambulance will report Entraining Officer at HOPOUTRE Station at 4.30am on 30th inst. One large car from H.Q. Field Ambulance will report to Entraining Officer at 3.30pm at 30th. 8. D.A.A.M.G. (Green) at PROVEN will station so as to be in rear of area & ready to load train when they will remain in depot until departure of Train. 9. A.D.M.S. then moves to B.H.Q. BAPAUME for details this afternoon. 10. Whereabouts of all units of Column will be reported to A.D.M.S. BAPAUME Office or at BAPAUME after 1/c Motor Amb Ambulance for instructions was disposed of column of Staff Assistant Officer (D.A.A.G.) 62 R.T.O. BAPAUME. (Signed) Green A.D.M.S. Received Staff Arrival of Field Ambulances. Two large cars and one Staff Car left for COOTHAVE near PROVEN POPERINGHE Road at 7am 29/J21.a.2.6. Report to O/C Ambulance Column A Pres 20 Division 62 Field Ambulance will entrain at HOPOUTRE Station 17 train. (sgd) F.L. Grange Lieut. Col. Comdg.	M.O.
	30-9-17			

Army Form C. 2118

WAR DIARY
or
INTELLIGENCE SUMMARY
(Erase heading not required.)

CONFIDENTIAL

WAR DIARY

OF

62nd Field Ambulance

From 1st Oct 1917   To 31st Oct 1917

COMMITTEE FOR THE
MEDICAL HISTORY OF THE WAR
Date —8 DEC. 1917

B.E.F.

SUMMARY OF MEDICAL WAR DIARIES OF
62nd F.A., 20th Divn. 14th Corps, 5th Army.
3rd Corps, 3rd Army from 2/10/17.

WESTERN FRONT Oct. 1917.

O.C. Lt. Col. E.F. L'Estrange.

SUMMARISED UNDER THE FOLLOWING HEADINGS.

Phase "D" 1. Passchendaele Operations July-Dec. 1917.

(b) Operations commencing 1/10/17.
Canadians attacked Passchendaele Oct. 30th.
Canadians took Passchendaele Nov. 6th.

B.E.F. 1.

62nd F.A., 20th Divn. 14th Corps, 5th Army. WESTERN FRONT.
O.C. Lt. Col. E.F. L'Estrange.   Oct. 1917.
3rd Corps, 3rd Army from 2/10/17.

Phase "D" 1. Passchendaele Operations July-Dec. 1917.

    (b) Operations commencing 1/10/17.
        Canadians attacked Passchendaele Oct. 30th.
        Canadians took Passchendaele Nov. 6th.

1917.   Headquarters. At Panama Camp E.18.b.2.8. (Sheet 27)

Oct. 2nd.   Moves and Transfer. Unit transferred with 20th Divn. to 3rd Corps, 3rd Army and moved to Bapaume en route for new area.

B.E.F.

SUMMARY OF MEDICAL WAR DIARIES OF
62nd F.A., 20th Divn. 14th Corps, 5th Army.
3rd Corps, 3rd Army from 2/10/17.

WESTERN FRONT Oct. 1917.

O.C. Lt. Col. E.F.L. Estrange.

SUMMARISED UNDER THE FOLLOWING HEADINGS.

Phase "D" 1. Passchendaele Operations July-Dec. 1917.

(b) Operations commencing 1/10/17.
Canadians attacked Passchendaele Oct. 30th.
Canadians took Passchendaele Nov. 6th.

B.E.F. 1.

62nd F.A., 20th Divn. 14th Corps, 5th Army. WESTERN FRONT.
O.C. Lt. Col. E.F. L'Estrange.   Oct. 1917.
3rd Corps, 3rd Army from 2/10/17.

Phase "D" 1. Passchendaele Operations July-Dec. 1917.

    (b) Operations commencing 1/10/17.
        Canadians attacked Passchendaele Oct. 30th.
        Canadians took Passchendaele Nov. 6th.

1917.   Headquarters. At Panama Camp E.18.b.2.8. (Sheet 27)

Oct. 2nd.   Moves and Transfer. Unit transferred with 20th Divn. to 3rd Corps, 3rd Army and moved to Bapaume en route for new area.

WAR DIARY or INTELLIGENCE SUMMARY

Army Form C. 2118.

51. 62 Field Ambulance

Place	Date	Hour	Summary of Events and Information	Remarks and references to Appendices
PAYAMA Camp	1.10.17		62 Field Ambulance to entrain at 5.45 p.m. Camp to be handed over to Area Command and PROVEN. Instructions received from A.D.M.S. 20th Division.	Sht.
PROVEN AREA E18 F22 Sheet 17			to entrain under orders. 6.1 Major loaded instructions for unit to entrain at 2 a.m. unit left POPERINGE SIDING at 6 a.m.	
BAPAUME	2.10.17		Train arrived at 5 p.m. Transport ordered to march via BEUGNY. 2nd Division and Bears Divison 62 Field Ambulance marched from BAPAUME at 6.30 p.m. route via VILLERS au FLOS & BUS. Met LECHELLE. Took over camp 4. from 1/3 WEST LANCASHIRE FIELD AMBULANCE. Captain W. PICKUP R.A.M.C. reported for duty on 3.10.17 authority A.D.M.S. 20th Division.	Sht. Sht2
HAUT	4.10.17		Orders from A.D.M.S. 20th Division. to proceed to HAUT ALLAINES. C29 B. (62.0 map). Captain W.S. PICKUP Royal Ambulance	Sht.
ALLAINES C29 B (Sheet 62c.)	6.10.17		CAPTAIN PICKUP R.A.M.C. took over medical charge of 7 Somersetshire Light Infantry. CAPTAIN J CHANDLER R.A.M.C. posted to 62 Field Ambulance for duty from 7 S.L.I. Inspected box Respirators and P.H. Helmets of personnel Rank & File (H.T+M.T).	Sht.
	7.10.17		62 Field Field Ambulance to relieve 136 Field Ambulance at Corps Rest Station MOISLAINS. C.12 d.o.5 Sheet 62 E. 8.10. One Field Sub-Division with one Officer (Lieut. H. GAUSS U.S.M.R. to proceed to S.CC.S. TINCOURT prob. duty on 9.10.17.	Sht.

1577 Wt.W10791/1773 500,000 1/15 D.D.&L. A.D.S.S./Forms/C. 2118.

WAR DIARY
INTELLIGENCE SUMMARY

Army Form C. 2118.

52   62 Field Ambulance

Place	Date	Hour	Summary of Events and Information	Remarks and references to Appendices
III Corps C.R.S.	8-10-17		62 Field Ambulance relieved 136 Field Ambulance at III Corps Rest Station at MOISLAINS C 12 d.o.s' Sheet 62.C. One Section of 2/1st West-Lancashire Field Ambulance attached for duty at C.R.S. Captain RICHARDS R.A.M.C.T. in charge of Section. Handing over and Receiving over Receipts given. 12 Officers and 385 O.R.s Rank in Hospital. A.D.M.S. 20th Division visited Field Ambulance.	O.K.d.
MOISLAINS C12 d.o.s Sheet 62c			NO 45,755 Pte PRINGLE Raine. and NO. M2/105,187 Pte COOK. J.W. A.O.C. M.T. awarded the military medal under authority of the Corps Commander III Corps.	
	9.10.17		NO 35,293 Staff Sergeant J. WELLINGTON Raine took over duties as acting Sergeant Major from. 23-9-17. Remained Officers 12. O.R.s 365. Admitted Officers 2. O.R.s 84. Discharge to Duty 99. to C.C.S 3. to C. Conv. Depot 1. Remaining Officers 14. O.R.s 366. Commences putting up Remaining Adrian huts for personnel Camp. Repairs to roofing of existing Adrian huts carried out.	Sh.P.
	10.10.17		Remained Officers 14. O.R.s 366. Admitted Officers 1. O.R.s 41. discharge to Duty. Officers nil - O.R.s 1. to C.C.S 5. Remaining Officers 15 O.R.s 401. A.D.M.S 20th Division visited 62 Field Ambulance. Advance repair Columns reports to O.Dues III Corps. huts. Assents for material forwarded to O.Dues III Corps.	Sh.P.

WAR DIARY or INTELLIGENCE SUMMARY

Army Form C. 2118

53 62 Field Ambulance

Place	Date	Hour	Summary of Events and Information	Remarks and references to Appendices
III Corps Rest Station MADISLAIN C.a.d.o.S. Sheet 62E	11.10.17		Remained. Officers 15. ORs. 401. Admitted Officers nil ORs 7. Discharges to duty ORs 42 – to C.C.S. 3. and I.C.T. Remaining Officers 15. ORs 423. Prevailing diseases P.U.O. and I.C.T. Number of sick from 58th Division increasing	S.R.2
	13.10.17		No 50329 Pte CORNES V. Rank & Duties acting Sgt without pay from 13.10.17 A.D.M.S. Laundry Officer 62 Field Ambulance Rewarding Baths Pictures in B° Division visited. Mrs Corps Mobile Corps Rest Station. Sedimentation tanks and filter beds inspected. Number of admissions increasing. 55th Division influenza not Captain P. BENNETT RAMC granted 10 days leave in United Kingdom from 14.10.17	S.R.2
	14.10.17		to 24.10.17. Inspection of Box Respirators and P.H. Helmets of personnel RAMC and ASC in the XXX Depot. Building of Huts Wards owing to lack of material. Indents for material forwarded to D.D.M.S. III Corps. Checker Investigation Equipment 62 Field Ambulance. Biscuits for depraved	SR.2
	16.10.17		founder. D.D.M.S. III Corps and D.D.M.S. VII Corps inspects Corps Rest Station. Question of hand of letter applications for dealing with fire suspected stairs pipe with heights of fire buckets not available and was at a setting state. Arrangements made for water. Evacuations from Corps Rest Station increasing. Pte CROSS J. RAMC 4 per Aux. J.C.T. case with Medical Baths no 80 to 117 market issued to brought Chiropodist to 62 Field Ambulance – Patient detailed One Mule to be handed to No 32 Mobile Veterinary Section	S.A.
	19.10.17		No MS/2722 Sgt MASON G.F. ASC (MT) granted 10 days leave 19.10.17 to 29.10.17 VII Corps Headquarters relieves III Corps Head Quarters at 12 noon on the 18.10.17. III Corps Rest Station becomes VII Corps Rest Station from 12 noon. Issue of dubbin and Corps under the attention relation of VII Corps – Office of DDMS VII Corps at TEMPLEUX LA FOSSE	S.A.2

WAR DIARY
or
INTELLIGENCE SUMMARY
(Erase heading not required.)

Army Form C. 2118

54
62 Field Ambulance

Place	Date	Hour	Summary of Events and Information	Remarks and references to Appendices
VII Corps Rest Station	20.10.17		D.D.M.S. VII Corps inspected Corps Rest Station. No 19281 Pte NORTHCOTT. T. Rane granted 20 days leave 30.10.17 to 20.11.17. Col Tennant 12 years AEI, No 1328. on 3.7.16 Corps Commander VII Corps visits Rest Station. No 34643 acting Serjeant GLANCY. T. Rane S.M.E.	
MIDHAINS C2 do 55 Shelter C	21.10.17		Granted permanent rank from 14.9.17. Authority Rane Order No 20.1917. Army Clothing issued to personnel Rane and W.C. 62 Field Ambulance by Lt. ZIMMHAN. Lt. U.S.M.R. Reports 62 Field Ambulance from 20 D.S.C. on arrival Inst. for personnel Rane completio - Commences making pit places in Wash house of annexure of 2nd Division increasing heavy sick parade arriving from many Drewry Station at BERNES. B.4. A.O.6. Shed 62.C. annexed. Precautions against fire Carts up in all buildings - and tents.	S.M.E.
	24.10.17		A.T.M.S. 58th Division visits 62 Field Ambulance - Prepare forms for planting applies to A.C. Corps. Commenced depot for planks -	R.R
	26.10.17		D.D.M.S. III Army and A.D.M.S. 20th Division acting D.D.M.S. VII Corps inspect Corps Rest Station - No 435485 Sgt Majr WHEELDON. H.O. Rane reports his arrival for duty to 62 Field Ambulance. -	R.R
	28.10.17		No 435485 Sgt Majr WHEELDON Rane was admitted to Hospital on the 27.10.17 and discharged on the 28.10.17. Dental treatment at 55 C.C.S.	R.R
	29.10.17		Corps Rest Station comes under the Administration of III W Corps from now to-day. Captain L.J. JACOB. Rane, proceeds to No 5. C.C.S. for duty. In relief Lt. Reid. GAUSS. Jr. U.S.M.R. who rejoins 62 Field Ambulance for duty. III Corps Rest Station. Captain J.S. PRIDHAM Rane Proceeds on 10 days leave to U.K. 30.X.17 to 9.XI.17. Captain P. BENNETT Rane rejoins unit from 10 days leave -	R.R
	30.10.17		D.D.M.S. III Corps visits Corps Rest Station. Number of patients for C.C.S. to be increased. 2 A.A - 55th Division to discontinue sending sick to Corps Rest Station.	R.R
	31.10.17		A.D.M.S. 20 Division visits 62 Field Ambulance and presents ribbons to No 327.31 Sgt CURRIE M.	

Army Form C. 2118.

WAR DIARY
or
INTELLIGENCE SUMMARY.   55   62 Field Ambulance

(Erase heading not required.)

Instructions regarding War Diaries and Intelligence Summaries are contained in F. S. Regs., Part II. and the Staff Manual respectively. Title pages will be prepared in manuscript.

Place	Date	Hour	Summary of Events and Information	Remarks and references to Appendices
III Corps Rest Station	31-10-17		Casualties	
			37194 Sergt. ROLLO. L.	
			32031 Pte CARTER. G. ⎫ Wounded in Nosfield (U.K.) ⎫ RAMC	
			39457 Pte OWERS. W.H. ⎬	
			45756 Pte PRINGLE. A. ⎭	
			M2/10587 Pte COOK. S.W. A.S.C.(M.T.)	Ok?
NEUSLAINS Cados Shed 62C			The Divisional Commander congratulates the recipients.	
			G.F.K. Chaves Lieut Col RAMC	
			O.C. 62 Field Ambulance	

140/2578

No. 62. 7.O.

COMMITTEE FOR THE
MEDICAL HISTORY OF THE WAR
Date 17 JAN. 1918

Army Form C. 2118

WAR DIARY
or
INTELLIGENCE SUMMARY
(Erase heading not required.)

Confidential

War Diary
of
62nd Field Ambulance

From 1st Nov 1914
to 30 Nov 1914

Army Form C. 2118.

WAR DIARY
or
INTELLIGENCE SUMMARY.

(Erase heading not required.)

5b

62 Field Ambulance

Instructions regarding War Diaries and Intelligence Summaries are contained in F. S. Regs., Part II. and the Staff Manual respectively. Title pages will be prepared in manuscript.

Place	Date Hour	Summary of Events and Information	Remarks and references to Appendices
IIIrd Corps Rest Station	1-11-17	Small NISSEN huts for Officers Ranks completed & one Influenza Compound in ADRIAN and Marie huts. 1:11 Officers and 537 O.R.s in hospital - Inspection of Princh for Reception and R.A. Wounds by Personnel Ranks and A.N.C. Dynamo for Electric Lighting of Hospital working satisfactorily.	MC
NOISLAINS 62/p.Cordos	2-11-17	Telegram 957 from 3rd CORPS - SECRET. addressed IIIrd CORPS REST STATION VIIth CORPS. D.D.M.S. V.Q. dated 1-11-17. Order the Section 2/1st Wed Lancashire Field Ambulance attaches to you to report its unit. Attach A.A.A. addressed IIIrd CORPS REST STATION - Captain H. RICHARD S. RAIN(?) and 47 Other Ranks 2/1st West Lancashire Field Ambulance left IIIrd Corps Rest Station at 2pm to report unit.	PMC
	3-11-17	Completed disposition in case of fire also type to be erects at a central spot. Hose pipes to be attached. 10 Officers 340 Other Ranks remaining. D.D.M.S. IIIrd Corps visited Rest Station. Tent the taken down	MC
	4-11-17	Personnel Ranks moves into ADRIAN hut. Tents occupied by personnel. Struck and sent to O.C. 20 Divisional Main Dressing Station at Finis. Instructions from DD M.S. III Corps to Evacuate patients of 55th and 24th Division and reduce number of patients at III Corps.	PMC
	5-11-17	No 71030 PTE H. MURPHY Ranks awarded 90 days F.P. No 1. by Field General Court Martial held on 3.11.17. succeeding head at or School/MAPS. Additional NAMES 3rd Division 16.20 Parade - and Districts IIIrd Division No S. 5A. the following have been approved Winter's Nov. 1917. ADMS 2nd Division R 20 d 50.65 - R 20 d 15.90 - R 20 t 30.30 GAME SUPPORT, New entrant Trench. R 20 d. 15.90 - R 20 d 55.15. RIFLE ALLEY. New G.T. R 14 d 2.3 - R 14 d 55 45 PARTRIDGE ROAD. Ricord ad R 14 C 50 b 60 CAATE N R14 C 50 100 PARTRIDGE ROAD.	SM

Army Form C. 2118.

WAR DIARY
or
INTELLIGENCE SUMMARY.

(Erase heading not required.)

39/ 62 Field Ambulance

Instructions regarding War Diaries and Intelligence Summaries are contained in F.S. Regs., Part II. and the Staff Manual respectively. Title pages will be prepared in manuscript.

Place	Date	Hour	Summary of Events and Information	Remarks and references to Appendices
III Corps Rest Station	6.11.17		9 Tents Circ. pattern handed over to I/C of O.C. 61st Field Ambulance at D.M.D.S. Finis & 18C. authority D.D.M.S. III Corps. Box Respirators drill for all available personnel. Same of A.S.C. practice in carrying stretchers and drawbar patients - Officers posted to various duties and ordering orders - Dinner A.S.C. Officers messed in division with formation for the inspection dejeuner.	P/Q
MOISLAINS 62c/c,12.d.0.5	7.11.17		150 Stretchers and 560 Blankets handed over to O.C. 21 M.A.C. authority D.D.M.S. III Corps. above being surplus to requirements at III Corps Rest Station - D.D.M.S. III Corps Walker Rest Station.	Sh.R.
	8.11.17		No 34263 Pte. Williams. J. Rand awarded 14 days F.P. no 1. for the following Offence. When in active service absenting himself without leave from 6 p.m. 6.11.17 until he reported himself to the N.C.O. i/c of Police at 8.15 p.m. 7.11.17. 26 hours 15 minutes.	OR
	9.11.17		No. 34263 Pte. J. Williams Rand awarded 14 days Field punishment no 1 Offence. Absent without leave from 10 a.m. to 8.55 p.m. 7.11.17, 22 hours 55 minutes.	OR
	11.11.17		A.D.M.S. 20th Division visit 62" Field Ambulance. Issued instructions that 1 N.C.O. and 20 bearers to report to O.C. 60" Field Ambulance at Finis type new 15.12th No 3524 Pte H.R. Tilbury Ramc. awarded 7 days field punishment no I Offence. Absent without leave from the 7.11.17 to 9.11.17. two days. Regimental No 352 Great Zirkmann 08R. Promulgated Fighting Precautions in accordance with III Corps No 0.5.9.9/3.	OR
	12.11.17		3. G.S. Waggons. 3 Mules act. H.T. and 6 heavy draught horse to report to O.C. 69 Field Ambulance for temporary duty - authority ADMS 20th Division.	P/R
	13.11.17		D.D.M.S. III Corps Walker Rest Station - Number of patients 2nd Division. 33rd Division and other Formations to be retained -	P/R

WAR DIARY or INTELLIGENCE SUMMARY

Army Form C. 2118.

58. 62 Field Ambulance

Place	Date	Hour	Summary of Events and Information	Remarks and references to Appendices
III Corps Rest Station	14.11.17	6.18	3rd early Parade Order No. 231. Reference Maps 57 C.1/20,000. GOUZEAUCOURT 1/20,000. Scale 1/2.11.17 The 7 KOYLI will relieve the 12th KING'S in FRONT LINE on night 16/17 November 1917. D. Coy on front Burghe Way be disposed as follows:— 2 R. KOYLI LIVE Hois R and 2.3.6. 12th KINGS Support Cos. HEUDECOURT W. 26.8.8. 6 & 7 M. Bde — No change — 8 D and 6 11th S.L.I. SOREL 6. 11 M.C. Co. HEUDECOURT W. 26.8.8.	O.K.
	16.11.17		No 3032 Cpl Bolton came to this unit from 6 secs — 1 NCO and 6 men proceeded to hospital and transferred to 5 secs, No 5 CCS for temporary duty 2 NCO and 8 men returned to 62 field ambulance to CCS from 5 CCS for cases and 7 R. Penn. Ferries to 60 th.	O.R.
Mouslans C.C.A.D.S	18.11.17		Reply to Medical Arrangements 111th Corps Medical No.7 Received on 18.11.17 Amendment No.1	O.R.
			Medical Arrangements 111th Corps Medical No.7 A Dm S. 20th Division on S S.2 S.A.2 dated 18.11.17 Received — Four Letter Stations CoE. CALLS will be taken over by ZERO DAY by all units as their call and address - 23 ORS RANK. TOPMS to LES Quarters 2nd Div. to report	
	19.11.17		A D M S. 20th Div on No 3509 Received — CENTRAL OF TRAFFIC. APM 111 Corps ADDENDUM No. 1 to Medical arrangements 111 - Corps Operation Q 117 received. ADMS. 20 Div. No. S 504 Reserve Of had been noticed that Main Line BRIGADES in the Line English BRIGADE will have Battalions in the TRENCHES The Battalion in Support and Reserve Battalion will be in WED ESCORT and ESSART WOOD	
	20.11.17		LIEUT COL. R S TAYLOR Ranc. and Captain H Haydon Ranc. 3 ORs came 3 TR's to J.S. CROMIE - F.E. 62 Field Ambulance and Captain P.G. BENNETT Ranc 2 ORs Ad Hi. CHANDLER Ranc. and Captain A. MULLS 1 hotel Wal. and 2 H.A. Walkins with 4 H. Draft and 2 R.A.S. conductors to 60 field Ambulance a The 194 H Heavy Draft to Mules. Unities WAC H. 100 frd Ambulances and 2 WVR cols Ambulance and 4 Nurses WAC Ht personnel and 3 ORS Ranc in Orderlies For Ambulances with 4 A.D.S. GOUZEACOURT. LOCATION of MEDICAL UNITS succeeded to A.D.S GOUZEACOURT. MEDICAL ARRANGEMENTS dated 15th Nov. 1917. LOCATION of MEDICAL UNITS. 20th DIVISIONAL OPERATIONS A PRIOR TO ZERO. Sheet 57c (1/40000). (1) BATTLE AID POSTS — LEFT. R 20 a 2.9 (XVI RAVINE) (2) RELAY POSTS (1) R 26 a 8.4 (HOTEL CECIL). RIGHT 25 d 4.9 (2) R 19 d 3.7 near XVI RAVINE. (3) A.D.S. GOUZEACOURT B. 36 6.9. (4) DIV WALKING WOUNDED. COLLECTING STATION. GOUZEACOURT BATHS. Q 36 6.1.4. (5) H.Q. 60 F.A. (O.C. BEARERS) & BEARER CAMP. FINS. V 12 C.6.6. (6) Corps MAIN DRESSING STATION. V 18 C.07 FINS - NURLU ROAD. & CORPS SICK COLLECTING POINT V 18 C.07 FINS. NURLU ROAD. (7) F.O.S. (1) YTRES GR.63P. (2) FINCOURT GR.6P.	O.R.

WAR DIARY or INTELLIGENCE SUMMARY

Army Form C. 2118.

59 Oxfield Auchlane

Place	Date	Hour	Summary of Events and Information	Remarks and references to Appendices
III Corps Rest Station	20/11/17		(Continued) B. at ZERO:- (a) An ADVANCED BATTLE AID POST (Right) at R 20 d 7.4 will be taken over as an Aid Post by 61st Brigade. The QUARRY (R 25 d 4.9) will continue to be used for the Reserve Battalion of the 59 Bde until it is ordered to be moved up by B.G.C. 59 Infantry Brigade. (b) A Forward ADS (LEFT) will be established at Infantry Left Battle Aid Post R 20 a 2.9 (SURREY RAVINE). (c) An ADVANCED BATTLE AID POST (LEFT) will be established at R 14 a 8.9 (SURREY RAVINE) eventually to become one of the chain of F.A. RELAY POSTS (d) AFFORWARD ADS (Right) will similarly be established later at the ADVANCED BATTLE AID POST R 20 d 7.4. On account of [?] The move open [?] of the [?] of the initial positions it has been found inadvisable to make arrangements for [?] until then [?] are arranged that these will be as follows. The initial MO's Area of F.A. will be intensively arranged that these will be as follows. Thrown at ZERO (a) ADVANCED LEFT BATTLE AID POST R 14 a 8.9 (SURREY RAVINE) (b) Infantry LEFT BATTLE AID POST R 20 a 2.9 XVI Corps [?] MO's of 60th Brigade in Reserve until orders up. (c) ADVANCED BATTLE AID POST R 20 d 7.4 The (RIGHT) (1) one of more MO's of 61st BRIGADE (1) One MO, 61st Bn BUCKS. MO in Reserve until ordered up. A Original Right BATTLE AID POST (QUARRY) Remaining in position remaining in reserve until ordered up. R 25 d 4.9 The MO's of 59 Brigade remaining in reserve. The B.G.S.C desire troops both the exception of the MO of each Brigade when the RAMC's with all RAMC's will be required to establish RAP's as situation demands. The LIVE RIF CENTRAL - R.S central in Suggested as suitable Relieving Stations, whilst it may be found convenient to establish an ROUTE the evacuation of wounded. Heavy Bombardment commenced at 6.30 am.	ZI.7
Moislains C.12 d 0.5 62.C West	21/11/17		Both of the two [?] mentioned. Nearest Right ADVANCED BATTLE AID POST at R 20 d 7.4 - CAPTAIN CHANDLER Roads, and Captain BENNETT Roads of 62 Field Ambulance Both at Corps Rest Station. DDMS during evacuation W. CARNES Roads for duty at III Corps Main Dressing Stations. BDMS Lethro Certain cases to 41 Stationary HOSPITAL BARILLY unable to take cases. Evacuate Convalescent Depot TINCOURT Corps Convalescent Depot. A Battle Aid Post at R 20 d 7.4. 50 [?] wounded Casts arrived from FA. Numbers of lists suitable to III ERS including 2 manged with 2 Dms S. [?] for transport to evacuate Cases to 41 Stationary Hospital BARILLY, 2 Dundu A/dl, 1 Corporal Field Ambulance	ZI.7

Army Form C. 2118.

WAR DIARY
or
INTELLIGENCE SUMMARY.

(Erase heading not required.)

62 Field Ambulance

Place	Date	Hour	Summary of Events and Information	Remarks and references to Appendices
In Corps Rest Station	21.11.17		No M.2/2727 Lt-Mason. A.S.C. (M.T.) proceeds to 62 Field Ambulance for traffic control duty. Packed equipment of section A. Inspects hired car. Responsible for P.O. Vehicles & removing of Camp Road. etc.	CM1
Moislains C.12.d.05 Shelters	22.11.17		Visits Relay post at R.20.b.7.4. Checks particulars for transport loads. 62th pitches tents and two marquees. D.S. of III Corps visits III ERS. all marquees, machines to have ready 200 stretchers. Explains P.W. M. Arm attached. 1 M.O. proceeds to 62 FA to take up A.P.S. at R.39.d.7.0. Debus RT4203-7 Captain A. Chandler. Rand and Captain P. Bennett hand over B.P. 4-R-20 Captain A. Chandler. Rand took out. 6.28.c9.B.578 Captain J. Pritcham Rand a 7.9. to new Relay post at R.20 A.7.4. 195 195 Rand proceeded to Bead Camp on Relay Post at R.20 A.7.4. 08.d.05 Ruifill 4 MID horses obtained for 62 Field Ambulance - Moislains - 08.d.05 Ruifill	RY9
	23.11.17		Completed second Advance Hospital, perronnel Rand out two Bearer camps 62 Field Ambulance moves to 16 Ravine at R.14 C.3.1. Auto C Captain Seddon 62 Field Ambulance relieving Bearer Camp of this unit at Rise. Captain Morcrieff Muir. Rand. 67 Field ambulance front to duty at III Rds. Captain Hunt, Rostrum Act. M.T. returns from leave in U.K.	RS
	24.11.17		No 3280. Pte Tilbury. Rand whilst from 21 CCs. wounded G.S.W. Head punctuating at ERS. Early. G.M.D.S. FMIS Quirk Road - Average numbers of sick farrated cases K.36 CCs in edge hill. V.18 C. returning from F/y Ambulance from dept: 11 Caps Infantries	CM1
	25.11.17		Captain P. Bennett Rand returns to 62 Field Ambulance from 16 Ravine. (Villiers Flowsk). Bearer Camp. Notified from 21 CCs at TRs. 11 the death of No 33260. Pte Tilbury H. Rand. of Res. Head. V Sanctuary. 15 Ravine. Villiers Jewish. R.14 C.D.4. R4 Bearn Camp at 16 Ravine Cl Edge Hill. 639 Reinway.	SP
	26.11.17	8 OM.	Rank & Rains (Kingsman) reports for duty from V Tly.S. 20 Div S.9.1.36 Ph. unsung to 36/P/ca Captain W Carnes Aue to report to Divisional Park-H. in according with instructions from S. Div. III Corps	

A.702   Wt. W28594/M1293   750,000   1/17   D.D. & L., Ltd.   Forms/C2118/14.

Army Form C. 2118.

WAR DIARY
or
INTELLIGENCE SUMMARY.

(Erase heading not required.)

61
62 Field Ambulance

Place	Date	Hour	Summary of Events and Information	Remarks and references to Appendices
III Corps Rest Station	27.11.17		D.D.M.S. III Corps visits Corps Rest Station - Copy of Education Programme for hutment Units to 12 noon 25th November 1917. Reference MAPS. 57.d and 62 d.	Sh. 2.
MOISLAINS C.12.0.5			20th Division ADVANCED DRESSING STATIONS - MANIERE BREWERY G.26.d.1.6.- GOUZEACOURT Q.36.d.6.9. " " LA VACQUERIE RELAY POST. " RELAY Post and BEARER CAMP. XII RAVINE (R.20.a.2.9). Walking Wounded Collecting Post GOUZEACOURT BATHS G.36.(1.1.4). FIELD AMBULANCE 4th. 60th FA FIRS V.12.C.8.8.- 6th F.A. COFFEE MAIN DRESSING Station V.18.C.- 62. FA MOISLAINS (C.R.S.) C.12.0. A.D.M.S. SOREL LE GRAND W.18.a. Lieut. T. GAUSS. M.O.R.C. U.S.A. returns from Corps Prisoners of War Cage.	
	28.11.17.		A.D.M.S. 12th Division visits III CCS 3 O/Rs proceed to no 5 CCS TINCOURT for duty. Pvt.	
	29.11.17.		1st Lieut. M ZINKHAM. M.O.R.C. U.S.A. proceeds to 5 CCS TINCOURT. Relieves Captain LG JACOB Captain LG JACOB Reuel rejoins 62 FA from 5CCS TINCOURT. Inspects Rail Rest Station of Personnel Reinf and R.A.C. (H.T-M.T).	P.R.T.
	30.11.17		Captain L.G. JACOB Reuel. proceeds on 14 days leave to The United Kingdom. Authority- A.Tubs. 20th Division. M.F. 1st December 1917. Large number of transit cases arriving from hutment units of 29th.12th and 6th Divisions. Notifies B Dun III Corps.	

E.F.K Schrauge
Lieut.Col. Rauer.

COMMITTEE FOR THE
MEDICAL HISTORY OF THE WAR

Date -1 FEB. 1918

No. 62 7. a.

Army Form C. 2118.

Vol 25

WAR DIARY
or
INTELLIGENCE SUMMARY.

Confidential

War Diary

of

62nd Field Ambulance

From Dec 1914 To 31st Dec 1914

WAR DIARY
or
INTELLIGENCE SUMMARY.

Army Form C. 2118.

62 Field Ambulance —

Place	Date	Hour	Summary of Events and Information	Remarks and references to Appendices
III Corps Rest Station	1.12.17		Captain J. PRIDHAM R.A.M.C. reports at 62 Field Ambulance from 6 Field Ambulance A.D.S. at G.25.d.2.6. Proceeds on duty to heavy shelling by the enemy. 5 O.R's Bearer (Bearers) reports for duty from LA VACQUERIE A.D.S. LA VACQUERIE A.D.S. Proceeds on 12-30 "" Bearer Station — 16 RAVINE R20.a.2.9. PRD.P.&T. Bearer Camp Salvage. Captain P. Bennett R.A.M.C. 5 O.R's Bearers (Bearing) proceeds to 6 Field Ambulance at FINS. DD In S III Corps orders Capt Red Station	PRA
MONCHNS Cm. d. 0.8. 62.e.	2.12.17		Captain R. STAGG becomes purveyor to U.K. on the expiration of Dec. to 15 December 17. Authority A.Div. 20 Division. D Wess. M Corps wires Coho Red Station – instructions to prepare to hand over 62 Field Ambulance to 20 Division.	PN
	3.12.17		Captain P. BENNETT R.A.M.C. and one O.R. Pack left 82 Bezin Court transport billeting officer 61st Infantry Brigade. Bearer Division and havesport at its home on the 4 inst. Remanded to Sutrain — at YTRES Station to be at MAULTE at 5 pm on twenty transport and tent division to hand over to incoming Field Ambulance by 12 noon on 5 inst. by 5 inst.	RY
	4.12.17		Tent Subdivision and one Officer to join up Headquarters & field Ambulance from 5 CCS at MAULTE. One Sergeant-clerk and personnel from Subtrain 21 CCS at YTRES. Captain F. CHANDLER R.A.M.C. T and bearer Division 62 Field Ambulance entrained at YTRES station at 1.30pm. heavy area BUZINCOURT distribution station BORRÉ Bearer Division arrived at BUZINCOURT at 1.30 am. transport personnel removed from BURÉ A Vers. 20 Division wires instructions tent Division to leave MOISLAINS III ○ CRS on 5 and join up with Bearer Division at 5 pm at MAULTE. 108 Field Ambul. area arrived at III ○ CRS	RL
	5.12.17		Hand over buildings and tents etc. are equipment of III CRS B.O.C. 105 F.A. Red Station of 62 Field Ambulance and with transport marched from MOISLAINS to MEAULTE starting at 7 am arriving at MEAULTE at 4pm contents	CRL

WAR DIARY or INTELLIGENCE SUMMARY. 62 Field Ambulance

Army Form C. 2118.

Place	Date	Hour	Summary of Events and Information	Remarks and references to Appendices
BOULINCOURT W.16 central Sheet 57D	5.12.17		Field Service kits transported in march to AVELUY W.16. C Ref 57D. Advance Guard – Officers and Transport included. Orderlies to night transport picked up by Field Ambulance. Orders from 6th Infantry Brigade – Z.A. 101. 5.12.17 say 2A.100 Cyclists – 6th Inf Battn billeted at AVELUY 6.10 am 6 Infantry Brigade. You will be at Station No.1 later than F.30 am. A.D.M.S. 3rd Division Staff Ravine Junction Nos 95 but 5th Dec 1917. Moves Field Ambulance: (1) 62 Field Ambulance personnel (11 Officers and 161 O.Rs) will proceed by 181 train leaving AVELUY for HESDIN at 10 am. Transport of Field Ambulance 11 O.Rs to move 9 miles – 13. T. ambs at transport left included in the above train with march in billets 6th Inf. Battn PIERS – and DOULLENS met BOUVERS – SUR – CANCHE 8th instant. PRISES. 4 Personnel entraining will arrive 2 hours before time of leaving. Transport will arrive 2 hours before time of leaving. Wagons entrained and loft the animals outspanned to units applying to senior officer by the Railway authorities Women will be returned after entrainment. Should Costs and hood fuel unusual to reach Kingstown by time stated transport sent by home Royal Baggage party to behicle be sent. Reminder – Transport March of 9.30 am for PRUGES. (2) 62 Fld Ambulance cars transport entrained at 9.30 am AVELUY. Arrived at 12.30 am HESDIN. at 7 pm.	
COUPELLE NEUVE LENS SHEET 36.108 NW	6.12.17 7.12.17		Transport arrived at COUPELLE NEUVE at 6 am. to-day – Captain & Ambulance Corps.	
	8.12.17		Cap'n R. BENNETT – proceeded to report to 6th Infantry Brigade. Assumed for futter duty in new area. 6th Infantry Brigade Nov. 1916 2.38 – Mat ok to D.R.E. 49.7 (1) the Division (less artillery) to send transport from X 16 IX Corps on Dec 11th 12th trans from Troops area to BLAIRINGHEM on Dec 11th may moves from Troops area to BLAIRINGHEM 3 weeks (2) personnel of the 61st infty Bde group will move by Bus to the more to be notified as soon as practible. Continued –	

WAR DIARY or INTELLIGENCE SUMMARY

Army Form C. 2118.

62 Field Ambulance

Place	Date	Hour	Summary of Events and Information	Remarks and references to Appendices
COUPELLE NEUVE	10.12.17	2.17	(3) Transport of the Group. Unit move by road under the orders of the Brigade. T.O.(W) Radhead will be in F. ESLINGHEM from PRO 12.F until (5) Brigade transport unit elsewhere at PREBOY- at 7am on the 12th inst. and then in rest area in Artois — No 8.499 Pte STERWOOD P. 19 DLI attached RAC NT two aus- th- 14 days F.P. Pvt 1. Officer Conduct to the prejudice of good order and military discipline the tooth. Neue. Creating a disturbance in a Detaineraufs ADM.S. Division Operation Orders S.362 +363.	A.J.
LENS SHEET 1.100,000	11.12.17		Lt.Col. E.F. L'ESTRANGE RAMC departed on leave to U.K. date 12.12.17 - 26.12.17. Capt J.A. PRIDHAM assumed Command of 62 F.AmB. Lt GAUSSEN, DOR (CR reinforcements) rejoined from unit.	J.P.
WALLON CAPPEL	12.12.17		62 F.AmB. two transport provided by lorry from COUPELLE NEUVE to BLARINGHEM AREA (MR HAZEBROUCK TOWER). Billets on road WALLON CAPPEL - BOIS DES HUIT RUES. Transport 62 F.AmB under Capt. CHANDLER RAMC proceeded by road, leaving COUPELLE NEUVE 10.50am to arr. 612 Bde TRANSPORT TRANSPORT & billets for night in THIEMBRONNE AREA.	J.P.
HAZEBROUCK plast 1 100,000	13.12.17		Lt. ZIMMERMAN U.S.M.O.R.C. and 18 O.R. returned to unit from 3 C.C.S. Transport under Capt. CHANDLER RAMC arrived 6 p.m.	J.P.
	14.12.17		Leave 7 Lt. Col. L'ESTRANGE to October 6 11/11/18	J.P.
	16.12.17		12th Lieuts. E.F. PHELAN, L.A. RYAN, & L.A. KANE attached for dut of U.S. M.O.R.C. strike to this unit for duty.	J.P.
	26.12.17		The MILITARY MEDAL is given to Pte H. PRESCOTT RAMC & Pte E. TAYLOR RAMC. Capt. P. Bennett RAMC & Lt Ganso USAMORC are appointed to perform medical	J.P.

Army Form 2118.

WAR DIARY
or
INTELLIGENCE SUMMARY. 62 Field Ambulance

(Erase heading not required.)

Instructions regarding War Diaries and Intelligence Summaries are contained in F. S. Regs., Part II. and the Staff Manual respectively. Title pages will be prepared in manuscript.

Place	Date	Hour	Summary of Events and Information	Remarks and references to Appendices
WARLOY	11/10/17		Medical charge of XII Kings Liverpools & XII Sion Basters regt Inds on return of this unit	YA
CAPPY				
SUZ HEDICOURT	24/10/17	6+8 PM	Lt J.O. Kenyon RAMC Proceeded on 14 days leave to U.K.	YA
WOOD			1st Lt Zverkoff proceeded (for 14 days leave to Paris	YA YA
	25/11/17		1 N.C.O. & 12 O.R. proceeded to 11 CCS at Godnesvelot for temporary duty	
	25/10/17		Being away from the headquarters for temporary duties. No new Positions Taken place.	YA
	28/11		Capt L.G. Jacob RAMC proceeded to 18th Bde. R.G.A. for temporary duty as M.O. to	YA

[signature]
CAPT. R.A.M.C
O/C 62ND FIELD AMBULANCE

WAR DIARY
or
INTELLIGENCE SUMMARY

CONFIDENTIAL

WAR DIARY
OF
62nd Field Ambulance

FROM 1st January 1918 TO 31st January 1918

COMMITTEE FOR THE
MEDICAL HISTORY OF THE WAR
Date -4 MAR 1918

Army Form C. 2118.

62 F Ambulance
766

WAR DIARY
or
INTELLIGENCE SUMMARY.

(Erase heading not required.)

Place	Date	Hour	Summary of Events and Information	Remarks and references to Appendices
WALLON CAPPEL Shut S.A. HAZEBROUCK	JAN. 1918 3.		C.O. inspected hutments & m/t motors, ride & addressed the new drivers. 1 LT. LAKANE U.S.M.O.R.C. returned from C.R.S. 30 Div. 1 LT. H. GOVSS U.S.M.R.C. transferred to permanent medical chgs. 1/XII K.I.N. 65. CAPT. CHANDLER R.A.M.C. & 1st LT. RYAN U.S.M.O.R.C. proceeded 5 motor ambulance cars to WOODCOTE HOUSE 28/I 200.S.3 to ascertain & to what T.	JPR
	4.	O.C. 9/15 Amb proceeded to BAILLEUL en route for NOUDEZE HOUSE All transport of 9/51st M.I. return from 61st Bch transport at L&S C.M.G. Rues Shut S.A. at 9.30am & proceeded to GODWAERSVELDT and 2 hour motor proceded from BAILLEUL to WOODCUTS HOUSE 1st LT. KANE U.S.M.O.R.C. took 6 O.R. R.A.M.C. proceeded to EBBLINHEM Shut S.A. at 10.30am for entraining leaving EBBLINHEM at 12.30pm A word at BAILLEUL 4.30 & proceeded by lorry to NOVOCUTS HOUSE Report to O.C. 57 F. Amb.	JPR
	5.	LT. COL. E. F. L'ESTRANGE R.AM.C. & CAPT. CHANDLER R.A.M.C. 7.F. returned to Despatches. Two letter of appt & protos sent. remember 1 F. Amb 38 O.R. with 1 LT. PHELAN U.S.M.O.R.C. proceeded to EBBLINCHEM arriving 6.30am nothing entrained at 9am arriving	JPR

A 1092. Wt. W285.9/M1293. 750,000. 1/17. D. D. & L., Ltd. Forms/C2118/14.

WAR DIARY or INTELLIGENCE SUMMARY

Army Form C. 2118.

62 Field Ambulance

67

Place	Date	Hour	Summary of Events and Information	Remarks and references to Appendices
HALLO N - JUN 1918	5.		and arrived at DICKEBUSCH & proceeded to WOODCOTE HOUSE 28/I.20.c.4.3. - 62 F Amb H.Qrs. established at WOODCOTE HOUSE from 12 noon. Transt 62 F Amb. arrived LA CLYTTE 28/N.7central Bhm T from their lines Lewis 8" militia.	9/WP
5th HAZEBROUCK	6.		T/F.Amb Capt WOODCOTE HOUSE 10AM. The Main Dressing Station at No 6 CLYTTE House billets at BEDFORD HOUSE 27/I.26.a.52. He Advanced dressing stations at CANADA STREET 28/I.30.a.5.k and CLAPHAM JUNCTION J.13.d.9.8 also posts at BODMIN J.19.d.8.1 OBSERVATORY RIDGE 28/I.24.c.9.3. TANK VIEW 28/I.24.a.7.6 JACKDAW CRATER 28/I.19.b.9.1.3. were shown was from 9 a.m.	9/WP
WOODCOTE HOUSE 28/I.20.c.4.3			At 12 noon O.C. 62 F Amb became responsible for arrangements and evacuation from 30 Div. Front.	
	7		Reliefs of 30 Div by 20 Div were completed	9/WP
	8		Lt.Col. S.A. STOCK RAMC took over command of 62nd Field Ambulance vice Lt.Col. F.G. LESTRANGE appointed O.C. No. 5. C.C.S.	9/WP

WAR DIARY or INTELLIGENCE SUMMARY

62 F. AMB

Place	Date	Hour	Summary of Events and Information	Remarks and references to Appendices
WOODCOTE HOUSE I.20.6.4.3 Sheet 28	JAN 8 1918		The following is a précis of hand over & remarks we evacuated from 20 DIV. front E of the line YPRES — WOOMEZEELE (Sheet 28) MAR Sht 28 HOURS Division Line front with four battalions in line. Left Brigade 61 Bde. RA Brigade on its right. Left Bde. Left Batt. R.F.P. (The TOWER) J.14.d.5.3 Pronounced by O.C. R.A.M.C. Evacuations by hand cars down "E" MENIN ROAD duckboard track to CLAPHAM JUNCTION. Personnel at CLAPHAM JUNCTION (I.13.d.9.2) On April 150 Collecting point. This is in connection with A.D.S. EUCLIDES (5 tarred camp) to HOOGE CRATER (I.18.b.4.5.) There was trench to can be to 3 N.Z. Fd A.B. & ECOLE Enter YPRES. On horse relay to Asylum. Right Batt. Left Bde. CENTRAL R.B.P. J.20.b.8.2. Pronounced 9 a.R. A.M.C. Evacuates the dugouts from E. BODMIN (Field hold T.19.b.8.1) followed at Asylum 13 F A.D.C.	

Army Form C. 2118.

WAR DIARY
or
INTELLIGENCE SUMMARY.

(Erase heading not required.)

Place	Date	Hour	Summary of Events and Information	Remarks and references to Appendices
WOT 20E HOUSE I30&43 Sh.t 28	7 PM 13/8 6.		Evacuations from B.13 min by hand carry in wheeled stretcher slings. "A" Advanced Troops to A.D.S. CANADA STREET. CANADA STREET A.D.S. = I.30 a.8.2. housing 2 officers 10 NH sjt. 9.19 O.R. RAMC. (accomodation for 24 hrs) Cases 50 sitters.) EVACUATED 5 wheeled stretchers in FORD car, & CPs. STAND down, post always went round. CMB STAND I28 b.4.9. passed to OP RAMC. (accommodation for 12 lying cases.) Thence by motor ambulance to M.D.S. at WORDERTE HOUSE. LOCAL POSTS. JACKDAW CRATER. I.19 d.1.9. 40R APTP covements by "E" in "A" duckboard. From L.A.D.S. on VIA EN ROUTE of PLUMERS DRIVE to TANK VIEW. TANK VIEW I 24 d.7.8. 40R RPRE covements to OBSERVATORY A.D.S.	

Army Form C. 2118.

WAR DIARY
or
INTELLIGENCE SUMMARY.

62 F AMP

(Erase heading not required.)

Place	Date	Hour	Summary of Events and Information	Remarks and references to Appendices
WOODCOTE HOUSE ICC CAMP	Tue 7th 1918		OBSERVATORY RIDGE 12Y C.1.3 from C 4 OR 12pm. Enemy via PLUMER'S DRIVE & CMB STAND	JR
Sun 28	8. 10.		On Pte Rennie (1F Amb) was wounded by machine gun bullet near CLAPH AM JUNCTION 7-11AM. 62 F Amb Govt Camp and Hospital Accommodation at LA CLYTTE 28/ inspected from 1F Amb. 62 Tunnelling Co's T C. 25 S.B. were sent from Buttsnotshi Capt. J.A. PRIDHAM R.A.M.C. S.R. was nominated the Military Rep	JH YMC
"			1/LT PHELAN U.S. M.O. R.C. taken over medical charge of I. D.C.L.I. vice Lt WOLNER R.A.M.C. who is under instructions to proceed to ENGLAND.	YMC
	14. 16.		180.RO. RDMC 62 F Amb returned from No.11.CCS. 1LT L. A. KANE US.M.O.M.C. ## took over Medical Charge of 7th CYLI vice Lt Connery Donnely on leave. E.F. CAPT G.A. Stark proceeded to CANADA ST ADS & M.O. I/c	YR YR

WAR DIARY
or
INTELLIGENCE SUMMARY.

62nd F. Amb   Army Form C. 2118.

71

Place	Date	Hour	Summary of Events and Information	Remarks and references to Appendices
WOODCOTE HOUSE	7/1/8 7pm/7		CAPT. L.B. JACOB R.A.M.C. returned from 50 Bde R.F.A.	app
	19		LT.COL. G.H. STACK R.A.M.C. returned from A.D.S. CANADA ST.	app
Ivorans	"		Ahmts 13 French Officers reexamined & 2 Staff officers 94th Army inspected WOODCOTE HOUSE.	
Sept 24 1918	19		Capt. J.P. QUINN M.C. R.A.M.C. 61F. Amb's reported & is attached for duty	app
			LT./A. D. ZINNIHAN U.S.M.O.R.C. left this unit to report to E.V.C. Lge A.E.F.	
			LIEUT J.T. HILL R.A.M.C. reported for temporary duty from 49F. Amb.	
	20		CAPT. J.P. QUINN R.A.M.C. 61 F. Amb returned to 61 F. Amb.	app
			CAPT. S.H. STALLARD R.A.M.C. 61F. Amb returned to temporary duty. ENEMIES movements	
	5		CAPT. S.H. STALLARD R.A.M.C. 61F. Amb & 50 O.R. 61F. Amb. reported for temporary duty.	app
	t		CAPT. MARBURY 60 F-Amb & 50 O.R. 60F Amb reported to his unit for temporary duty.	app
	13		CAPT. C.J. STALLARD R.A.M.C. 11 F. Amb. returned to his unit	app
			CAPT. H.S. APPINGTON U.S.M.O.R.C. 61 F Amb. reported for temporary duty	app

WAR DIARY or INTELLIGENCE SUMMARY

Army Form C. 2118.

62 F. Amb

72.

Place	Date	Hour	Summary of Events and Information	Remarks and references to Appendices
WOODCOTE HOUSE	1918 JAN 23	15	CAPT. W. MARBURY U.S.M.R.C. & V.F. Amb returned to his unit.	
EPSOM Staff 8	24/1/18		Weather fine. Usual of Boards in the later part of the Afternoon	
	25/1/18		4 Field Service Coy R.E. arrived hut for officers in the grounds of Woodcote House arrived.	
	26/1/18		Inspection by A.D.M.S. and engineers to arrange work O.C. 4 Field Survey Coy R.E. for hut to harness foundary. Weather mild.	
	27/1/18		Bright sunshine with frost at night. Day	
	28/1/18		Sharp frost at night. Two officers attd 96 Mobile V.S. section. Lieut Lee of Woodcote House 2 & A.D.S. Canada street by Major Wilson M.C. (U.S.)	
	29/1/18		Day mild & bright. Received part of orderly R.A.P. left in care of Scott signals. 20 cases to Red Cross only R.R.t to A.D.M.S.	

Army Form C. 2118.

WAR DIARY
or
INTELLIGENCE SUMMARY.
(Erase heading not required.)

62 F. Amb.

page 73

Instructions regarding War Diaries and Intelligence Summaries are contained in F. S. Regs., Part II. and the Staff Manual respectively. Title pages will be prepared in manuscript.

Place	Date	Hour	Summary of Events and Information	Remarks and references to Appendices
WOODCOTE HOUSE	30/1/18		Mng. with white frost at night. Div transfers at 10 A.M. from IX to XXII Corps. This is of 76 C.M. on C.H. BOLTON reduced to 115. (rank & file) owing to gales.	
WOODCOTE HOUSE	31/1/18		Cold cloudy with white frost at night. Inspection of WOODCOTE HOUSE by DDMS XXII Corps.	

Capt. A. McBrown

Army Form C. 2118.

WAR DIARY
or
INTELLIGENCE SUMMARY.
(Erase heading not required.)

CONFIDENTIAL

WAR DIARY

OF

62nd FIELD AMBULANCE

FROM 1st February 1918. TO 28th February. 1918.

COMMITTEE FOR THE
MEDICAL HISTORY OF THE WAR
Date -8 APR. 1918

Army Form C. 2118.

62 Field Amb.

WAR DIARY
or
INTELLIGENCE SUMMARY.
(Erase heading not required.)

Page 74

Place	Date	Hour	Summary of Events and Information	Remarks and references to Appendices
WOODCOTE HOUSE	1/2/18		Whereabouts & strength as at. Col.H. J.H. PRIDHAM	
I.BOC.4.1 Sheet 1/20 Ypres	2/2/18		Gen Sir E. Bulfin A.D. night inspection of Woodcote House. AAJ	
	3/2/18		Gen E. Capt J.W.L. BLAMEY R.A.M.C. S.R. reports for duty. No 336122 Pte HORAN W.17.A. attached to wrong S.S.S (Basses) Lieut RYAN posted to 92B52 R.F.A in lieu of Capt T.E. ROBERTS. AAJ	
	4/2/18		Weather fair. Lieut. L.A. RYAN returns from duty with 92/B52 R.F.A. AAJ	
	5/2/18		Weather fair. Capt F.L.P.G. BENNETT from Rouen O.K. reports to the unit. Conference at ADMS office ref handing over the evacuation route in the left section by 61st F.A. AAJ	
	6/2/18		Weather fair. Capt F.L.P.G. BENNETT to 12A Kings on relief of Capt L.D. MACOB (blues on sick list) Medical arrangements for XII Corps to replace troops of IX Corps. C.C. Scales being transferred to the Remy Group of C.C. Stns via Ypres Poperinghe & via Pesces Junct Pickelaich	

Army Form C. 2118.

62nd Field Amb

WAR DIARY
or
INTELLIGENCE SUMMARY.
(Erase heading not required.)

Instructions regarding War Diaries and Intelligence Summaries are contained in F.S. Regs., Part II. and the Staff Manual respectively. Title pages will be prepared in manuscript.

Place	Date	Hour	Summary of Events and Information	Remarks and references to Appendices
WOODIOT HOUSE 2. IDOLTUS. SH.Y.28 Y60000	7/2/18		Bright sunshine, information now at night. Relief of bearers up the line. 61 9A bearers being posted to deft Sec for 1 NCO & 10 OR to CLAPHAM in excess. 1 NCO 5 men to 6 ADS MENIN ROAD 19 c 66. Lieut gt Hill RAMC to Scabies IP CAESTRE for duty YHt	
	8/2/18		Rain in morning fine afternoon. O.C. 12 MAC called for consultation ret evacuation system. Capt. S J BEALE RAMC having reported his arrival for duty is taken on the strength of this unit YHt	
	9/2/18		Weather fine. Evacuation of the Northern Sector (81 Bde) taken over by 61st YA. CLAPHAM JUNCTION J.13.d.9.9 & JACKDAW Post J.19.6.1.9 being duty hand over. 62 YA being responsible for the remaining lines of evacuation 1 NCO & 5 OR of 61 sent to ADS MENIN ROAD also 1 SOR of 60 YA to own. 2 PM. Capt CW STALLARD RAMC & Capt w SAPPINSTON MORC U.S. return to their unit 61 YA. YHt	
	10/2/18		Rain overnight & day. Report HMS, my promotion of special cases Counter with OC 61 YA, re arrangements for serial cases from ADS Capt H G JACOB Evacuated B5 from Dys B(?) can cee Shn. YHt	

A. 7092. Wt. W285.9/M1293. 750,000. 1/17. D. D. & L. Ltd. Forms/C2118/44.

WAR DIARY
or
INTELLIGENCE SUMMARY

Army Form C. 2118.

6975 Field Amb.

Place	Date	Hour	Summary of Events and Information	Remarks and references to Appendices
MooSeeK House	11/2/18		Weather fine. OR of 60 to 61 rgt at ADS MERVIN. An officer of 30/4 reported for particulars of ADS & bearer posts & general sanitary scheme of Woodcote House. GM.	page 96.
120 c.43 May 1.25 Ypres	12/2/18		Slight rain over night. Fine & warmer. Mr Say. One officer & 20 OR of 30th YA reported at noon, & proceeded to Canada shift & ant stations with the bearers of this unit at the various relay posts etc. GM.	
	13.2.18.		Transport moves by road with transport of 697 BS, starting La Clytte 10.45AM via LOCHRE & BAILLEUL arriving in billets STRAZEELE 4 PM. Lt Ryan Transport officer. Capt Beale & orderly relay party by amb. car to EBLINGHEM 60 YA arrive 2 P.M. Signal to me of 60 YA leaving personnel C moves up this to relieve personnel C of this unit. Relieved of this late & administration of Woodcote House taken over by 30 YA. Rained all day, fine after 5 P.M. GM.	

WAR DIARY
or
INTELLIGENCE SUMMARY

Army Form C. 2118.

62 Field Amb.

Page 144

Place	Date	Hour	Summary of Events and Information	Remarks and references to Appendices
ERUNGHEM T.26.8.3	14/2/18		Weather fine. Unit packed up preparatory to entraining. Dickebusch 3 p.m. arriving Elvingham 6.30 p.m. HQ Ors. established at Shf. 29 Z.0000 T.22.6.83	
Shf/27 T.0.0.0	15/2/18		ROC.S.S. Reconnoitred S for Adv. camp & sch collects from 59th Inf B.D. Taps. Prep. cd for 20 patients stabld S at a barn at T.22.6.8.3. Cases for evacuation to No 15.C.C.S. T.18.central. Whose height 4.048	
	16/2/18		Yesterday night say four Russians with 01 disease for bath. At present office in S.Ms. baths. Capt Ryan proceeds to sortie to Musset offrs Sch. Sergt Dalton joining account 40.25.S. Capt Blaney to report CRE 24.B. as me i/c of Coy.	
	18/2/18	4.0 a.m.	O.R.me Marched to 15 CCS for temporary duties. Capt F.C.Chandler RAMC assumed duties temporary I/D & DMS XX Division via Capt A.d Hammond - Saddle Borne in linen	Mc
	19/2/18		Lt Ryan US MO Rt returns from XX II Corps School. Capt. Blaney RAMC Sn apptomed thrown' 2/M acting no M.O. Mc Doull, R.E.o.	Mc

Th Mannin nun has granted "1914 STAR" ribbon. —
T/19004 Sgt Maj. G. Rositen ASC HT. cAH 12 F. Amb. M.5/2727 Sgt S.F. Mason ASC M.T. c A 62 F.A.M. 19281 PL North O.T.F.T. RAMC, 7/04 Pt Henderson A.

WAR DIARY
INTELLIGENCE SUMMARY

Page 78

Place	Date	Hour	Summary of Events and Information	Remarks and references to Appendices
EBBLINGHEM	18		15113 Pte. LINES T.A. R.A.M.C. 6664 Pte. TURFREY E.H. R.A.M.C.	
T2268.3	21/2/18		LT.COL. G.H.S.JACK R.A.M.C. his extra Mr. E.i.S C.C.S. CAPT J.P.POISHAM R.C.R.M.C. took on temporary command. CAPT J.S. BEAUFORD being absent on leave. 15g, + 2 o.r. 62 F Amb. proceeded in Motor Ambulance car to new area XVIII Corps II Army. They proceeded to NESLE (S Lof AMIENS) in large charge of Driven with ambulance cars left at 10am for NESLE when he reported at	
	22/2/18		LT & 8 M. J.R. KENSHOLE R.A.M.C. 60 F. Amb. OMENCOURT (Sheet 66 D N.24) 62 F. Amb. including transport left billets at EBBLINGHEM 9am T moved via WALLON CAPPEL & MURBECQUE ESTEENBECQUE STATION arriving 6 p.m. Ambulance entrained there. TRAIN left 9 pm	
LE PLESSIS 66D W.I.C.9.I.	23/2/18		Train arrived NESLE (AMIENS) 7:30am Ambulance detrained. B.R.C.M.C. who crossed near station. Ambulance marched off 11am via 4 AM to billets at LE PLESSIS Sheet 66 D W.I C.9.I. arriving 4 pm. Weather on whole journey fine. MEN - Animals entrained journey well. MOTOR AMBULANCE CARS & CYCLIST clan LT 9.8.M. J.R. KENSHOLER R.A.M.C. Obtained with CAPT J.S.BEALE M.C.R.M.C. UNIT of 20 DIV. now in XVIII CORPS II ARMY	

WAR DIARY
or
INTELLIGENCE SUMMARY.
(Erase heading not required.)

Army Form C. 2118.

Place	Date	Hour	Summary of Events and Information	Remarks and references to Appendices
LE PLESSIS W1 C9.1/66D.	24/2/18	25 O.R.	D.A.D.M.S 62 F. Amb. located at 10 a.m. to 41 CCS CUENY (SM.15.6d) to report for temporary duty with CCS CORPS TROOPS. FOOT WASHING & INSPECTION gear - BILLETS cleared up. Incinerator & disinfectors constructed. Bath huts, ante latrines during moves arranged. ADDENDUM.	PPbE 79 9/2
	21/2/18		Pte GILLISPIE W. reported back from CENTRAL MEDICAL OFFICE.	9/2
	22/2/18		LT R. AN V.S. MORC located to V Army RAM school in structure at 61 CCS. Syllabus of training & F.Amb. commenced. Squads confined with lectures & stretcher drill.	9/2
	23/2/18		Instructed by D.D.M.S. XVIII Corps Col A.K. PRYNNE & A.D.M.S. Ex Div. St Col. Sgt. STARK R.A.M.C. reported unit. A.D.M.S. Inspected billets. Capt. LOW R.S.C. hyperchaeupinstitut	9/2 9/2
		2 pm	Horse arranged for a 1 hour as Riemannes School Court to Cultivate. 9 pm Orders stand by ready to move in 2-4 hours were received. Immediately all arrangements made to more to be ready to Move at 7 & hours notice	9/2

Army Form C. 2118

WAR DIARY
or
INTELLIGENCE SUMMARY
(Erase heading not required.)

Vol 31

140/2902-

Confidential.

WAR DIARY
OF
62nd FIELD AMBULANCE

From 1st March 1918.
To 31st March 1918.

COMMITTEE FOR THE
MEDICAL HISTORY OF THE WAR
Date 16 JUN. 1918

62nd Field Ambulance

WAR DIARY
or
INTELLIGENCE SUMMARY.

Army Form C. 2118.

(Erase heading not required.)

Page 80

Place	Date	Hour	Summary of Events and Information	Remarks and references to Appendices
LE PLESSIS W.I.C.9.b. Sheet 66D 1/40,000	1/3/18		Weather cold & cloudy with slight rain. Local affairs in progress & consult't rest. Wk. Start marking out of boundary of "Regimental Garden". Conference of O.A. Commanders at ADMS office. Temp. Capt. O. HEATH reports for duty. Substituted O.C.	
"	2/3/18		Heavy fall of snow. In acc with 61st Bde M.O. 246. Rear Zone of defences reconnoitred ie DURY area. M.A.Batt. DCLI move from FRESNICHES (P.8.a.) to CURCHY H.9.b. GHS	
"	3/3/18		Day dull with fine rain in early morning & showing there all day. Temp. Capt. HEATH. R.A.M.C. ordered to report for duty MDS 92nd Bde R.F.A. GHS	
"	4/3/18		Light mostly now all day. 61st Inf Bde instructions received re more & location of ADSs in support of Cavalry Corps. GHS only	
"	5/3/18		Weather fine. 6.O.R. trained in trench foot treatment & duties to units of 61st Bde. Capt Chandler & Capt Pickham ADMS D.V. badges of act Major with GOC ADMD.V. GHS	

WAR DIARY
INTELLIGENCE SUMMARY

68a? Field Ambulance
Army Form C. 2118.

Page 81

Place	Date	Hour	Summary of Events and Information	Remarks and references to Appendices
LE PLESSIS HUT C.21 SHEET 36D 1/40,000	6/3/18		Warm and bright Sunshine. Inspection of camp by A.D.M.S. 5th KSLI 60th Bde. move to CUGNY arrangements made to collect sick by this unit. GHH	
"	7/3/18		Warm with bright Sunshine slight frost at night. Maj CHANDLIER proceeds to UK 14 days leave 8th-22nd inst. Inspection & Gas drill all ranks by Bde Gas Officer. 1st Lieut RYAN returned from 61 CCSts. School of Instruction Paris. GHH	
"	8/3/18		lost 15 at VILLESELVE. Warm with frost at night. 5/3 Squadron Frenguons a medical officer to investigate an outbreak of Measles. Capt BLAMEY & Lieut S to report inspect contacts daily — two cases evacuated to 54 CCS to 026 D near GHH	
"	9/3/18		Bright Sunshine all day. 20th Div. Rees passing held at 026D near ERCHEU. All ranks march to the courses & back. GHH	
"	10/3/18		Fine day with whili? frost at night. 2 cases of measles from 5/3 Sqn RFC reported to go.	
"	11/3/18		Conference of A.D.M.S. YFA Commanders at DDMS. 4 OR to 61 CCS. School of Instruction Paris for a course. 2 SOR to 4 CCS to wr in to of 25 — at present attache's to that unit. MT My potom, Bruns? supply? motor transport of the unit GHH	

Army Form C. 2118.

62 Field Ambulance
Page 82

WAR DIARY
or
INTELLIGENCE SUMMARY.
(Erase heading not required.)

Place	Date	Hour	Summary of Events and Information	Remarks and references to Appendices
LE PLESSIS Mil C.C.S.	12/3/18		Bright fine day with a slight frost at night. 1st Lieut L.A.Ry? on MORC U.S. attached as M.O. to 92 Bde R.G.A. Reinf. See O.C. Report. RFC at PILLESELVE & arrange for M.O. in charge of the Battalion there to see his sick (as is done there as reports to for Post Masters. GHQ)	
"	13/3/18		Inspection of transport by O.C. Dir Train & A.D.S. Weather warm & fine. GHQ	
"	14/3/18		Dull morning bright afternoon no rain. Div Gas Officer on lects will (accompany) gas box respirators of all ranks. GHQ	
"	15/3/18		Bright warm day, dull afternoon followed by rain at night. GHQ	
"	16/3/18		Bright southerly wind, slight frost at night. GHQ	

Army Form C. 2118.

WAR DIARY
or
INTELLIGENCE SUMMARY.

(Erase heading not required.)

625th Field Ambulance 6a Page 8 C

Place	Date	Hour	Summary of Events and Information	Remarks and references to Appendices
Le Plissis W.I.C.9.1. Sh.11/66D 1/40,000	17/3/18		Warren brig & 1 Say Unit athletic sports held. Gas	
"	18/3/18		Genl. SEE Agricultural officer of Corps re seeds for Regimental Garden.	
"	19/3/18		Inspect present Medical sites with NCOs Parade Day #8.	
"	20/3/18		Transport stand by ready to move.	
		5 pm	Hospital evacuated and dismantled	
		6.30 pm	Orderly for fees marching out.	
		8.30 pm	Unit and transport Parade moves off 3 Kilometres and returns at 9 p.m. Transport remains loaded. Gas	
"	21/3/18		Orders "Man Battle Area" received at 2 p.m. Units will march independently to their areas.	
		2.30 pm	Unit complete parades and moves via BERLANCOURT – VILLESELVE – EAUCOURT – OLLEZY – to DURY and bivouacs at X.30.C.5.5. /66D Advanced Brigade Headquarters established at OLLEZY. Conference of Unit Commanders at Brigade Headquarters. Patients evacuated through 98th Field Ambulance.	

WAR DIARY
or
INTELLIGENCE SUMMARY.

Army Form C. 2118.

62nd Field Ambulance

Page 84

Place	Date	Hour	Summary of Events and Information	Remarks and references to Appendices
	22/3/18		Report 61st Bde 11.0 a.m.	
		11.30am	Orders to move to BROUCHY. Bridge at R.1.a.9.9./66D Blown up.	
		12 noon	Unit moves to via SONNETTE-EAUCOURT — Q.6.a.7.0 — HAM — K.31.d.4.3. AUBIGNY — BROUCHY. A.D.S. formed at CUGNY. Bearer Posts manned. R.A. Posts at L.25.a.2.2.; R.H.C.4.0.2; R.7.a.3.7. Orders to come under administration of A.D.M.S. 36th Division. O.C. 110th Field Ambulance established at Q.10.c.9.3./66D. Report A.D.M.S. 36th Division and consult O.C. 110th Field Ambulance giving our locations.	
		4 pm	Evacuations of wounded from 36th Division, 20th Division and 14th Division cases 61 B.C. 6th found closed. Cases evacuated by Ambt Cars & M.A.C. to ROYE	
BROUCHY	23/3/18	2 a.m	Sergt Smith R.A.M.C. and 8 Other Ranks R.A.M.C. not reported at A.D.S. after Bridge at SONNETTE-EAUCOURT blown up, last been evacuating cases from DURY.	
		10-30am	Orders to move unit to LE PLESSIS. Posts withdrawn from SONNETTE-EAUCOURT O.C. 110 R Field Ambce carries on evacuations from EAUCOURT to BROUCHY. A.D.S. to be formed at VILLESELVE Q.35.a.8.d./66D. Bearer Relay Post at Q.30.C.2.3. and R.20.c.9.4.	

Army Form C. 2118.

62nd Field Ambulance
Page 85

WAR DIARY
or
INTELLIGENCE SUMMARY.
(Erase heading not required.)

Place	Date	Hour	Summary of Events and Information	Remarks and references to Appendices
BROUCHY	23/3/18		Report Medical Officers of the Battalions 61st Inf. Bde., placing 2 Gunners at each Headquarters and informing M.O.'s location.	
		10-30am	Unit moved to LE PLESSIS via NILLESELVE and BERLANCOURT arriving 11-30am CUGNY becomes untenable. A.D.S. withdrawn to VILLESELVE.	
		2-30pm	Unit moved to GUISCARD site of IIIrd Corps Rest Station occupied by 54 Fld Amb 61st Inf. Bde. and 62nd Fld Ambce attached to 36th Division.	
		9pm	54 Field Ambulance moves from GUISCARD.	
GUISCARD	24/3/18		Receiving and evacuating Wounded and Sick from IIIrd Corps and XVIIIth Corps. Number of Wounded treated; English, Officers 8, Other Ranks 279. French " 3 " " 186.	
		2pm	A.D.S. withdrawn to BERLANCOURT.	
		6-30pm	GUISCARD becomes untenable by shell fire, all patients rapidly evacuated. Unit assembles on the NOYON Road at D.22.c.2.2/40E. Units bivouacs 3 men unaccounted for believed stragglers. No orders received from 36th Division of 61st Inf Bde.	
	25/3/18		Unit moves after midnight through NOYON to C.12.a./40E on the NOYON-ROYE Road. O.C. proceed to "G" Office XVIIIth Corps for orders in location of unit. Referred to A.D.M.S. 36th Division at AURICOURT CHATEAU. Orders to be attached to 61st Inf Bde and to march to PARVILLERS. PARVILLERS arrived at 9pm Capt. Blamey R.A.M.C. reports to A.D.M.S. 20th Division for duty.	

WAR DIARY or INTELLIGENCE SUMMARY.

Army Form C. 2118.

62nd Field Ambulance

Page 86

Place	Date	Hour	Summary of Events and Information	Remarks and references to Appendices
	26/3/18	6:00am	Marched from PARVILLERS to LE QUESNIL. Starting from VILLERS-LE-ROYE. Evacuating sick of Division and collecting Stragglers en route. Unit came under administration of A.D.M.S. 20th Division. Headquarters established at VILLERS-AUX-ERABLES. Walking W'ded Post at FRESNOY manned by 1 Officer and 9 Other Ranks. 1 Officer and 26 Other Ranks report to O.C. 61st Field Ambulance A.D.S. at LE QUESNIL. Sick and wounded evacuated to HARGICOURT by 31 M.A.C. 193 W'ded through A.D.S.	
VILLERS AUX ERABLES	27/3/18		A.D.S at HARGICOURT closed. Evacuations to NAMPES. 94 W'ded Cpl W Morris Pte E Taylor R.A.M.C. missing.	
SAINS-EN-AMIENOIS	28/3/18		Unit moves to DOMART SUR-LA-LUCE concentration of Division, thence at 4 p.m. to SAINS-en-AMIENOIS arriving 10 p.m. Heavy rain during the evening. All OMT vehicles, personnel and equipment attached to 61st Field Ambulance. Capt BANBURY RAMC attached to 61st Field Ambulance to limit. Capt PROCTOR RAMC to 61st Field Ambulance for duty. Weather cold with heavy rain in the evening	

WAR DIARY
INTELLIGENCE SUMMARY

62nd Field Ambulance

Army Form C. 2118.

Place	Date	Hour	Summary of Events and Information	Remarks and references to Appendices
	29/3/18		Weather cold but mild.	
		2pm	62nd Field Ambulance with 60th Field Ambee, 59th Bde transport and 61st Bde transport moves SEUX to billets under command of O.C. 62nd Fld Ambce	
WARLUS	30/3/18		Unit moves from SEUX to WARLUS to billets. 7/8	
			Heavy rain during the day.	
ABBEVILLE	31/3/18		From WARLUS to ABBEVILLE arriving 5 p.m. Bearers to Batt Details Camp. Transport to A.D.M.T. Browns Camp. Report A.A.B.M.G. L. of. C. and D.M.S. L. of. C. Officers HWt Mame	

Army Form C. 2118.

WAR DIARY
or
INTELLIGENCE SUMMARY.
(Erase heading not required.)

War Confidential Diary
of
62nd Field Ambulance

From 1st April 1918
to 30th April 1918

160/900

Vol 32

COMMITTEE FOR THE
MEDICAL HIST...
Date — 6 JUN 1918

62nd Field Ambulance

Army Form C. 2118.

WAR DIARY
or
INTELLIGENCE SUMMARY.
(Erase heading not required.)

Page 88

Place	Date	Hour	Summary of Events and Information	Remarks and references to Appendices
ABBEVILLE	1/4/18		Weather fine. Orders for putting ambulance cycles for prisoners. Transport requested by another Unit started 1.5 by O.C. A.D.M.T. Capt. Banbury RAMC. RANBURY rank having reported sick departure for Calais is fixed off. Mr. Scargett Supplies transport of 62 & 60 Fd (Sols) taken over by O.C. 62nd Fd Train to men.	
"	2/4/18.		Weather fine. Lucie & aircraft Boots Clothing & Harness Waggons unpacked & a full complement of drivers & waggons now at S of horses. A.V.C. officer inspecting horses – One Heavy Draft Cas'f. dis.	
"	3/4/18.		This morning light train survey of horses. Harness cleaned & Hayracks & Saddles oiled. 62 & 60 Fd H. to Jornets 1st Sy to QUEVAUVILLERS. Stormy night of W.W – 5 Fd at SOREL	
SOREL	4/4/18.		62 & 60 Fd moved from ABBEVILLE to SOREL (5 killed) 0.6. proceeds to OURAU. called to A.Div. for further instructions. Orders to remain at SOREL. Reported A.D.M.S. Heavy rain during afternoon & evg. Gas	
"	5/4/18.		4 AS refreshed at SOREL. Reported 60st/Bde H.Q. & reconnoitre LABOISSIERE for Dr.W.18. & light rain all day	

Army Form C. 2118.

WAR DIARY 62nd Field Ambulance

INTELLIGENCE SUMMARY.

(Erase heading not required.)

Page 89

Place	Date	Hour	Summary of Events and Information	Remarks and references to Appendices
LABOISSIERS	6/4/18		60 F.A. marches under orders under O.C. unit. 62 F.A. marches to LABOISSIERS. 20 Kilometer trek covering. 3.30 P.M. Capt. (Br) Lt. Beck reconnoiters to report W.O. 9 issues of am. Equ. struck off strength. My Chaston, from L.ieuts & Capt. Blaney from 61 F.A. reported for duty. My Chaston, from Lieuts & Capt. Blaney from 61 F.A. reported for duty. Our trip from GHQ.S from 61 F.A. reported for duty. Hospital established horses in a barn & 60 PR sick collects came in the afternoon. Major Chaston Sr. takes the charge. appointment of reg n.o. to CMDs	
"	7/4/18		All troops at rest after 3 & chickens. Visit My under Maj. met Major sent for medical way and equipment. Day fair with heavy rain at night.	
"	8/4/18		Weather cold & rain all day. Waggons Stores & supplies reported. WOMP & master W.8121 for S.Sgt Norris, Sgt Brazier, Dvr Youens & Edwards ph page the Hinton & Thompson (went Sick v.s. m.m.) also Cpl Beck (bar & m.c.)	

WAR DIARY or INTELLIGENCE SUMMARY

Army Form C. 2118.

62nd Field Ambulance

Page 40

Place	Date	Hour	Summary of Events and Information	Remarks and references to Appendices
LABOISSIERE	9/4/18		Rain all day. Maj Chandler with BSr Commander view area for billets. Visited HQ RS & Inspection by ADMS.	
MORIVAL	10/4/18		Unit marches with 61st (Bch) from LABOISSIERE to MORIVAL starting 10 AM arriving 3.30 PM. 60 mr RO stragglers chiefly sore feet upon 13 mi keys collected en route. Pts fed, seen established in a barn. Sgt Bell commander & observer collection finding obscure billeting of stragglers some 15 yr? not rung rain up to arrival in the L. 9pm.	
AULT	11/4/18		Orders received just after midnight to entrain meant. Unit marches tr his BSE to AULT starting 8 AM arriving 2.30 PM. Maj R. Sheen & party by lt btwns to Doullens & transpt conv from Pt & Acit arrive 8.30 am & 2 pm. Some 15-20 cases of sore feet, bronchitis & inst. Cases & others to wait for billets - another billet secured in the village had of province patients not to make room for patched in warm quarters.	

Army Form C. 2118.

WAR DIARY 62nd Field Ambulance

or

INTELLIGENCE SUMMARY.

page 91

(Erase heading not required.)

Place	Date	Hour	Summary of Events and Information	Remarks and references to Appendices
AULT	12/4/18		Day fine & bright. Got Sanitation to open room at the Casino & got the water turned on. Have difficulty of obtaining a tin for kitchen wash hand's latrines &c.	
"	13/4/18		Asked i.e. ADMS of GAMACHES. See O.C Div. Col. at service time of dinner as to Bar. Our ration can arrived. S. Lieut. Inspection by DDMS XXth Corps marked in pen.	
	14/4/18		Mr. M.n burns cold, high wind all day. 62 FA becomes the DRS. 1st visit Hamater ADRC reports for duty. Gas taking in the strength Have beds to obtain, & held 2 sick men. Then increasing hospital accommodation in Casino	
	15/4/18		Weather cold and wet. See opinion of District Officer R.E. would be to fix up the building of Potopan church schools by Maxwell Bry.	
	16/4/18		Day looking rain. See 9 to 10. Warning issued to be in preparedness for hospital shortly sick to be got ready by OBS Commander. Mng 40 sick evacuated quite to give room in case ordered.	

62nd Field Ambulance

Page 92

WAR DIARY
INTELLIGENCE SUMMARY

Place	Date	Hour	Summary of Events and Information	Remarks and references to Appendices
AULT.	17/4/18		Warning orders "Be ready to move" received. Billeting party to new area. Transport moves by road. Starting 8PM & marching all night. Weather cold with showers of rain.	
MARQUAY Seine Inf.	18/4/18		Personnel entrain at EU at 8 A.M. under Div orders - detrain at TINQUES 9.30 PM. arrive billets of MARQUAY after midnight. Div in GHQ Reserve under 1st Army. Transport arrives EAUCOURT S.E. of Abbeville 11 A.M. & for 8½ hrs halt moves to WILLENCOURT N.W. of AUXI LE CHATEAU. Cold wind with showers.	
	19.4.18		Personnel of unit arrives MARQUAY 12.15 A.M. Transport marches from WILLENCOURT to OCOCH! arriving 6 PM. Inspection by ADMS. Weather cold with showers of hail. 12 N.C.O.s & O.Rs Hospital & 1 nurse sick evacuated to No 12 Stationary on St Pol.	

WAR DIARY 62nd Field Ambulance or INTELLIGENCE SUMMARY.

Army Form C. 2118.

page 98

Place	Date	Hour	Summary of Events and Information	Remarks and references to Appendices
MARQUAY	20/4/18		Lecture by Corps Commander (XVIII) to Officers NCO's & left of Div. Orange for stretcher bearer classes for Battalions. Visit by DDMS Corps. reconnoitre for other billets nearer to hospital in Div area. Weather cold with snow showers in morning.	
	21/4/18		Visit by Div Q. ref to moving of unit to another site. Also all regimental medical officers met with stretcher bearers. Weather fine.	
	22/4/18		ADMS lectures regimental medical officers. Orange for taking of 60 TMB stretcher bearers to be billeted in BAILLEUL and lectures by the unit. Weather cold with some rain in eve. Inspection of horses & mules by Box Veterinary officer in MASSON in Infantry by OC. 161 Coy ASC.	

WAR DIARY 62nd Field Ambulance   Army Form C. 2118
or
INTELLIGENCE SUMMARY   Page 9 K

Place	Date	Hour	Summary of Events and Information	Remarks and references to Appendices
MAROUAY	23/4/18		Call on OC 12 Shr.P ref return to duty of 83 Div cases. Day fair.	
"	24/4/18		Inspect of Hosps by ADMS Div. ADMS inspects men of 182 proposed for lower categry at 62 FA. 61 F.A. open a scabies R/for cases from Div. Daughter & but survey Transfr. showers 9PM	
"	25/4/18		Reconnoitre with ADMS site for Ambulance & Hospital accommodation. Showers during the day. Egypt. Stables Camp exercises	
"	26/4/18		Wreath of fire. Orders prepare to receive scabies patients of Div.	
"	27/4/18		Inspection of transport by OC Div Train & ADMS. Orders to officers by Div Educational officers. Orders reserve supply to move to LE QUESNEL as soon as possible. Scabies cases & transport 55 from 61st & 60 FAs. Bath Parade to LE QUESNEL. Scabies Camp partially disinfected. Ordered to detail officer to see sick of New Cape Cyclists at PENIN vicinity.	

WAR DIARY 62nd Field Ambulance

INTELLIGENCE SUMMARY

Page 96.

Place	Date	Hour	Summary of Events and Information	Remarks and references to Appendices
MARQUAY	28/4/18		Col. K. Blaney Detailed, who arranged for the early inspection & evacuation of Sick. Day wet & misty.	
LE QUESNEL	28/4/18		Unit moves complete to LE QUESNEL. Hospital with Scabies Section established & holds 15 from MARQUAY transferred there. Report ADMS. 9 Sgt. 63 San. Sect. inf. consistency of village quts. Weather fine with cold winds.	
"	29/4/18		Orders to move to new area with 61 Bar. Group & transfer scabies cases to 61 94 batts to Unit to be clear of Billets by 11.30 AM. Hospital Sid over HS. Scabies cases which transferred to DRS 61st Field Amb. Unit billets/Mainparty CAMBLAIN L'ABBE area. Unit Parades and transport at 11.45. when orders to return to Bn. HQ. Arranges for sick of 94 by RE received. Reported to Bn. HQ & ADMS. On moving with heavy heavy was at MARQUAY to be seen daily. Your morning with heavy was showers in afternoon.	

Army Form C. 2118

WAR DIARY
or
INTELLIGENCE SUMMARY 62nd Field Ambulance
(Erase heading not required.)

Page 96.

Place	Date	Hour	Summary of Events and Information	Remarks and references to Appendices
LES VENTS	30/7/18		Orders "Move at once to thus area" received 11.30 AM. Billetting party sent in advance. Unit moved 1.30 PM from Le Quesnel by roads arriving LES VENTS at 5.30 with odd 9 A Sick. Rain all day. Officers detach Hotel Rome	

140/983.

62nd F.A.

COMMITTEE FOR THE
MEDICAL HISTORY
Date 9 JUL 1918

Aug 1/18

Army Form C. 2118

WAR DIARY
or
INTELLIGENCE SUMMARY
(*Erase heading not required.*)

Vol 33

Secret

War Diary
of
62 nd Field Ambulance

From 1st May 1918 to 31st May 1918

WAR DIARY or INTELLIGENCE SUMMARY

Army Form C. 2118

62nd Field Ambulance

Page 97

Place	Date	Hour	Summary of Events and Information	Remarks and references to Appendices
QUARTRE VENTS	1-5-18		6th Infy Bde relieves 9th Canadian Bde on left of Divisional Front.	
		12 noon	Orders received to move and to take over of A.D.S. and posts from 9th Canadian Field Ambce.	
			Posts taken over and relief completed by 6 p.m.	
			Major J. Prydhoes R.A.M.C. and bearers from "B" section proceed thither by lorry: remainder of unit thy road, arriving 6 p.m.	
			Disposition: Headquarters JENKS'S SIDING. 36c/S.2.c.8.3.	
			A.D.S. WHITE HOUSE 36c/M.28.8.7.1.	
			Left R.A.P. 36c/M.18.d.8.1.	
			Right R.A.P. 36c/M.24.c. central.	
			Consult O.C. 9th Canadian Field Ambce re disposition of Posts, and reliefs.	
			Weather fine.	
S.2.c.8.3. Sheet 36c Jenks Siding	2-5-18		Colonel's Post (36c/M.33.a.1.9.) taken over. Visit from A.D.M.S.	
			(b) 2nd Field Ambce moves to and becomes D.M.Dsg Stn at ABLAIN-ST. NAZAIRE.	
			See O.C. Gramways at LENS, functions re trams service for evacuation.	
			Weather bright.	

62nd Field Ambulance

WAR DIARY
or
INTELLIGENCE SUMMARY
(Erase heading not required.)

Army Form C. 2118

Page 98

Place	Date	Hour	Summary of Events and Information	Remarks and references to Appendices
S.2.C.8.3 Shed 36c Jonas Souding	3/5/18		Visit by A.D.M.S. Weather bright and warm. Captain L. SATOW. R.A.M.C and 1st Lieut. E.R. WEBBER. M.O.R.C. USA, report for duty	
	4/5/18		60th Field Ambulance moves to CHATEAU-de-la-HAIE. 60th Field Ambulance take there at 20 Div/BAl Bn. Arrange for evacuations of 59th Infy Bde in reserve area:- 11th Rifle Bde. (36c/S.8.C.) 11th K.R.R.C. COLUMBIA Camp (36c/S.13.C.) 2nd Scotch Rifles ALBERTA Camp (36c/X.18.a), also evacuations from No 2 Canadian Infy Works Battalion. CARENCY. Inspect site in BOIS de la HAIE for transport lines. Weather fine.	
	5/5/18		Reconnoitre sites for unit transport. Inspection by D.M.S. XVIII Corps. Rained all day.	
	6/5/18		Arrange with O.C. 61st Field Amblce. re system of keeping No D. Books while evacuating to D.M.S. Inspect site for units transport at X.16.c Shed 36.B. and report to A.D.M.S. Rain in morning. Fine in evening.	
	7/5/18		See District Commandant and Lieut BOSTOCK re accommodation at BOSTOCK camp. 1st Lieut C.T. HAMAKER M.O.R.C. posted to 48th Army F.A. Bde for duty M.A.C. car withdrawn from A.D.S. Recommendations for 7/Pte 344154 Pte F.SMITH and No.329509 Pte T. Mc WHANNEL, R.A.M.C. submitted	

Army Form C. 2118

WAR DIARY
or
INTELLIGENCE SUMMARY

(Erase heading not required.)

62nd Field Ambulance Page 99.

Place	Date	Hour	Summary of Events and Information	Remarks and references to Appendices
S.2.C.8.3 Sheet 36C John's Siding	8/5/18		See proposed site for units transport with A.D.M.S. 20th Div and also proposed site for [Gas] Centre. "B" Section Bearers relieved "B" Section Bearers at A.D.S. and R.A.P's. Orders to establish Gas Centre forthwith at X.14 central 36 B. and remove all surplus transport to rear. Transport moves to BOSTOCK Camp CARENCY X.15.d. 36 B.	
	9/5/18		Conference of Fd Amb. Commanders at A.D.M.S. Office. 62nd Field Amb to form Walking Wounded Centre and emergency Gas Centre. Major J.A. PRIDHAM. R.A.M.C. detailed to establish emergency Gas Centre at BATHS with Y.M.C.A. Hut at Railway Siding. 36 B/ X.14. central. Left R.A.P. withdrawn to 36C/ M.10.d.9. Right R.A.P. withdrawn to 36.C/M.23.d.n.8. Increase the number of Bearer Squads up line by 3 extra squads. Arrange with O.C. Tramways at LENS Junction re evacuation from A.D.S. by train. 1st Lieut G.H. RICHARDS. U.S.M.C. 60th Fld Amb. reported for temporary duty.	
	10/5/18		59th Infy Bde relieved 61st Infy Bde. Weather fine.	
	11/5/18		See medical officers of 61st Infy. Bde groups on rest re evacuation of their sick. also M.O.'s 20 Div. M.G. Bathy R.A.P. Reconnoitre site for Right R.A.P. The Field Marshall Commanding-in-Chief, under authority granted by His Majesty the King awarded a Bar to the Military Cross to T/Capt. S.J.A. BEAKE. M.C. R.A.M.C. Weather fine. rain last night.	

62 and Field Ambulance
Page 100

WAR DIARY
or
INTELLIGENCE SUMMARY
(Erase heading not required.)

Army Form C. 2118

Place	Date	Hour	Summary of Events and Information	Remarks and references to Appendices
S.2.C.2.3. Sheet 36C Jonks Siding	12/5/18		Wet and cold in morning. Fine in afternoon. 1st Lieut G.H. RICHARDS. MC.U.S.A returned to 62 Field Ambulance. Major J.A. PRIDHAM. M.C. RAMC receives orders to establish Gas Centre. All tentage and the required personnel of unit placed at his disposal. Requisition for necessary ig? and Red Cross material submitted. Capt J.N.H. BLAMEY. RAMC detailed to assist in laying out the camp.	JHS
	13/5/18		Wet all day. Right R.A.P. is again established at 36C/M.24.C.5.6., structural improvements to be made. Col. O.C. Tramways re evacuation to and from new Gas Centre (36.B x.14. central) Plan of 20th Divisional Gas Centre drawn up.	JHS
	14/5/18		Recommendation for No. 34.4576 Cpl J. SMITH and 32950 Pte T. McWhannel returned. Plan of Gas Centre forwarded to ¾ A.D.M.S. 29th Div. Major F.C. CHANDLER. RAMC from D.A.D.S. placed on duty. Siding at E. WHITE HOUSE 36c/N.28.B.4. just out of action by shell fire.	JHS
	15/5/18		Weather fine and warm. 1 N.C.O and 24 men from 60th H.Fd Ambce report for duty. Relief of Stretchers in the line. Reconnoitring Artillery tracks and paths and reserve trenches between COLONELS POST (Sc. M.83.a.9) and Jonks Siding. Siding at A.D.S. WHITE CHATEAU reported damaged by shell fire.	JHS

62nd Field Ambulance

WAR DIARY
or
INTELLIGENCE SUMMARY

Army Form C. 2118

(Erase heading not required.)

Page 101

Place	Date	Hour	Summary of Events and Information	Remarks and references to Appendices
P.2.C.8.3 JENKS SIDING	16/5/18		Weather fine and warm. G.A.S. CENTRE established at 36B/X.14.C.62. Major F.C. CHANDLER. R.A.M.C. from sick list. Consult with D.A.D.M.S. 2nd Div and O.C. 61st Field Amb re car arrangements for evacuation of lying cases.	
		11.75	Weather fine & warm.	
		18.75	Weather hot. Some 40 gas (shell) cases admitted from 2nd Scottish Rifles, treated at N.H.61 Amb. No serious cases.	
		19.75	Institution of train service from Jenks Siding to Lievin Tn. Travel with Adjutant of Trainways on train for consultation and report. Relief of 59th Inf Bde by 61st Inf Bde.	
	20/5/18		Weather fine & warm. Inspection of Gas Centre by D.D.M.S. XVIII Corps.	

WAR DIARY
or
INTELLIGENCE SUMMARY

Army Form C. 2118
62nd Field Ambulance
Page 102

Place	Date	Hour	Summary of Events and Information	Remarks and references to Appendices
S2.c.8.3 36c Junks Siding	21/5/18		Interview with D.D.M.S. and A.D.M.S. at Corps Headquarters. Weather fine & warm.	
	22/5/18		Weather fine & warm. Arrange with M.O i/c 2nd Division R.E's for collection of units sick. Some 20 gassed cases admitted, from 2nd Scottish Rifles, 6 K.S.L.I. and 12 R.F's.	
	23/5/18		Weather stormy. Relief of Bearers in the line.	
	24/5/18		Weather fair.	
	25/5/18		Weather fine.	
	26/5/18		Weather warm. Visit from A.D.M.S. 20th Division. 84 gassed cases admitted from Y Huts X.9 & 12th Kings School Regt.	
	27/5/18		Gas Centre at CARENCY (36B/X.17.c.6.2) Visit from A.D.M.S. 20th Division. Shelling in vicinity of Junks Siding. Gas shell explodes in A.D.S. (36c/M.28.b.7.1) 2 Officers and 14 Other ranks gassed before gas masks on. Located by D.A.D.M.S Train.	
		10am	Monthly sanitation of transport by D.A.D.M.S Train. 72 Gassed cases 20 of 1st Corps troops admitted gassed. 84 OR's & 2 Offrs Corps troops admitted gassed	

WAR DIARY
or
INTELLIGENCE SUMMARY
(Erase heading not required.)

Army Form C. 2118

62nd Field Ambulance
Page 103

Place	Date	Hour	Summary of Events and Information	Remarks and references to Appendices
A.D.C.B.3 Jenks Siding	28/5		Weather fine. See A.D.M.S. re evacuation of sick at Jenks Siding. See O.C. Tramways re train service to CARENCY. Major F.C. CHANDLER admitted to hospital "gassed" (Wounded) also 8 O.Rks R.A.M.C. duty of Bearers at A.D.S. R.A.M.C.	
	29/5		Units headquarters move to GAS CENTRE CARENCY. Capt J. EATON. M.C. R.A.M.C. admitted to hospital "gassed" (Wounded) also 9 O.Rks R.A.M.C. 32 Gassed Cases Corps troops + 13 2nd Division admitted. A.D.S. reports 5 O'clock of gas.	
CARENCY K.19.C.2 Sheet 36B	30/5		A.D.M.S. 90 Div & N.D.M.S. 52nd Division inspect camp. See O.C. Rds Construction Coy re roadway to hospital, and standings for motor transport. R.E's start laying water pipes into camp. Weather warm	
	31/5		LT. C.T. HAMAKER M.O.R.C. U.S.A reports for duty from 4th + 3rd bde R.F.A. Major F.C. CHANDLER R.A.M.C. from sick list. Capt. Downs R.A.M.C. from 52 Div. attack is to visit ward 6 H.S. for instruction. Lt. HAMAKER to 1/10am & 5 p.m. trip in reinforcement. S.22.O.C.6.17 A.M. re wave of gas through these Quarters Etc.	

SECRET.

ADDENDUM NO.2 to OPERATION ORDER NO.109.
(59th Infantry Bde.).

Reference 59th Inf. Bde. O.O.109, para 6, sub-para (a) "The trenches are all clear" will be notified to Brigade Headquarters by the code word "WENT"

The Brigade Gas Officer will notify units when the trenches are fit for re-occupation.

Para.6, sub-para. (d) "Re-occupation of trenches" will be notified to Brigade Headquarters by the code word "DUN".

ACKNOWLEDGE.

                                              Captain,
                               Brigade Major,
18th May 1918.   59th Infantry Brigade.

Issued to all recipients of OO.109.

SECRET.   Copy No. 7

61st. INFANTRY BRIGADE ORDER No. 6.
****

Ref:Maps- Sheets 36B.and) 1/40,000
              36C.   )   17th.May, 1918.

1.   The 61st. Inf. Bde. will relieve the 59th. Inf. Bde. in the LENS Section of the Divisional front on the night 19/20th. May in accordance with the attached Table.

2.   Details of Reliefs will be arranged between Commanding Officers concerned.

3.   Details of work in hand and projected will be taken over from outgoing Battalions of the 59th. Brigade in such a way that continuity of work is not interrupted.

4.   Special maps, plans, photographs, and Trench Stores will be taken over and a list forwarded to Bde. H.Q. 24 hours after relief.

5.   The same dispositions as those of units of the 59th. Inf. Bde. will be taken over.

6.   B.G.C., 61st.Inf.Bde. will assume command of the LENS Sector on completion of the relief on night 19/20th. May.

7.   Completion of reliefs will be reported to Bde. H.Qrs. by the code word:- "KALAS".

8.   Brigade H.Qrs. will close at ABLAIN ST.NAZAIRE at 9.0 P.M., and open at M.27.b.6.7. at the same hour.

9.   All information, orders, Maps and schemes regarding the action of Battalions of the Brigade in Corps Reserve will be handed over to Battalions of the 59th. Inf. Bde. and a receipt obtained.

10.   ACKNOWLEDGE.

                                            E P Combe
                                                        Captain,
                              Brigade Major, 61st. Infantry Brigade.

Issued at 12:15 p.m.

Copies to:-   7. 62nd.Field Amb.   14. 59th.Inf.Bde.
  1. G.O.C.   8. 161st.Coy.A.S.C.   15. 60th. ,,   ,,
  2. King's.   9. Bde,Supply Offr.   16. 72nd. ,,   ,,
  3. Som.L.I.   10. ,, Sig. Offr.   17. Bde. Major.
  4. D.C.L.I.   11. ,, T.O.   18. Staff Capt.
  5. 61st.T.M.BtyM   12. 20th.Div."G".   19. War Diary.
  6. 84th.Fd.Co.R.E.   13. ,,   ,, "Q".   20. File.

TABLE OF RELIEFS.

(Issued with 61st. Infantry Brigade Order No. 6 of 17th. May, 1918.)

Serial No.	Unit.	From.	To.	Relieving.	REMARKS.
1.	7/D.C.L.I.	COLUMBIA CAMP.	LINE. (Right Sub-Sector.)	11/K.R.R.C.	By train from LENS Junction.
2.	7/SOM.L.I.	SOUCHEZ HUTS.	LINE. (Left Sub Sector.)	2/SCOTTISH RIFLES.	-do-
3.	12/KING'S.	ALBERTA CAMP.	SUPPORT.	11/RIFLE BRIGADE.	By March Route. Leave Camp 7-45pm. 500 Yds. interval between Coys.
4.	61st.T.M. BTY.	S.7.d. 5=5.	LINE.	59th. T.M. BATTERY.	By Train from LENS Junction.
5.	61st.ECE. H.Q.	ABLAIN St. NAZAIRE.	LINE.	59th. ECE. H.Q.	Separate instructions have been issued.

Details of movements by train will be issued later.

SECRET.   Copy No. 6.

61st. INFANTRY BRIGADE ORDER No. 7.

Ref. Map- Trench Map, LENS 1/10,000.   22nd. May, 1918.

1. 12/King's will relieve 7/D.C.L.I. in the Right Sub-Sector of the Brigade Front on night 25/26th. May.

2. On Relief, 7/D.C.L.I. will become Battalion in Brigade Reserve, taking over the same dispositions as those at present occupied by 12/King's.

3. All details of Relief will be arranged direct between Commanding Officers concerned.

4. 7/D.C.L.I. will take over all instructions regarding Working Parties provided by the Battalion in Reserve in such a way that continuity of work is not interrupted.

5. All Maps, Trench Stores and details of work in hand and projected will be handed over.

6. Completion of Relief will be wired to Brigade H.Q. by the code-word " SLAB ".

7. ACKNOWLEDGE.

E.P. Combe.

Captain,
Brigade Major, 61st. Infantry Brigade.

Issued through
Signals at 10.45 P.M.

Copies to:- 1. 12/King's.   8. Bde. Sig. Offr.
            2. 7/Som.L.I.   9. 20th. Div. "G".
            3. 7/D.C.L.I.   10. 59th. Inf. Bde.
            4. 61st.T.M.Bty.   11. 72nd. Inf. Bde.
            5. 84th.Fd.Coy.R.E.   12. War Diary.
            6. 62nd.Field Amb.   13. File.
            7. Supply Officer.

COPY NO. 13   SECRET

59th INFANTRY BRIGADE OPERATION ORDER NO. 109.

1. A "Gas Beam" attack is being carried out on the XVIII Corps front from T.9.b. to N.25.b. on the night of May 16/17th, or the first night after on which the wind is favourable.

2. On the Divisional Front the gas will be discharged from trucks on which the cylinders are loaded from the two tram-heads.

3. On the 59th Inf. Bde. front the gas will be discharged from N.25.b.92.88 to N.25.b.50.58.

4. "B" Special Coy. R.E. will perform the operation.

5. **TRUCKS & CYLINDERS.**

Each line is being allotted 75 trucks, each containing 21 cylinders, i.e. 1575 cylinders to each tram-head. The 75 trucks will be sent up each line in 7 trains of 10 trucks and 1 train of 5 trucks.

5. Trucks will be   pushed from the Power-heads to discharge points and back by infantry pushing parties.

6. **PRECAUTIONS FOR TROOPS IN THE LINE.**

If the "Gas Beam" attack is ordered :-
(a) The Outpost Line from the Right Boundary of the 59th Inf. Bde. as far North as N.20.a.0.4., and troops in the Main Line of Resistance between N.25.d.9.7 and N.19.c.5.5 in AGUE and N.19.b.1.6 in AMULET will be withdrawn by 12 Midnight.

(b) Troops forward of a line drawn through N.25.c.0.8 - N.13.c.0.0 - N.13.b.5.5. will wear Box Respirators from 12 Midnight until orders for their removal are given by an Officer. This should in no case be given until Zero plus 30 minutes, and then only if the trench system is reported clear of gas.

(c) The Divisional Gas Officer, assisted by the anti-gas personnel of units, will make arrangements for :-
(i) Clearing dugouts and cellars by means of fires, etc. immediately after completion of discharge.
(ii) Clearing trenches, saps, etc. by means of flappers immediately after discharge.
(iii) Troops will not re-occupy trenches until the Battn. and Bde. anti-gas personnel have reported them to be safe.
Anti-gas curtains will be securely fastened down in all evacuated dugouts and cellars, in order to minimize the danger of their becoming filled with gas.

(d) The evacuated trenches will be re-occupied on the first opportunity. Further details regarding the reoccupation of trenches will be issued later.

7. **ARTILLERY & MACHINE GUNS.**
                                              draw
Artillery action which might   retaliation is to be avoided, otherwise Artillery fire and Machine Gun fire will be normal until two hours after the discharge.

– Page 2 –

Arrangements have been made for sufficient firing by Artillery and machine guns to take place between the hours of 10 p.m. and 12 Midnight or such time as the gas is to be discharged so as to cover the noise of the discharge from the cylinders, and the noise made by the trucks.

8. **WIND LIMITS.**

Cylinders can be discharged in any wind between W.N.W. and S.W., velocity not less than 6 m.p.h. nor more than 15 m.p.h.

A decision will be given at 1 p.m. daily as to whether the operation will be carried out.

Code words to be used as follows :-
"Gas Beam attack will take place tonight" ..... ASTI.

No message will be sent at 1 p.m. if no attack is to take place.

To cancel "Gas Beam attack previously ordered" the word CHIANTI will be sent.

9. **ZERO HOUR.**

Zero hour will be 12 Midnight or as soon after as the trucks are reported to be in position. The order for the discharge will be given by Major BUNKER, M.C., O.C. Special Coys. He will be in telephonic communication with each of the three railheads.

10. **RATIONS.**

On the day upon which it is decided to discharge the "Gas Beam" the Light Railways will be closed to ammunition and food supply from 12 Noon onwards.

Two days rations will, therefore, be taken up today, May 15th. There will then be one day's supply in hand for use on the day following the night upon which the gas is discharged.

11. **ACKNOWLEDGE.**

Captain,
Brigade Major,
59th Infantry Brigade.

May 15th 1918.

Copy No.		Copy No.	
1	20th Dvn.G.	13	62nd F.Amb.
2	20th Dvn.Q.	14	159th Co.A.S.C.
3	60th I.Bde.	15	S.T.O.
4	61st I.Bde.	16	S.O.
5	72nd I.Bde.	17	"B" Special Coy.R.E.
6	92nd Bde.R.A.	18	D.T.M.O.
7	2nd Sco. Rif.	19	Loft Group, 20th Bn.M.G.C.
8	11th K.R.R.C.	20	Liason Off'r. H.A.
9	11th Rif.Bde.	21	Bde. Gas Officer.
10	59th T.M.Bty.	22	Office.
11	84th F.Co.R.E	23)	
12	96th F.Coy.R.E.	24)	War Diary.
		25)	

COPY NO. 17   SECRET

59th INFANTRY BRIGADE OPERATION ORDER NO.111.

Ref.Maps. Sheets 36.b)
              30.c) 1:40,000   May 17th 1918.

1. (a) The 59th Inf.Bde. will be relieved by the 61st Inf.Bde. in the LENS Section of the Divisional front on the 19th and night of 19/20th May.
   (b) The 59th Inf.Bde. will relieve the 60th Inf.Bde. in the AVION Section of the Divisional Front (Bde.H.Qrs. S.5.d.9.4) on the 20th and night of 20/21st May.
   (c) All moves will be carried out in accordance with attached Table "A".

2.   All details of relief will be arranged between Commanding Officers concerned.

3.   Command of the AVION Section will be taken over by B.G.C. 59th Inf. Bde. at 9 a.m. on 21st May.

4. (a) In the event of an alarm or enemy attack during reliefs, troops will halt and man the nearest defences, reporting their dispositions to Bde. H.Qrs.
   (b) Officers Commanding Battns. will remain with their opposite numbers, and await instructions.

5.   Details of work in hand and projected will be handed over in the LENS Section and taken over in the AVION Section.
   There will be no hiatus in the work.

6.   Special maps, plan & photographs, trench stores, anti-gas appliances, etc. will be handed over on relief and taken over when relieving.

7.   Completion of relief will be reported to Bde.H.Qrs. by the code words :-

           May 19/20th   - "MIKE".
           May 20/21st   - "GOOSILA".

8.   ACKNOWLEDGE.

                                                      Captain,
                                  Brigade Major,   59th Infantry Bde.

Issued through Sigs. at
    9.30 p.m

                    Copy No.1 20th Dvn.G.
                          2 20th Dvn.Q.
                          3 60th I.Bde.
                          4 61st I.Bde.
                          5 72nd I.Bde.
                          6 92nd Bde.R.F.A.
                          7 2nd Sco. Rif.
                          8 11th K.R.R.C.
                          9 11th Rif.Bde.
                        10 59th T.M.Bty.
                        11 Left Group, M.G.Bn.
                        12 62nd F.Amboe.
                        13 159th Co.A.S.C.
                        14 84th Fd.Co.R.E. (Adv).
                        15 96th F.Co.R.E.
                        16 S.T.O.
                        17 S.O.
                        18 Signals.
                        19 Office.
                 20/ 22 War Diary.

TABLE "A" issued with 59th INFANTRY BRIGADE OPERATION
ORDER NO. 111

Serial No.	Date MAY.	Unit	From	To	Relieving Unit	Remarks
1.	19/20	11th K.R.Rif.C.	LINE (Right)	COLUMBIA CAMP, AS.14.a.2.9	7th D.C.L.I	
2.	"	2nd Sco. Rifles.	LINE (Left)	ALBERTA CAMP, X.17.b.5.1	7th Som. L.I.	
3.	"	11th Rifle Bde.	Support, M.22.b.b.1.0	SOUCHEZ HUTS; S.C.C.	12th King's L.R.	
4.	"	59th L.T.M.Bty.	LINE, M.23.a.0.1.	S.7.d.5.5.	61st L.T.M.Bty.	
5.	"	59th Brigade H.Q.	M.27.b.6.7.	ABLAIN ST.NAZAIRE, X.10.b.0.2 (Corps Reserve)	61st Bde. H.Qrs.	

Serial No.	Date MAY.	Unit	From	To	In Relief of	Remarks
6.	20/21st	11th K.R.R.C.	COLUMBIA CAMP	Support, S.5.b.7.8	12th Rif.Bde.	
7.	"	2nd Sco.Rifles.	ALBERTA CAMP	LINE (Left Subsection), SOUCHEZ R.- N.32.d.35.50.	6th K.S.L.I.	
8.	"	11th Rif. Bde.	SOUCHEZ HUTS	LINE (Right Subsection); T.3.d.4.f - N.32.d.35.50.	12th K.R.R.C.	
9.	"	59th L.T.M.Bty.	S.7.d.5.5.	LINE, N.31.d.2.0.	60th L.T.M.Bty.	
10.	"	59th Bde.H.Qrs.	ABLAIN ST. NAZAIRE	S.5.d.9.4.	60th Bde. H.Qrs.	

NOTE. - Train arrangements will be notified later.

COPY NO. 26   SECRET

59th INFANTRY BRIGADE OPERATION ORDER NO. 108.

1. (A) Refer. 59th Inf.Bde. Warning Order No. ZI.740/54 of the 6th inst., on the night 13/14th May 11th K.R.R.C. will relieve the 2nd Sco. Rifles in the Right Sub-Sector of the Brigade Front.
   (B) On relief, 2nd Sco. Rifles will move into Brigade Support, with H.Qrs. at M.22.b.15.10.

2. All details of relief will be arranged direct between C.O's concerned.

3. All trench stores, maps, aeroplane photographs, gas appliances and A.A. positions will be handed over. Work in hand and projected will also be handed over.

4. Completion of relief will be wired to Bde.H.Qrs. by the Code Word "KAATGES".

5. ACKNOWLEDGE.

                                                    Captain,
May 12th 1918.   Brigade Major, 59th Infantry Bde.

                    Copy No. 1   20th Dvn.G.
                            2   20th Dvn.Q.
                            3   60th Inf.Bde.
                            4   61st Inf.Bde.
                            5   72nd Inf.Bde.
                            6   91st Bde.R.F.A.
                            7   2nd Sco. Rif.
                            8   11th K.R.R.C.
                            9   11th Rif.Bde.
                           10   59th T.M.Bty.
                           11   96th F.Co.R.E.
                           12   84th F.Co.R.E.
                           13   60th F.Amb.Co.
                           14   159th Co.A.S.C.
                           15   S.T.O.
                           16   S.O.
                           17   Signals.
                       18/ 20   War Diary.
                           21   Office.
                           26   62 Bde Ambulance

COPY NO. 13   SECRET

59th INFANTRY BRIGADE OPERATION ORDER NO.110.

1.   On the night May 16/17th 2nd Sco. Rif. will relieve 11th Rif. Bde. in the Left Sub-Section of the Brigade Front.
        On relief, 11th Rif. Bde. will move into Brigade Support.

2.   All details of relief will be arranged direct between Battalion Commanders concerned.

3.   All trench stores, maps, aeroplane photographs, gas appliances and A.A. positions will be handed over, also work in hand or projected.

4.   Completion of relief will be wired to Bde. H. Qrs. by the Code Word "NIGHTINGALE".

5.   ACKNOWLEDGE.

                                                        Captain,
May 15th 1916.   Brigade Major, 59th Infantry Bde.
Issued through Sigs. at 11 p.m.

                    Copy No. 1 20th Dvn. G.
                         2 20th Dvn. Q.
                         3 60th I. Bde.
                         4 61st I. Bde.
                         5 72nd I. Bde.
                         6 92nd Bde. R.F.A.
                         7 2nd Sco. Rif.
                         8 11th K.R.R.C.
                         9 11th Rif. Bde.
                        10 59th T.M. Bty.
                        11 84th F. Co. R.E.
                        12 96th F. Coy. R.E.
                        13 62nd F. Amboe.
                        14 S.T.O.
                        15 S.O.
                        16 159th Co. A.S.C.
                        17 Signals.
                        18 Office.
                     19/ 21 War Diary.

SECRET.   Copy No. 24
                    61st. INFANTRY BRIGADE ORDER No.4.
Ref. Maps:- 36 B)
            36 C) 1/40,000.   9th. May 1918.

1.   61st. Infantry Brigade will be relieved by 59th. Infantry
       Brigade in the LENS Sector on the night 10th/11th. May.

2.   Reliefs and moves will be carried out as laid down in
       attached Table.

3.   On completion of Reliefs, 61st. Infantry Brigade will with-
       draw to the Reserve Brigade Area (SOUCHEZ - CARENCY), and will be
       in DIVISIONAL RESERVE.

4.   Details of Relief will be arranged between Commanding
       Officers concerned.

5.   O's.C. King's and Som. L.I. will be prepared to leave behind
       one Officer per Company for 24 hours should relieving Battalions
       so desire it.

6.   All Maps, Defence schemes, trench Stores, Reserve Rations, Gas
       appliances, and such aeroplane photographs as were handed over by
       7th. Canadian Infantry Brigade, will be handed over to units of
       the 59th. Infantry Brigade, and a receipt obtained. A copy of
       handing over List will be forwarded to Brigade H.Q. by 6pm. 12th.
       instant.

7.   Details of work in hand and projected will be handed over
       in such a manner as to ensure continuity.

8.   Completion of reliefs will be reported to Brigade H.Q. by
       the Code word - "PLUM".

9.   Command of the Brigade Sector passes to the B.G.C. 59th.
       Infantry Brigade at 9-30am. 11th. May.

10.   Administrative instructions are attached.

11.   ACKNOWLEDGE.
                                                E.P. Coombe.
                                                Captain,
Issued through No.4   Brigade Major, 61st. Infantry Brigade.
Signal Section at -
         pm.

1. G.O.C.   10. Bdo. Supply Officer.
2. King's.   11. ,,   Sig. Officer.
3. Som. L.I.   12. ,,   Transport Offr.
4. D.C.L.I.   13. 20th. Div. "G".
5. 61st. T.M.B.   14. ,,   ,,   "Q".
6.   M.G.Bn.   15. 60th. Inf. Bde.
7. 84th. Field Co. R.E.   16. 72nd. Inf. Bde.
                                        17. 8th. Army Bde. C.F.A.
                                        18. Bde. Major.
                                        19. Staff Captain.
                                        20. War Diary.
                                        21. File.

TABLE OF RELIEFS.

(Issued with 61st. Infantry Brigade Order No. 4, 9/5/18.)

Serial No.	Unit.	From.	To.	Relieved by-	Remarks.
1.	7/D.C.L.I.	Support.	COLUMBIA CAMP S.14.a.2.9.	11/K.R.R.C.	H.Q. and 3.Coy. via CITE de ROLLENCOURT and RED MILL SIDING, (M.27.d.8.0.) One Company via main LENS - LIEVIN Road. 500 Yds interval between Coys. No movement to take place before 8-0pm.
2.	12/King's.	Line (Right Sub-Sector.)	ALBERTA CAMP, X.17.b.5.1.	2/Scottish Rifles.	By train from RED MILL SIDING, commencing at 10-30pm. (See Administrative Instructions.)
3.	7/Som.L.I.	Line (Left Sub-Sector).	SOUCHEZ HUTS. S.8.c.	11/Rifle Bde.	By train from RED MILL SIDING, commencing 11-45 pm.
4.	61st.T.M. Bty	LINE.	S.7.d.5.5.	59th.T.M.Bty.	-Ditto-
5.	61st.Bde.H.Q.	LINE.	X.10.b.0.2.	59th.Bde.H.Q.	Separate instructions have been issued.

SECRET   20th Division No.G.351

ADDENDUM No.1

To 20th (LIGHT) DIVISION ORDER No.240.

Reference 20th Division Order No.240 para 2 (d), The B.G.C. 61st Inf.Bde. will assume command of the LENS Section on completion of relief on night of 1st/2nd May. B.G.C. 7th Canadian Inf.Bde. will, howvever, remain at his H.Q. until completion of relief in the AVION Section on night 2nd/3rd May.

                                                  (sd) A.F.Hunt, Captain
                                                    for Lt.Col.General Staff,

30/A/18
                                                            20th Division.

                       (2)

O.C.
60, 61, 62, Field Ambulance.

        For information reference para 2(d) of RAMC O.O.No.1.

        Please acknowledge.

                                                      Captain, R.A.M.C.,
                                            for Colonel, A.D.M.S.20th Division.

1/5/1918.

SECRET

R.A.M.C. Operation Order No. 1.
by Colonel B.F.WINGATE, DSO, Commanding
Refce. Maps. 36B 1/40,000 **R.A.M.C. 20th Division.**
36C

1. (a) The XVIII Corps is relieving the 3rd Canadian Division and a portion of the 4th Canadian Division as far South as approximately T.3.d.4.1 . The 24th Divn. will be on the left and the 4th Canadian Divn. remains for the present on the right of the 20th Division.

   (b) The 20th Div.(less Artillery) will take over the LENS-AVION Section from T.3.d.4.1. (BETTY TRENCH) exclusive to N.13.d.7.9 in accordance with the programme of moves and reliefs on attached Table "A".
   All reliefs (except Machine Gun reliefs in the AVION Section) to be completed by 6.0 a.m. 3rd May.
   61st Inf.Bde. relieve portion of 7th Canadian Inf.Bde.(3rd Can.Div.) from the SOUCHEZ River to N.13.d.7.9.(LENS Section). The SOUCHEZ R. is inclusive to 61st Inf.Bde.
   60th Inf.Bde. relieve portion of 7th Canadian Inf.Bde.(3rd Can.Div.) from T.3.b.4.0 to the SOUCHEZ River (excl.). On completion of this portion of the relief 60th Inf.Bde. will extent its right to T.3.d.4.1, taking over the line between T.3.b.4.0 and T.3.d.4.1 from the 11th Canadian Inf.Bde.(4th Can.Div.) and this will then be included in the AVION Section.
   59th Inf.Bde. will be in Divl. Reserve in the SOUCHEZ-CARENCY Area (H.Q. will be notified later).

2. (a) Details of reliefs, subject to the provisions of this order, will be arranged between Brigadiers concerned.

   (b) Details of reliefs of R.E., Pioneers, and the Medical Units will be arranged by the C.R.E. and A.D.M.S. respectively.

   (d) B.Gs.C. 61st and 60th Inf.Bdes. will assume command of the LENS and AVION sub-sectors of the Divl. front on the completion of relief on night of 2nd/3rd May.

   (e) Until 10 a.m. 3rd May Units of the 20th Divn. whilst in 3rd Canadian Div. area will be under the orders of the G.O.C. 3rd Canadian Div.

3. Pending the issue of further instructions telephone conversations East of the ARRAS - SOUCHEZ - AIX NOULETTE Road are forbidden.

4. The command of the LENS - AVION Section will pass to the G.O.C. 20th Division at 10.0 a.m. on 3rd May.1918.

5. Completion of all movements and reliefs will be reported to 20th Division H.Q. by wire.

6. 20th Division H.Q. will close at VILLERS CHATEL at 10.0 a.m. on 3rd May and open at VILLERS AU BOIS at the same hour.

over

R.A.M.C. Operation Order No. 1 continued:-

MEDICAL :

1. 62nd Field Ambulance will be prepared to move with 61st Infty. Brigade and take over collection and evacuation of sick and wounded from the Brigade Sector of the line from any Medical Units that may be ordered to be relieved.

2. 60th and 61st Field Ambulances will be prepared to move with their respective Brigades in accordance with Table "A".

3. Detailed orders will be published as soon as possible.

ACKNOWLEDGE

1/5/1918.

A C Hammond Searle
Captain, R.A.M.C.,
for Colonel, A.D.M.S. 20th Division.

Copies to :-
60th Field Ambulance.
61st Field Ambulance.
62nd Field Ambulance.

TABLE "A" to accompany 20th Divisional Order N° 240 of 30.4.18

Annex N°	Date	Formation	From	To	Route	Remarks
1	May 1st	61st Inf Bde	Sandikourt & Ablainhourdry	Lens-Lieve Section	—	Bn. at Sourchez to be clear of Sourchez by 5 am. Gun at Cambrai to be clear of Cambrai by road under orders of Q
2	"	2 Bns. 7th Can. Inf. Bde.	LENS section	Caucourt area	—	—
3	"	60th Inf Bde (South)	ESTREE CAUCH -IE	Sourchez area	Villers au Bois	Not to enter SOUCHEZ before 5 am
4	2nd	60th Inf Bde	Sourchez area	Lens-AVION section	—	To be clear of Sourchez by 5 am
5	"	7th Can. Inf. Bde. less 2 Bns.	AVION section	Caucourt area	—	—
6	"	Sqn. 2nd Bde	Villers Brulin area	Sourchez & Villers au Bois	—	Not to enter Sourchez before 5 am
7	3rd	20 Dm. H.Q.	Villers Chatel	Villers-au-Bois	—	—

NOTES 1. Further orders for moves of Field Ambulances will be issued as soon as possible.

SECRET.   A.D.M.S., No.M30/1811.

MEDICAL ARRANGEMENTS IN CONNECTION WITH 20TH DIVISION O.O.NO.240.

1st May, 1918.

1. (a). 24th Division will be on the left and the 4th Canadian Division remains for the present on the right of the 20th Division.

   (b). The 20th Divisional front will extend from T.3.d.4.1. BETTY TRENCH to exclusive to N.13.d.7.9.

   (c). The 61st Bde. will be on the left, the 60th Bde. on the right. The SOUCHEZ River inclusive to 61st Bde. being the inter-brigade boundary.

2. Medical. Location of Medical Units.

   A. Left Sector
      (62nd Fd.Amb.).

      R.A.Ps.   (1) CROCUS HOUSE (N.23.d.4.8.)
                      (2) N.19.c.9.7.
                      (3) N.24.c.5.6. (if required).

      Relay Post.   N.24.c.5.6.

      A.D.S.   WHITE HOUSE (LIEVIN) N.28.b.7.2.

   B. Right Sector.
      (61st Fd.Amb.).

      R.A.Ps.   (1) LA COULOTTE.
                      (2) T.1.b.2.1.

      A.D.Ss.   (1) LA COULOTTE (N.31.c.5.1.).
                      (2) PAULINES (S.4.a.2.8.)(accessory)

   C. H.Qs. 62nd Fd.Amb. JENKS SIDING- S.2.c. (SOUCHEZ).

   D. H.Qs. 61st Fd.Amb. & Divl.Main Dressing Stn. - ABLAIN-ST-NAZARRE.

   E. H.Qs. 60th Fd.Amb. & Divl.Rest Stn. - CHATEAU de la HAIE.

EVACUATION.

Left Sector - Wounded are evacuated by hand carry along CROCODILE and CROCUS trenches to R.A.P. at CROCUS HOUSE - from where they are conveyed by wheeled stretchers to the A.D.S. at WHITE HOUSE (LIEVIN). From R.A.P. at N.19.c.9.7. wounded are evacuated by hand carry down ADROIT and ABSALOM trenches to Relay Post at N.24.c.5.6., thence by wheeled stretcher to A.D.S.
From the A.D.S. at WHITE HOUSE wounded are evacuated by means of light railway to M.D.S. at ABLAIN-ST-NAZARRE - whence they are evacuated by M.A.C. Car to C.C.S. (1 Divl. and 1 M.A.C. Car are kept constantly at the A.D.S. WHITE HOUSE for evacuation of urgent cases.)

Right Sector - Wounded are taken from the R.A.P. at T.1.b.2.1. by hand carry to the A.D.S. at LA COULOTTE. From here they are taken by light railway by night to PAULINES, JENKS SIDING or M.D.S., ABLAIN-ST-NAZARRE. Wounded from right sector, dressed at LA COULOTTE or PAULINES, will not as a rule be off-loaded at JENKS SIDING, but will proceed direct to M.D.S. at ABLAIN-ST-NAZARRE. From here they will be evacuated to C.C.S. by 8 M.A.C.
Urgent cases are evacuated by hand trolley in the day time along light railway to PAULINES - where they are dressed and conveyed on to M.D.S. at ABLAIN-ST-NAZARRE.
Urgent cases can also be evacuated direct to C.C.S. from PAULINES by ambulance car being always kept there for this purpose.

3. There is a good supply of blankets & stretchers at the R.A.Ps., A.D.Ss. and M.D.S.

4. ACKNOWLEDGE.

                                              [signature]
                                              Captain, R.A.M.C.,
                                              for Colonel, A.D.M.S., 20th Div.

Copy to recipients of O.O.No.2.

SECRET.   Copy No. 3

20TH DIVISION R.A.M.C. OPERATION ORDER NO. 2.
by COLONEL E.F. WINGATE, D.S.O., A.D.M.S.

1st May, 1918.

Reference 20th Division O.O. No. 210, dated 30th April, 1918.

1. A. (1). 62nd Field Ambulance will relieve 9th Field Ambulance (3rd
Canadian Division) in the left sector of the line by the evening of
1-5-18. They will proceed by road.
H.Qs. of 62nd Field Ambulance will be established at JENKS SIDING
(S.3.C.)- H.Qs. of 9th Field Ambulance at AIX NOULETTE being outside
the Divisional Area.

    (2). An advance party will be sent as soon as possible to take over
advanced posts and learn the line. Lorry accommodation will be provided.

    B. (1). 61st Field Ambulance will move under Brigade arrangements from
HOTEL CAUCHIE on the afternoon of 1-5-18, being accommodated in the
BOUCHEZ Area.

    (2). 61st Field Ambulance will take over the evacuation of wounded
from the right sector of the Divisional front from 9th Field Ambulance
(3rd Canadian Division). Relief to be completed by the evening of 2nd.

    (3). H.Qs. 61st Field Ambulance will be established at ABLAIN-ST-
NAZAIRE which will be opened as a Divisional Main Dressing Station.

    (4). An advance party will be sent as soon as possible to learn the
line.

    C. (1). 60th Field Ambulance will take over the Field Ambulance site at
CHATEAU de la HAIE from a Field Ambulance of the 4th Canadian Division
by 6 p.m. on 3rd instant.

    (2). An advance party of 1 Officer and 25 O.R. will proceed by road
on the morning of the 2nd instant in partial relief of the Field
Ambulance in occupation.

    (3). H.Qs. 60th Field Ambulance will be established at this site on
the 3rd instant and will be prepared for the reception of patients as
a Divisional Rest Station.

2.   Details of reliefs will be arranged between O's.C. of units concerned.

3.   All blankets, stretchers and other Area stores will be taken over,
receipts given and forwarded to this office.

4.   A.D.M.S. office will close at MAGOVAL at 5 p.m. on the 2nd instant
and open at the same hour at VILLERS-AU-BOIS.

5.   Acknowledge.

                                           A C Hammond Searle
                                              Captain, R.A.M.C.,
                                    for Colonel, A.D.M.S., 20th Division.

Distribution overleaf.

Copies to:-

1. 60th Bde.
2. 61st " "
3. 62nd " "
4. B.G.R.A., VIII Corps.
5. B.G.R.A., First Army.
6. C.R.A., 3rd Canadian Division.
7. " " 4th "
8. " " 34th Division.
9. 20th Division 'G'.
10. " " 'A'.
11. 59th Inf.Bde.)
12. 60th " ") through 'L'.
13. 61st " ")
14. D.D.O.
15. Signals.
16.) for Diary.
17.)
18. File.

COPY. NO. 12.   SECRET

59th INFANTRY BRIGADE OPERATION ORDER NO. 115.

1. (a) 2nd Sco. Rif. will relieve 11th Rif. Bde. in the ~~Left~~ Right Subsection of the Brigade front on May 27th and the night May 27/28th.

   (b) On relief 11th Rif. Bde. will move into Brigade Support in RED TRENCH (H.Qrs. S.6.a.5.2).

2. All details of relief will be arranged direct between Commanding Officers concerned.

3. All work in hand or projected, working parties, etc. will be handed over. There must be no break in the continuity of work, and as far as possible the usual working parties will be found on the night of relief.
   Special arrangements should be made to prevent there being a break in the continuity of work on dugouts. For this purpose the 96th Field Co.R.E. will get into touch with the O.C. Battn. being relieved.

4. All trench stores, anti-gas appliances, etc. will be handed over.

5. Completion of relief will be wired to Brigade H.Qrs. by the Code Word - "ZONKA".

6. ACKNOWLEDGE.

                                                        Captain,
                                        Brigade Major, 59th Infantry Bde.

May 26th 1918.
Issued through Sigs. at 2.30 p.m.

                Copy No. 1 20th Dvn.G.
                        2 20th Dvn.Q.
                        3 60th I.Bde.
                        4 61st I.Bde.
                        5 155th I.Bde.
                        6 2nd Sco.Rif.
                        7 11th K.R.R.C
                        8 11th Rif.Bde
                        9 59th T.M.Bty.
                       10 B Coy.M.G.Bn.
                       11 96th F.Co.R.E
                       12 62nd F.Amb.ce.
                       13 159th Co.A.S.M.
                       14 S.T.O.
                       15 S.O.
                       16 91st Bde.R.F.A.
                       17 Signals.
                       18 Office.
                    19/21 War Diary.

War Diary

Army Form C. 2118

WAR DIARY
or
INTELLIGENCE SUMMARY

(Erase heading not required.)

Vol 34
140/3076

CONFIDENTIAL.

WAR DIARY.

of

62nd FIELD AMBULANCE

From 1st June 1918.
To 30th June 1918.

COMMITTEE FOR THE
MEDICAL HISTORY OF THE WAR
Date 7 AUG 1918

WAR DIARY
or
INTELLIGENCE SUMMARY

62nd Field Ambulance Army Form C. 2118

Page 104

Place	Date	Hour	Summary of Events and Information	Remarks and references to Appendices
CARENCY X.17.c.6.2 3 & B.	1/8		Gas shelling occurred in neighbourhood of A.D.S. Weather fine. Road from SOUCHEZ Corner to CARENCY closed from 8-0 a.m. to 8 p.m. to all Ambulance traffic. Capt TODD from 42 C.C.S. sick with gas patients. At 9 P.M. L.R.C. temporary evacuation of WHITE HOUSE (36c/M28.B.7.1.) and arrange with O.C. Tramways KENS JUNCTION for alteration in train system of evacuation. 10 Casualties from Shell Gas in personnel. Capt T.H. HOUSTON and Capt BLAMEY FNL. RAMC join sick list Capt L. SATOW. RAMC from sick list. G.H.S.	
"	2/8		Weather fine. Visit A.D.S. with D.D.M.S. 20th Division and consult re system of evacuation after evacuation of WHITE HOUSE. A.D.S. temporarily withdrawn to COLONEL'S POST (36c/M33.a.1.0) as result of gas infections. WHITE HOUSE became car relay post. Evacuation by car to COLONELS POST. From relay post to W. FIELD AMBULANCE (ABLAIN-ST-NAZARRE) by train or car. CAPT KIRTON. J. RAMC.M.C. and 9 O.Rs left 61st Field Ambce to A.D.S. for temporary duty. 1 N.C.O. and 2 men to KENS JUNCTION as train orderlies. Holding party withdrawn from JENKS SIDING. 6 Casualties from Shell gas in personnel. G.H.Slack	
"	3/8		Weather fine. Tram tipply at KENS JUNCTION came under orders of O.C. 61st Field Ambulance. Personnel of this 62nd Field Ambulance relieved by 60 Field Ambulance. See O.C. VIII M.A.C. re cars. 2 to be stationed with 1st Field Ambulance. Telephone communication with VIII M.A.C. established. Capt DOWNS RAMC returns to 1/1st LOWLAND Field Ambulance. 4 Casualties from Shell gas in personnel. G.H.Slack Rev E.N. CARTER C of F hosted to unit.	

WAR DIARY
or
INTELLIGENCE SUMMARY

Army Form C. 2118.

62nd Field Ambulance Page 105

Place	Date	Hour	Summary of Events and Information	Remarks and references to Appendices
CARENCY X.14.C.6.2 36.B	4/8		Weather fine. Rev M.S. INGRAM. C.F. posted to 20 Div Hqrs. Capt A.N.L. BLAMEY from sick lst. Lieut. C.T. HAMAKER. U.S M.O.R.C. reports for duty from 51st Division.	
	5/8		Weather fine. Visit from A.D.M.S. 20 Division.	
	6/8		Capt J.N.L. BLAMEY relieves Major F.C. Chandler at A Post Sh. Capt. T.H. HOUSTON. RAMC from sick list. Weather fine.	
	7/8		Major F.C. CHANDLER. R.A.M.C.(T) awarded Military Cross by His Majesty the King. Weather fine.	
	8/8		All wounded from LEFT SECTOR, with the exception of stretcher cases to be admitted to 62nd Fld Ambce. See O.C. Tramways, re COLONEL'S SIDING at M.33.a.45.65. Sheet 44A.	
	9/8		Weather mild. Rain in evening. Capt J. KIRTON. M.C. RAMC attached to 60th Field Ambulance. Capt L. BATOW. M.C. RAMC to 7/Son 2 L for temporary duty as M.O/c.	
	10/8		Weather fine in evening, rain in morning.	

WAR DIARY or INTELLIGENCE SUMMARY.

Army Form C. 2118.

62nd Field Ambulance

Page 106

Place	Date	Hour	Summary of Events and Information	Remarks and references to Appendices
CARENCY XM.c.6.2. Sheet 36b	11/6		Weather dull in morning. Fine evening. 7th Lieut HAMAKER. U.S. M.O.R.C. to medical charge of 23rd Labour Group. JWB	
	13/6		Weather fine. Capt L. SATON M.C. RAMC returned to unit from 7th Som L Inft Bde. JWB	
	16/6		59th Inf Bde relieved in line by 61st Inf Bde. Capt L. SATON. M.C. RAMC at A.D.S. 60th Fld Amb bearers returned to their unit. JWB	
	17/6		Weather fine in morning. Capt T.H. HOUSTON. RAMC. to medical charge of 12th King's pool Regt. JWB	
	18/6		Weather fine. 59th Inf Bde relieve 60th Inf Bde in right sector of line. JWB	
	19/6		Rain in morning. Fine in evening. Major F.C. CHANDLER M.C. RAMC relieves 1st Lieut WEBBER. U.S. M.O.R.C. at A.D.S. 5 extra stretcher squads to reinforce A.D.S. Capt J N L BLAMEY RAMC reports to 61st Inf Bde for duty at R.A.P. 10 Wounded 20th Division passed through A.D.S. JWB	
	20/6		Dull morning. Rain in evening. Capt J.N.L. BLAMEY RAMC returned to unit from 61st Inf/Bde. JWB	

62nd Field Ambulance

WAR DIARY
or
INTELLIGENCE SUMMARY
(Erase heading not required.)

Army Form C. 2118.

Page 107

Place	Date	Hour	Summary of Events and Information	Remarks and references to Appendices
CARENCY X.11.C.6.2 AMB.	21/6/18		Capt J.N.K.BRAMEY reports to D.D.M.S. XVIIIth Corps for duty at Special P.U.O. Hospital. Interviews D.D.M.S. XVIIIth Corps re 20th Divisional arrangements for P.U.O. cases. Interview with D.M.S. First Army. GHS	
	22/6/18		Interview A.D.M.S. 20th Division re arrangements for 20th Div. P.U.O. cases. Capt and Q.M. J.R.KENSHOLE RAMC, Major F.C.CHANDLER MC RAMC and S/M H.WHEELDON RAMC admitted to hospital with P.U.O. 1st Lieut WEBBER U.S.M.O.R.C. to sick list with P.U.O. R.O.R. readmitted to hospital with P.U.O. A.D.S. established at SATOW'S POST M.26.d.8.2 Sheet 44A Central R.A.P. established at ORDEUS HOUSE Left R.A.P. established M.19.c.65.35.	GHS
	23/6/18		Weather fine. 10 other ranks RAMC admitted to hospital with P.U.O.	GHS
	24/6/18		Capt A.T.HOUSTON RAMC to sick list with P.U.O. 5 other ranks RAMC admitted to hospital with P.U.O. Weather cold & rainy	GHS
	25/6/18		Weather fine Lt WEBBER U.S. MORC evacuated to 42 CCS. Capt.J.T.HOUSTON RAMC from sick list. 13 other ranks admitted to hospital with P.U.O. Major J.R.PRIDHAM M.C. RAMC to sick list with P.U.O.	GHS
	26/6/18		Weather fine. Major F.C.CHANDLER M.C. RAMC from sick list. 10 other ranks admitted to hospital with P.U.O.	GHS
	28/6/18		Weather fine Capt T.HOUSTON RAMC relieves Capt L.SATOW RAMC at A.D.S.	GHS

62nd Field Ambulance
Page 108

WAR DIARY
or
INTELLIGENCE SUMMARY.

Place	Date	Hour	Summary of Events and Information	Remarks and references to Appendices
CARENCY X.17.c.6.2 3rd H.H.B	29/8		Weather fine. Left R.A.P. established at M.17.e.65.35. Allied H.H.A. Relief of O.R.D & Staff. Major J.A. PRIDHAM. M.C. RAMC from sick list.	

Lt. Col. R.A.M.C.
O.C. 62nd FIELD AMBULANCE

SECRET.　　　　　　　　　　　　　　61st Bde G.322/18

62nd Div Arty.

Amendment No.1 to 61st Bde Order No. 11.

1. Para: 3 (a), line 4.

　　for "14. 3" Hows." read "14. 6" Hows".

18/6/18

Copies to all Recipients of B.O. No. 11.

　　　　　　　　　　　　　　　　　　　　[signature]
　　　　　　　　　　　　　　　　　　　　Captain
　　　　　　　　　　　　　　　　　　　　BRIGADE MAJOR,
　　　　　　　　　　　　　　　　　　　　61st LIGHT INFANTRY BRIGADE

SECRET.   Copy No. 12

61st. BRIGADE ORDER No. 11.

16th. June, 1918.

Ref. 1/10000. Map. 41.A.S.W. 1.

1.   The 7/SOM.L.I. will carry out a raid with one Company of Infantry on the night 19/20th. instant, with the object of capturing and killing as many Germans as possible and obtaining identifications.

2. **OBJECTIVES:-**
   (a)   The Railway Embankment from N.14.c.25.92. to N.14.c.05.60.
   (b)   The Road from N.14.c.41.13. to N.14.c.45.60.

3. **ARTILLERY**
   (a) The Artillery covering the raid is as follows:-

91st Bde. R.F.A.	12.	18 pndrs.	
92nd. Bde. R.F.A.	12.	18 pndrs.	6. 4.5 Hows.
1st. Bde. C.G.A.	14.	3" Hows.	6. 9.2 Hows.
Y/20 Battery.	3.	6" Newton Mortars.	
V/XVIII Battery.	1.	9.45" Heavy Mortars.	
61st. T.M. Battery.	9.	3" Stokes Mortars.	

   (b) The Artillery arrangements are as follows:-
   (i)   A hurricane barrage on the first objective for 2 mins.
   (ii) Creeping barrage lifting off the first objective at Zero plus 6 minutes. This barrage is fired by 3. 18 pndrs. 92nd. Bde. R.F.A. and 9. 18 pndrs. 61st. Bde. R.F.A.

   Rates of fire:- Zero to Zero plus 6 -   INTENSE.
                   Zero plus 6 to Zero plus 40 - NORMAL.
                   Zero plus 40 to Zero plus 60. SLOW

   Shrapnel is being fired until the barrage commences to creep, after which 50 % H.E. is used.

   (iii) Standing barrage fired by 18 pndrs. and 4.5 Hows. and H.E. on certain fixed points.

   (iv) An enfilade barrage found by 2. 18 pndrs. 92nd. Bde. R.F.A. from N.14.c.25.92. to N.14.c.05.60. These guns do not lift until Zero plus 10 mins. After zero plus 10 mins. they are superimposed on the whole length of the Creeping barrage.

   The Raiders will creep up within 50 yds. of this enfilade barrage and then rush the first objective.

   The Signal to the Raiders that these two guns are on the point of lifting will be a golden rain rocket fired from the vicinity of the guns at the order of the Officer in charge at Zero plus 10 minutes. The guns are in action at about M.C.d.50.30.
   On this signal going up the Infantry will advance to the first objective.

(v) All fire opens at Zero and ceases at Zero plus 60 mins.

Details of the Standing and Creeping Barrages have been communicated to units concerned.

4. At Zero plus 2 minutes the Raiders will advance to their objectives from ALOOF TRENCH. To assist in gauging the correct time a GREEN/RED/GREEN Grenade will be fired by a Brigade Staff Officer from the Coy. H.Q. in APPROACH TRENCH. At Zero plus 30 mins. a similar grenade will be fired under arrangements made by 7/SOM.L.I. from Coy. H.Q. COW TRENCH, M.12.d.80.10 to denote that raiding Party will commence to withdraw.

AT Zero to zero plus 30 mins -

5. The 61st. Brigade Machine Gun Company will place a barrage with 8 guns on the line N.20.c.15.75. - N.20.a.60.20. This barrage will be INTENSE from Zero to Zero plus 10. From Zero plus 10 to plus 40, it will be intermittent.

6. All posts, except ST. LOUIS CRATER, in the Observation Line, will be withdrawn at Zero minus 10 to places under cover but not west of AMULET TRENCH. As soon as the bombardment has died down, the posts will be immediately reoccupied.

Except for the necessary Sentries, the remainder of the garrison in the defences will remain under cover from Zero until it is ascertained that the locality of their posts is not being shelled.

7. Watches will be synchronised at 61st. Bde. H.Q., M.27.b.6.7. at 6.0 P.M. on 19th. instant.

Representatives from Som. L.I., 61st. T.M. Battery and those detailed in 20th. Div. Artillery O.305 of 15th. inst. will attend.

8. All prisoners will be sent to Brigade H.Q.

All papers should be brought in from any German that is killed and any portion of his uniform that will assist in identifying the unit to which he belongs.

Papers must be taken from prisoners as soon after capture as possible and sent to Brigade Headquarters.

9. Zero hour will be notified later.

10. ACKNOWLEDGE.

EPCombe
Captain,
Brigade Major, 61st. Infantry Brigade.

Issued at 5-30 PM.

Copy No.			
1.	G.O.C.	7.	C.R.A.
2.	Som. L.I.	8.	D.T.M.O.
3.	Kings.	9.	59th. Inf. Bde.
4.	D.C.L.I.	10.	60th. Inf. Bde.
5.	T.M.Bty.	11.	72nd. Inf. Bde.
6.	20th. Div. "C".	12.	62nd. Field Amb. ✓
		13.	20th. Dn. M.G.C

6/1 Inf Bde
Raid 19/20 June 18

S E C R E T.   20th Division No. G.121.

AMENDMENT NO. 2 TO
DISPOSITION AND LOCATION REPORT NO. 8.

Locations as for 6 a.m. 6th June 1918.

Amend D. & L. Report No. 8 as follows:-

   Serial No. 17, Col. 2 -

      for "12th R.B." read "12th K.R.R.C."

   Serial No. 18, Col. 2 -

      for "12th K.R.R.C." read "12th R.B."

                        (Sd) A.F.HUNT, Capt.,

5th June, 1918.
                        for Lieut. Colonel,
                General Staff, 20th Division.

S E C R E T.   20TH (LIGHT) DIVISION.   20th Division No. G.996.

DISPOSITION AND LOCATION REPORT NO. 8.

Reference Maps:- Sheet 36B) 1/40,000.
                 Sheet 36C)

Serial No.	Unit.	Location of Headquarters 6 a.m. 31-5-18.	Remarks. Moving during next 24 hours.
1.	DIVISIONAL HEADQUARTERS.	CHATEAU DE LA HAIE.	
2.	DIVISIONAL ARTILLERY H.Q.	CHATEAU DE LA HAIE.	
3.	91st Bde. R.F.A.	ANGRES, M.33.d.2.5.	
4.	92nd R.F.A.(Bde.)	ANGRES, M.27.c.9.4.	
5.	D.A.C.	GOUY SERVINS (No. 3 Secn. ABLAIN ST. NAZAIRE).	
6.	C.R.E.	CHATEAU DE LA HAIE.	
7.	83rd Fld. Coy. R.E.	SOUCHEZ, X.17.b.4.2.	
8.	84th Fld. Coy. R.E.	ABLAIN ST. NAZAIRE, X.10.b.6.3.	
9.	96th Fld. Coy. R.E.	ABLAIN ST. NAZAIRE, X.10.b.3.9.	
10.	59TH INF BDE. H.Q.	ABLAIN ST. NAZAIRE, X.10.b.0.2.	
11.	2nd Scottish Rifles.	COLUMBIA CAMP, S.14.a.2.9.	Corps Reserve.
12.	11th K.R.R.C.	SOUCHEZ HUTS, S.8.c.	
13.	11th. R.B.	ALBERTA CAMP, X.17.b.8.1.	
14.	59th T.M.Bty.	S.7.d.5.5.	
15.	59th INF. BDE. H.Q.	S.5.d.9.4.	
16.	6th K.S.L.I.	S.6.a.5.2.	
17.	12th KRRC RB	S.5.c.central.	Line , AVION Section. Left Subsection, SOUCHEZ River to N.32.d.35.50.
18.	12th RB	S.5.b.7.8.	Right Sub-Section, T.3.d.4.6. to N.32.d.35.50.
19.	60th T.M.Bty.	N.31.d.2.0.	Support.
20.	61ST INF. BDE. H.Q.	M.27.b.6.7.	Line.
21.	12th King's (L'pool) Rgt.	M.25.d.6.5.	Line, LENS Section. Right Sub-Section, N.25.b.80.30. to N.19.b.95.25.
22.	7th Somerset L.I.	M.17.c.7.4.	Left Sub-Section, N.19.b.95.25. to N.15.b.50.00.
23.	7th D.C.L.I.	M.23.b.1.0.	Support. M.17.c.7.4.Line Left.
24.	61st T.M.Bty.	M.23.a.9.1.	Support.
25.	11th Durham L.I.	MATATA CAMP, X.16.d.1.4.	Line.
26.	20th Battn. M.G.C.	SCOTT'S CAMP, CARENCY, X.16.d.	

P.T.O.

-2-

Serial No.	Unit.	Location of Headquarters 6 a.m. 31-5-18.	Remarks. Moving during next 24 hours.
27.	A.D.M.S.	CHATEAU DE LA HAIE.	
28.	60th Field Ambulance.	CHATEAU DE LA HAIE.	
29.	61st Field Ambulance.	ABLAIN ST. NAZAIRE.	
30.	62nd Field Ambulance.	CARENCY, X.17.s.6.2.	
31.	DIVL. TRAIN H.Q.	CHATEAU DE LA HAIE.	
32.	158th Coy. A.S.C.	ABLAIN ST. NAZAIRE.	
33.	159th Coy. A.S.C.	ODILLON CAMP, X.17.c.	
34.	160th Coy. A.S.C.	ABLAIN ST. NAZAIRE.	
35.	161st Coy. A.S.C.	ODILLON CAMP, X.17.c.	
36.	D.A.D.V.S.	CHATEAU DE LE HAIE.	
37.	32nd Mob. Vet. Secn.	PETIT SERVINS, Q.29.c.4.1.	
38.	A.P.M.	CHATEAU DE LA HAIE.	
39.	D.A.D.O.S.	X.17.central.	
40.	Divl. Employment Coy.	CHATEAU DE LA HAIE.	
41.	Divl. M.T. Coy.	SAVY.	
42.	Divl. Grenade Officer.	OPPA DUMP, X.11.b.6.1.	
43.	Divl. Salvage Officer.	CARENCY, X.16.d.9.5.	
44.	Divl. Anti-Gas Stores.	X.16.d.central (opposite ODILLON CAMP).	
45.	Divl. Wing.	MAISNIL BOUCHE.	

Transport Lines.

	59th Inf. Bde.	ABLAIN ST. NAZAIRE.	
	60th Inf. Bde.	ABLAIN ST. NAZAIRE.	
	61st Inf. Bde.	ODILLON CAMP, X.17.c.	

(Sd) A.F.HUNT, Capt.,
for Lieut-Colonel,
General Staff, 20th Division.

29th May, 1918.

Reference O.O. 9. of 5th. June, 1918.

Reference Maps:-

    For "36.B"   read   "44.B".
    For "36.C"   read ~~XXX~~ "44.A".

                                                Captain,
Brigade Major, 61st. Infantry Brigade.

S E C R E T.   Copy No. 22

61st. INFANTRY BRIGADE OPERATION ORDER
No: 9.

Ref.Maps:- 44.B) 1/40.000.
44.A)   ,,
5th. June, 1918.

1. 61st. Infantry Brigade will be relieved by 59th. Infantry Brigade in the LENS Sector on the night 7th/8th. June.

2. Reliefs and moves will be carried out as laid down in attached Table.

3. On completion of reliefs, 61st. Infantry Brigade will withdraw to the Reserve Brigade area (SOUCHEZ - CARENCY) and will be in Corps Reserve.

4. Details of relief will be arranged between Commanding Officers concerned.

5. (a) All Maps, Defence schemes, Trench Stores, Reserve Rations, Gas Appliances and Special Aeroplane photographs will be handed over to relieving units, and a receipt obtained.
   (b) Details of work in progress and the general work policy on the Battalion front will be handed over. A copy of this Report (with a Map) is to be forwarded to Bde. H.Q. by 12 Noon 7th. instant. In handing over the work in hand, arrangements will be made that will ensure that continuity of work is not interrupted.

6. All information, orders and schemes regarding the action of the Brigade in Corps Reserve will be taken over from units of the 59th. Infantry Brigade.

7. In the event of an alarm or an enemy attack during the Relief, troops will halt and man the nearest defences, reporting their position at once to Brigade H.Q. O's.C. Battalions, in this event, will remain with their opposite numbers and await instructions.

8. Completion of Relief will be reported to Brigade H.Q. by the code-word "THRUSH".

9. Brigade H.Q. will be established at ABLAIN St.NAZAIRE on completion of relief.

10. Administrative Instructions will be issued later.

11. ACKNOWLEDGE.

E.P. Combe.
Captain,
Brigade Major, 61st. Infantry Brigade.

Issued through
Signals at :-
8.0 P.M.

Copy No. 1. G.O.C.   7. 84th.Fd.Coy.R.E.   15. 72nd.Inf.Bde.
        2. King's.   8. Bde.Supply Offr.   16. 92nd.Bde.R.F.A.
        3. Som.L.I.   9. ,, Sig.Officer.   17. Bde. Major.
        4. D.C.L.I.   10. ,, Transport Offr.   18. Staff Captain.
        5. T.M.Bty.   11. 20th.Div."G".   19. War Diary.
        6. M.G.Coy.LENS   12. ,,   "Q".   20. File.
           Sector.   13. 59th.Inf.Bde.
                            14. 60th.Inf.Bde.

TABLE -of- RELIEFS.

(Issued with 61st. Infantry Brigade Order No.9 of 5/6/18)

Serial No.	UNIT.	FROM.	TO.	RELIEVED BY-	REMARKS.
1.	7/D.C.L.I.	LINE (Left Sub-Sector.)	COLUMBIA CAMP, S.14.a.2.9.	11/Rifle Bde.	By train from M.16.d.9.2. commencing at 12 midnight.
2.	12/King's.	LINE (Right Sub-Sector.)	ALBERTA CAMP, X.17.b.5.1.	11/K.R.R.C.	By train from M.35.b.80.45 commencing in at 1-45 A.M.
3.	7/Som. L.I.	SUPPORT.	SOUCHEZ PITS, S.8.c.	2/Sco.Rifles.	By march route via ROLLENCOURT - ANGRES - SOUCHEZ (Main LENS-LIEVIN Road will not be used.)
4.	61st.T.M. Bty.	LINE.	S.7.d.5.5.	59th. T.M.Bty.	By train with 7/D.C.L.I.
5.	61st.Bde.H.Q.	LINE.	ABLAIN-ST-NAZAIRE. X.10.b.0.2.	59th.Bde.H.Q.	Separate instructions have been issued.

COPY NO. 12   SECRET

59th INFANTRY BRIGADE OPERATION ORDER NO. 118.

1. (a) 2nd Sco. Rif. will relieve 11th K.R.R.C. in the Right Sub-Section of the Brigade Front on June 10th and the night June 10/11th.

   (b) On relief 11th K.R.R.C. will move into Brigade Support with H.Qrs. at M.22.b.15.10.

2. All details of relief will be arranged direct between C.O's. concerned.

3. All work in hand or projected, working parties, etc. will be handed over. There must be no break in the continuity of work, and the relief must interfere as little as possible with working parties.

4. All trench stores, anti-gas appliances, etc. will be handed over.

5. Completion of relief will be notified to Brigade H.Qrs. by the Code Word :- "CHARLEMAGNE".

6. ACKNOWLEDGE.

                                                    Captain,
                                              Brigade Major,
June 10th 1918.   59th Infantry Brigade.
Issued thro' Sigs.
 at 1.30 p.m.

                    Copy No. 1 20th Dvn.G.
                             2 20th Dvn.Q.
                             3 60th Inf.Bde.
                             4 61st Inf.Bde.
                             5 72nd Inf.Bde.
                             6 2nd Sco. Rif.
                             7 11th K.R.R.C.
                             8 11th Rif.Bde.
                             9 59th T.M.Bty.
                            10 A Coy.M.G.Bn.
                            11 96th F.Co.R.E
                            12 62nd Fd.Ambce
                            14 150 Co.A.S.C.
                            15 92nd Bde.R.A.
                            16 S.T.O.
                            17 S.O.
                            18 Signals.
                            19 Office.
                       20/ 22 War Diary.

COPY NO. 11.   SECRET

59th INFANTRY BRIGADE OPERATION ORDER NO. 119

1. (a) 11th K.R.R.C. will relieve the 11th Rif. Bde. in the Left subsector of the Brigade front on the night June 13/14th.

   (b) On relief 11th Rif. Bde. will move into Brigade Support with H.Qrs. at H.22.b.15.10.

2. All details of relief will be arranged direct between C.O's. concerned.

3. All work in hand or projected, working parties, etc. will be handed over. There must be no break in the continuity of work, and the relief must interfere as little as possible with working parties.

4. All trench stores, anti-gas appliances, etc. will be handed over.

5. Completion of relief will be notified to Bde.H.Qrs. by wiring the Code word :- "RICHELIEU".

6. ACKNOWLEDGE.

                                                    Captain,
                                            Brigade Major,
                                            59th Infantry Brigade.

June 12th 1918.

Issued through Sigs. at
    9.30 p.m.

                    Copy No. 1   20th Dvn.G.
                             2   20th Dvn.Q.
                             3   60th Inf.Bde.
                             4   72nd Inf.Bde.
                             5   2nd Sco.Rif.
                             6   11th K.R.R.C.
                             7   11th Rif.Bde.
                             8   59th T.M.Bty.
                             9   D Co. M.G.Bn.
                            10   96th F.Co.R.E
                            11   62nd F.Amboe.
                            12   159 Co.A.S.C.
                            13   92nd Bde.R.A.
                            14   S.T.O.
                            15   S.O.
                            16   Signals.
                            17   Office.
                        18/ 20   Diary.

S E C R E T.   Copy No. 7

ADMINISTRATIVE INSTRUCTIONS ISSUED IN CONNECTION WITH 61st. INF. BDE. ORDER No.10, dated 15. JUNE.1918.

1. **TRAINS.**
   Units travelling by Light Railway will entrain as shown below:-

Unit.	Entraining Point.	Time.	Detraining Point.
7/Som. L.I.	LENS JUNCTION.	9-0 P.M.	Constitution Hill.
7/D.C.L.I.	,, ,,	10-10P.M.	Kingston Line Junc.
T.M.BATTERY.	,, ,,	9-0 P.M.	CROW DUMP.
BDE. H.Q.	ABLAIN ST.NAZAIRE.	8-30P.M.	Australia Siding.

   Bde. H.Q. will entrain at a point 200 yds. North of the Y.M.C.A. Hut in ABLAIN ST. NAZAIRE.
   Each unit will detail an Entraining Officer to report to the Staff Captain at LENS JUNCTION 30 minutes before due departure of their respective trains.

2. **RATIONS.**
   Ration trains will be available as usual. Units requiring to use the ration trains will notify the Traffic Officer, LENS JUNCTION, of their requirements.

3. **TRANSPORT.**
   Bde. T.O. will arrange for the collection of stores and kits, and will detail wagons to remove H.Q. Stores and Baggage to O'DILLON CAMP.

4. **T.M. BATTERY.**
   Bde. T.O. will arrange to remove T.M. Battery Kit and Stores to O'DILLON CAMP.

5. **R.E. MATERIAL & AMMUNITION.**
   Indents for R.E. material and Ammunition must reach Bde. H.Q. by 8-0 P.M. daily.

6. **HORSES.**
   Bde. T.O. will arrange for the necessary change over of H.Q horses with the 59th. Bde. T.O.

7. **DETAILS.**
   Surplus personnel of units not required in the line will proceed to the Divl. Reception Camp at CHATEAU de la HAIE, and will be quartered in VANCOUVER CAMP.
   One Officer and N.C.O. from each Battalion will proceed to CHATEAU de la HAIE and report to the District Commandant on the morning of 16th. instant and obtain the necessary accommodation.
   Major Uniacke, 12/King's, will have command of the whole of the Bde. Details

8. **GUARDS.**
   The following guards will be detailed and will report to 59th. Bde. H.Q. at 10-0 A.M. 16th. instant-
   King's ...... 1 N.C.O. & 6 Men. Gas Guard, Bde. H.Q.

   D.C.L.I. .... 2 Men. Guards on LIEVIN DUMP.
   ,,   ---------------- 2 ,,   ,,   ,, SANDPIT ,,
   ,, ... 2 ,,   ,,   ,, SCOTT   ,,
   ,, ... 1 ,,   ,,   ,, BDE.H.Q.,,

   These details will be distributed by an N.C.O. of this Bde. H.Q.

9. **ACKNOWLEDGE.**

                                                    Chas.W.V. Webb,
                                                         Captain,
                                          Staff Captain, 61st. Infantry Brigade.

Copy. N° 1 G.O.C.   11 Bde. T.O.
       2 12/Kings   12 2nd Div. C
       3 7/Som L.I.   13
       4 7/D.C.L.I.   14 58th Inf. Bde
       5 61st : M. By.   16 Bde ...
       6 2nd Field Coy R.E.   17 Bde. Major
       7 6th Field Amb   18 Staff Captain
       8 161 Coy A.S.C.   19 War Diary
       9 Bde. Supply Officer   20 File
      10   "   Signal

COPY NO. 12   SECRET

59th INFANTRY BRIGADE OPERATION ORDER NO. 120.

Ref. Maps 56.b) 1/40,000   June 15th 1918.
         56.c)

1. (a) The 59th Inf.Bde. will be relieved by 61st Inf.Bde. in the LENS Section of the Divisional front on the 16th and night 16/17th June.
   (b) The 59th Inf.Bde. will relieve 60th Inf.Bde. in the AVION Section of the Divisional front on the 17th and night 17/18th June.
   (c) All moves will be carried out in accordance with attached Table "A".

2. All details of relief will be arranged direct between C.O's. concerned.

3. Command of the AVION Section will pass to B.G.C. 59th Inf. Bde. on completion of relief on the night 17/18th June.

4. (a) In the event of an alarm or an enemy attack during reliefs, troops will halt and man the nearest defences, reporting their dispositions to Bde.H.Qrs.
   (b) Officers Commanding Battalions will remain with their opposite numbers, and await instructions.

5. Details of work in hand or projected will be handed over in the LENS Section and taken over in the AVION Section.
There will be no hiatus in the work.

6. Special orders and instructions for units in Corps Reserve will be taken over from 61st Inf.Bde. and handed over to 60th Inf. Bde., receipts being given and obtained.

7. Special maps, plans, photographs, trench stores, anti-gas appliances, etc. will be handed over on relief and taken over when relieving.

8. Completion of relief will be reported to Bde.H.Qrs. by wiring the code words :-

          June 16/17th - QARI.
          "   17/18th - KAATJES.

9. ACKNOWLEDGE.

                                                    Captain,
Issued through Sigs   Brigade Major,
at 9 p.m.   59th Infantry Bde.

          Copy No.1   20th Dvn.G.   Copy No.11   D. Coy. M.G.Bn.
               2   20th Dvn.Q.   12   62nd F.Amboe.
               3   60th Inf.Bde.   13   159th Co.A.S.C.
               4   61st Inf.Bde.   14   96th F.Co.R.E.
               5   72nd Inf.Bde.   15   S.T.O.
               6   92nd Bde.R.A.   16   S.O.
               7   2nd Sco.Rif.   17   Signals.
               8   11th K.R.R.C.   18   Office.
               9   11th Rif.Bde.   19/20 War Diary.
              10   59th Tr.H.Bty.

TABLE "A" ISSUED WITH 59th INFANTRY BDE. OPERATION ORDER NO.120

No.	Date JUNE	Unit	From	To	Relieving Unit.
1	16/17th	2nd Sco. Rif.	LINE (Right Subsector)	SOUCHEZ HUTS, S.8.c.	7th Som. L.I.
2	"	11th K.R.R.C.	LINE (Left Subsector).	ALBERTA CAMP, K.17.b.5.1.	7th D.C.L.I.
3	"	11th Rif.Bde.	Support, H.22.b.10.00.	COLUMBIA CAMP, S.14.d.2.9.	.... 12th Kings.
4	"	59th T.M.Bty.	LINE, H.23.b.00.20.	S.7.d.50.50.	61st T.M.Bty.
5	"	59th Bde.H.Q.	H.27.b.60.70.	ABLAIN ST.NAZAIRE, K.10.b.00.20.	61st Inf.Bde.H.Q.

No.	Date JUNE	Unit	From	To	In relief of
6	20/18th	2nd Sco. Rif.	SOUCHEZ HUTS	Support, S.5.b.7.8.	7th K.S.L.I.
7	"	11th Rif.Bde.	COLUMBIA CAMP.	Line (Left) SOUCHEZ R. to N.32.d.35.50.	12th Rif. Bde.
8	"	11th K.R.R.C.	ALBERTA CAMP	Line (Right), T.3.d.4.6 to N.32.d.35.50.	12th K.R.R.C.
9	"	59th T.M.Bty.	S.7.d.5.5.	Line, N.31.d.20.00	60th T.M.Bty.
10	"	59th Bde.H.Q.	ABLAIN ST.NAZAIRE	LINE, S.5.d.9.4.	60th Bde.H.Q.

NOTE - Front Line Battns. will move by rail.
Train arrangements will be notified later.

//*/*/*/*/*/

S E C R E T. Copy No. 7.

61st. INFANTRY BRIGADE ORDER - NO. 10.

Ref. Maps:- Sheets 44.A. and) 1/40,000.
44.B.)

13th. June, 1918.

1. The 61st. Inf. Bde. will relieve the 59th. Inf. Bde. in the LENS Section of the Divisional Front on the night 16/17th. June, in accordance with Table overleaf.

2. Details of relief will be arranged between Commanding Officers concerned.

3. Details of work in hand and projected will be taken over from outgoing Battalions of the 59th. Brigade in such a way that continuity of work is not interrupted.

4. Special Maps, plans, photographs and Trench Stores will be taken over and a list forwarded to Bde. H.Q. 24 hours after relief.

5. The same dispositions as those of units of the 59th. Inf. Bde. will be taken over.

6. B.G.C., 61st. Inf. Bde. assumes command of the LENS Sector on completion of the relief.

7. In the event of an alarm or an enemy attack during the relief troops will halt and man the nearest defences, reporting their positions to Bde. H.Q.
Officers Commanding Battalions will remain with their opposite numbers and await instructions.

8. Brigade H.Q. will close at ABLAIN ST. NAZAIRE at 10.0 P.M., and open at M. 27.b.8.7. at the same hour.

9. All information, orders, maps and schemes regarding the action of units of the Brigade in Corps Reserve will be handed over to units of the 59th. Inf. Bde. and a receipt obtained.

10. Completion of Relief will be reported to Bde.H.Q. by the code-word "FOX".

11. ACKNOWLEDGE.

E.P. Combe
Captain,
Brigade Major, 61st. Infantry Bde.

Issued at 7 A.M.

Copy No. 1. G.O.C.
2. 12/King's.
3. 7/Som. L.I.
4. 7/D.C.L.I.
5. 61st.T.M.Bty.
6. 84th.Fd.Coy. R.E.
7. 62nd.Fd. Amb.
8. 161.Coy. A.S.C.
9. Bde. Supply Officer.
10. „ Signal Officer.
11. Bde. T.O.
12. 20th. Div. "G".
13. 20th. „ "Q".
14. 59th. Inf. Bde.
15. 60th. Inf. Bde.
16. 72nd. Inf. Bde.
17. Bde. Major.
18. Staff Captain.
19. War Diary.
20. File.

TABLE OF RELIEFS:

Issued with 61st. INFANTRY BRIGADE ORDER - No. 10 of 13th June, 1918.

Serial No.	Unit.	From.	To.	Relieving.	Remarks.
1.	7/ D.C.L.I.	COLUMBIA CAMP.	LINE (Right Sub-Sector.)	2/Sco. Rifles.	By Train from LENS Junction.
2.	7/ SOM. L.I.	SOUCHEZ HUTS & X.4.c.8.5.	LINE (Left Sub-Sector.)	11/ K.R.R.C.	-ditto-
3.	12/ KING'S.	ALBERTA CAMP.	SUPPORT.	11/Rifle Bde.	By March Route. Leave Camp 9-0 P.M. H.M. 500 yds. interval between Coys.
4.	61st.T.M.BTY.	S.7.d.5.5.	LINE.	59th.T.M.BTY.	By train from LENS Junction.
5.	61st.Bde.H.Q.	ABLAIN ST.NAZAIRE.	LINE.	59th.Bde.H.Q.	Special instructions have been issued.

Details of movements by train will be issued later.

SECRET.

WAR DIARY.

of the

OFFICER COMMANDING, 62ND FIELD AMBULANCE.

20TH (LIGHT) DIVISION.

1ST JULY, 1918 - 31ST JULY, 1918-

****

WAR DIARY
or
INTELLIGENCE SUMMARY.

62nd Field Ambulance   Page 109

Place	Date	Hour	Summary of Events and Information	Remarks and references to Appendices
X.15.c.6.2 Shell H.H.B	1/7/18		Weather fine. LIEVEN Heavily shelled with Gas. 123 Gas cases admitted.	—
	2/7/18		Weather fine. 40 Gassed cases admitted.	—
	3/7/18		Weather fine	—
	4/7/18		Weather fine	—
	6/7/18		Capt J.M.F. BIRNEY N/5 RAMC A.D.M.S. in relief of Capt L. SATOW. M.C. RAMC. Weather fine.	—
	9/7/18		Major G.H. STACK. R.A.M.C. takes over command of 35th Field Ambulance. Major R.G.S. GREGG. RAMC takes over command of 62nd Field Ambulance. Weather fine in morning. Rain in afternoon.	—
	10/7/18		Relief of Bearers in forward area. Weather Rained most of day.	—
	11/7/18		O.C. visits forward posts and A.D.Sh. Visit from O/C m.S & 20th Division. Capt L.L. SATOW. M.C. RAMC. to A.D.S. Capt C.S. TENNANT. RAMC. reports his arrival for duty.	—
	12/7/18		A.D.M.S. visits forward posts and A.D.S.	—

Army Form C. 2118.

62nd Field Ambulance

WAR DIARY
or
INTELLIGENCE SUMMARY.

(Erase heading not required.)

Page 110

Instructions regarding War Diaries and Intelligence Summaries are contained in F.S. Regs., Part II. and the Staff Manual respectively. Title pages will be prepared in manuscript.

Place	Date	Hour	Summary of Events and Information	Remarks and references to Appendices
X/5.c.6.2. Sheet 44B CARENCY	13/8/18		A.D.M.S. 20 Div instructs Gas Course and transport lines. Weather: rainy.	appx 92 acc1
	14/8		Weather rainy. Capt C.S. TENNANT. R.A.M.C. A.D.S. in relief of Capt J.N.L. BLANEY. R.A.M.C.	acc1
	15/8		Weather rainy. Major J.A. PRIDHAM. M.C. R.A.M.C. proceeded to U.K. on 14 days leave. Heavy thunderstorm at night.	acc1
	16/8		Weather Rainy. Thunderstorm in early morning. Capt C.S. TENNANT R.A.M.C. took over temporary duties of M.O. 1/c 91st Brigade R.F.A. in relief of Captain BENALL R.A.M.C. proceeding on leave to U.K.	acc1
	17/8		Weather: Fine. Relief of Bearers in forward area. Visit forward area and inspect routes of evacuation of wounded.	appx 88
	18/8		Weather: Fine. Major F.C. CHANDLER. M.C. R.A.M.C. to A.D.S. in relief of Capt L. SATOW. M.C. R.A.M.C. A.D.M.S. 20 Div Division visits A.D.S.	appx 90
	19/8		Weather: Fine.	appx 91
	20/8		Weather: Fine in morning, heavy thunderstorm in afternoon.	acc1

WAR DIARY
or
INTELLIGENCE SUMMARY

62nd Field Ambulance Army Form C. 2118

Page 111

Place	Date	Hour	Summary of Events and Information	Remarks and references to Appendices
X.15.c.6.2 Huts H4B (CARENCY)	21st		Weather: Dull.	a888
	22nd		Weather: Rainy. 61st Infy. Bde carried out bombing raid, 20 wounded passed through A.D.S. Lieut. I.E. HEMPSTEAD. M.O.R.C. U.S.A. attached viii Corps Headquarters taken on the strength of this unit.	a888
	23rd		Weather: Heavy rains during day. Capt. J.N.L. BLAMEY. R.A.M.C. to A.D.S. in relief of Capt. T.H. HOUSTON. R.A.M.C.	a888
	24th		Weather: Fine. Visit from A.D.M.S. 2nd Division. Capt. T.H. HOUSTON. R.A.M.C. to 61st Field Ambulance for temporary duty. Relief of bearers in forward area.	a888
	25th		Weather: showery. Capt. E.S. TURNER, Capt. G.S. ROBERSON, MORE and 3 N.C.O's U.S. Army attached for instructional purposes.	a888
	26th		Instruct. attached personnel of U.S. Army in methods of evacuation of wounded from front line. Enemy planes bombed Divisional area during night.	a888
	27th		Weather: rained most of the day. Capt. L. SATOW. M.C. R.A.M.C. to A.D.S. in relief of Major F.C. CHANDLER. M.C. R.A.M.C.	a888

WAR DIARY
or
INTELLIGENCE SUMMARY

Army Form C. 2118

62nd Field Ambulance

Page 112

Place	Date	Hour	Summary of Events and Information	Remarks and references to Appendices
X.15.c.6.2 Huts & Hub (CARENCY)	28/7/18		Weather: Fair. Col. E.S. TURNER. M.O.R.C., Capt. L.S. ROBERSON. M.O.R.C. and 3 N.C.O's U.S. Army departed for 61st Field Ambulance. Capt. C.P. MAJOR. M.O.R.C., Capt. C.W. VATES. M.O.R.C. and 2 N.C.O's U.S. Army reported for instruction in forward area work.	e.m.
	29/7/18		Weather: Fine. Capt. T.H. HOUSTON. R.A.M.C. returns from 61st Field Ambulance. Capt. J.N.L. BLAMEY. R.A.M.C. proceeded to 61st Field Ambulance for temporary duty. Instruct attached U.S. personnel in methods of evacuating wounded from forward area.	e.m.
	30/7/18		Weather: Very warm. Capt. T.H. HOUSTON. R.A.M.C. proceeded to A.D.S. for duty. Capt. C.P. MAJOR. M.O.R.C., Capt. C.W. VATES. M.O.R.C. and 2 N.C.O's proceeded to join their respective units. Bombing raid at night carried on by 61st Army Bde., eight wounded passed through A.D.S.	e.m.
	31/7/18		Weather: Very warm. Relief of beds in forward area. Visit R.A.G.P.8 and A.D.S. Bombing by enemy planes in divisional area at night.	e.m.

R.S. Hogg
Lt. Col. R.A.M.C.
O.C. 62nd Field Ambulance

CONFIDENTIAL.

WAR DIARY.

OF

62ND. FIELD AMBULANCE.

1st August, 1918 to 31st August 1918.

Army Form C. 2118.

WAR DIARY
62nd Field Ambulance
INTELLIGENCE SUMMARY.
(Erase heading not required.)

Page 113

Place	Date	Hour	Summary of Events and Information	Remarks and references to Appendices
X.15.c.6.2 h+B CARENCY	1/8/18		Weather fine & warm. 5 Other ranks granted 10 days leave to PARIS.	OM1
	2/8		Rained most of day. Capt Sherman. C.S. (R)AMC returns from 91st Bde R.F.A. and proceeds to A.D.Sh for duty. Major J.A. PRIDHAM. M.C. R.AMC returns from leave. Capt T.H. HOUSTON RAMC proceeds to clothes of medical charge of 11th D.L.I.	aff1
	3/8		Rain during morning. Fine in afternoon. Major J.A. PRIDHAM. M.C. R.AMC to A.D.S for duty. Visit A.D.Sh and R.A.P.s.	am1
	4/8		Weather fine	aff1
	5/8		Rain during day. Capt C.S. TENBRANT FRAME to ADS in relief of Capt L.A. SATON. M.C. R.AMC.	a ff1
	6/8		Rained most of day. Fine evening. Capt commander visits A.D.Sh. Enemy Planes dropped bombs in Divisional area at night.	a ff1
	7/8		Weather fine. Relief of Bearers in forward area.	a 111
	8/8		Weather fine. Visit from J.A.D. M.S. 2nD division.	a 115
	9/8		Weather fine. A.D.S. Raid forced with additional Bearers Road by 11 R13dc at night from N.13.d.98.42 to N.14.a.05.20. Sheet 44 A.S.W.	a 115

WAR DIARY or INTELLIGENCE SUMMARY

62nd Field Ambulance Army Form C. 2118.

Page 114

Place	Date	Hour	Summary of Events and Information	Remarks and references to Appendices
X.15.c.6.2. Sheet 44B. CARENCY.	10/7		Weather fine. Major F.C. CHANDLER. M.C. R.A.M.C. to A.D.M.S. in relief of Major J.A. PRIDHAM. M.C. R.A.M.C. Capt. & Q.M. KENSHOLE. J.R. R.A.M.C. proceeds to U.K. on 14 days leave.	App
	11/7		Weather fine. Visit from A.D.M.S. 20th Division. Enemy planes bomb D.D.S. area. 2 O.Rks. 159 Coy A.S.C. wounded. Major J.A. PRIDHAM. M.C. R.A.M.C. and 4 O.Rks R.A.M.C. proceed to First Army R.A.M.C. School for 14 days course of instruction.	App
	12/7		Weather fine. Visit from A.D.M.S. 20th Division. Capt. L.A. SATOW. M.C. R.A.M.C. to A.D.S. for duty.	App
	13/7		Weather fine. Enemy planes bomb D.D.S. area during night	App
	14/7		Weather fine. Relief of Bearers in forward area. Enemy planes bomb D.D.S. area during night.	App
	15/7		Weather fine. Major F.C. CHANDLER. M.C. R.A.M.C. proceeds to temporary duties of D.A.D.M.S. 20th Division	App
	16/7		Weather fine. Capt. N.L. BLAMEY. R.A.M.C. to A.D.S. in relief of Major F.C. CHANDLER. M.C. R.A.M.C.	App
	17/7		Weather fine.	App
	18/7		Weather fine. Enemy planes bomb divisional area at night.	App

WAR DIARY or INTELLIGENCE SUMMARY

Army Form C. 2118.

62nd Field Ambulance

Page 115.

Place	Date	Hour	Summary of Events and Information	Remarks and references to Appendices
X.15.c.6.2 Sheet 44B CARENCY	19/8		Weather dull. No 35295 S/Sgt F.C. WELLINGTON, RAMC transferred to 25th Field Amb.	APP M
	20/8		Weather dull.	APP M
	21/8		Weather fine. Relief of bearers in forward area.	APP O
	22/8		Weather fine. Enemy planes bomb Divisional area during night.	APP N
	23/8		Weather fine. Visit from A.D.m.S. 20th Division.	APP N
	24/8		Weather: Rainy during morning. VIII Corps Sports. Major J.A. PRIDHAM, M.C. and Lt. O.Rhe RAMC, return from 1st Army School of Instruction	APP P
	25/8		Fine in morning; Thunderstorm at night. Capt. & R/M. KENSADLE. J.R. RAMC returned from leave. Major J.A. PRIDHAM. M.C. and Capt. C.S. TENNANT. R.A.M.C. to A.D.S. for duty in relief of Capt. K. BATOW.M.C. and Capt L.N.L. BLAMEY. RAMC	APP P
	26/8		Weather: Dull and rainy. Major F.C. CHANDLER. M.C. RAMC proceeded on 10 days leave to PARIS—PLAGE.	APP S
	27/8		8th Division to take over ACHEVILLE SECTION from 8th Division. 24th Division take over KENS SECTION from 20th Division. O.T.O. Str and R.A.P. in LENS SECTION handed over to 40 th Field Amb.	APP S

WAR DIARY
INTELLIGENCE SUMMARY

62nd Field Ambulance Army Form C. 2118.

Page 116

Place	Date	Hour	Summary of Events and Information	Remarks and references to Appendices
X.16.c.6.2 Sheet 44B (ARRENCY)	27/18		Capt. J.N.L. BLAMEY. R.A.M.C. with 28 ORks proceeded to relieve 26th Field Amb. in forward area of ACHEVILLE SECTION. Posts taken over as follows:- M.D.Stn. B.2.b.0.4, A.D.S. Sheet 51B R.A.P's; T.19.c.2.7., T.20.b.6.3, and T.27.d.2.4. Sheet 44B. Left Relay Post. T.26.b.1.6. Right Relay Post T.26.d.9.9. 4 O.Rks R.O.M.C. (Nursing Section) attached to VIIIth Corps Rest Station. (30.C.C.S.)	a.m.
	28/18		Major J.A. PRIDHAM, M.C. R.A.M.C. to 87th Stn. for duty. T/1904/A/pm Major G. ROSTRON, A.S.C. M.T evacuated to No7 C.C.S. (sick)	a.m.
	29/18		Weather: Dull	a.m.
	30/18		Weather: Dull Capt. E. STENNANT. R.A.M.C. and 2 ORks proceeded to 20 Division Reception Camp for temporary duty. A.D.M.S. 20 Division visits posts in forward area.	a.m.
	31/18		Weather: Dull Capt. T.H. HOUSTON. returns from 11th Durham L.I. a.m.	a.m.

A.T.?.M
Col. R.A.M.C
O.C. 62nd FIELD AMBULANCE

Army Form C. 2118.

WAR DIARY
or
INTELLIGENCE SUMMARY.
(Erase heading not required.)

Instructions regarding War Diaries and Intelligence Summaries are contained in F. S. Regs., Part II. and the Staff Manual respectively. Title pages will be prepared in manuscript.

Place	Date	Hour	Summary of Events and Information	Remarks and references to Appendices
				18637
				149/3259
			(ORIGINALS.)	

WAR DIARY or INTELLIGENCE SUMMARY

Army Form C. 2118.

Place	Date	Hour	Summary of Events and Information	Remarks and references to Appendices
X.10.c.b.2. 2nd.C.H.H.B (CAPENGHY)	1/9/18		Capt. T.H. HOUSTON, R.A.M.C. proceeded to A.D.S. in relief of Capt. J.N.K. BLAMEY, R.A.M.C. transport ambulance active during day.	aff
	2/9/18		2nd. Lieut. R.G.S. GREGG, R.A.M.C. proceeded to A.D.S. in relief of Major J.A. PRIDHAM, M.C., R.A.M.C. Wounded during day.	aM
	3/9/8		Wounded during day.	aff
	4/9/8		Relief of Bearer Divisions cancelled at A.D.S. 2/Lt. [illegible] of Ca 29, 30th, 91st and 95th Field Ambulances	aff
			2/Lt. R.G.S. GREGG, R.A.M.C. evacuated during day.	aff
	5/9/8		Capt. J.N.K. BLAMEY, R.A.M.C. proceeded to United Kingdom on leave from 6th to 12th inst.	aM
			Capt. L. SATOW, M.C. R.A.M.C. proceeded to 1st D.C.L.I. in relief of 1/Lt. E.F. PHELAN, U.S.A.M.O.R.C. who was attached to U.S.A. from 1st to 18th inst. (A.A.6)	0
			[illegible handwriting]	
	9/9/8		[illegible] Capt. T.H. HOUSTON, R.A.M.C. [illegible]	aM

Major F.C. CHANDLER, M.C. R.A.M.C.
F.C. CHANDLER, M.C. R.A.M.C.

Army Form C. 2118.

WAR DIARY 62nd Field Ambulance
or
INTELLIGENCE SUMMARY.

(Erase heading not required.)

Instructions regarding War Diaries and Intelligence Summaries are contained in F. S. Regs., Part II. and the Staff Manual respectively. Title pages will be prepared in manuscript.

Place	Date	Hour	Summary of Events and Information	Remarks and references to Appendices
X.16.c.16.2. SH...1118. (CARENCY)	7/5/18		2nd Lieut R.G.S. GREGG, R.A.M.C. rejoined at O.B.2. Major J.A. PRIDHAM, M.C., R.A.M.C. S.O. Rendu reported for duties and taken on strength. Weather fine.	
	8/5/18		Weather warm.	
	9/5/18		O.P. 2. detailed O.B.2 and Posts.	
	10/5/18		Weather warm.	
	11/5/18		Relief of Bearers in forward area. Major F.C. CHANDLER, M.C., R.A.M.C. 2nd Lieut R.G.S. GREGG, R.A.M.C. rejoined dets. A.B.2. Weather raining.	
	12/5/18		2nd Lieut at O.P.M.2. Officers — commanding Officers, 20th Bde. R.G.S. GREGG, R.A.M.C. attached. Weather warm.	
	13/5/18		2nd Lieut R.G.S. GREGG taken on O.B.2. 2nd Lieut R.G.S. GREGG taken on O.P.M.2. Lt. B/R.C. DIXON, W.V., R.A.M.C. taken on strength Weather fine.	

WAR DIARY
or
INTELLIGENCE SUMMARY.

Army Form C. 2118.

Page 119.

Place	Date	Hour	Summary of Events and Information	Remarks and references to Appendices
X.16.C.b.2. 2nd MHS (CARENCY)	14/9/18		O.C. 2nd R.G.S. GREGG, R.A.M.C. visits 2.A.D.S. & B.O.P. MAJOR. J.A. PRIDHAM, M.C., R.A.M.C. takes over at B.D.S. 3 2nd MAJOR. F.C. CHANDLER, M.C., R.A.M.C. [illegible]	[illeg]
	15/9		Capt. C.S. TENNANT, R.A.M.C., [illegible]	[illeg]
	16/9		O.C. 2nd R.G.S. GREGG, R.A.M.C. visits [illegible] Capt. F.C. CHANDLER, M.C., R.A.M.C. [illegible]	
	17/9		[illegible] F.C. CHANDLER, M.C., R.A.M.C. [illegible] O.C. 2nd R.G.S. GREGG, R.A.M.C. visits [illegible]	[illeg]

Army Form C. 2118.

WAR DIARY
or
INTELLIGENCE SUMMARY.
(Erase heading not required.)

Page 120

Instructions regarding War Diaries and Intelligence Summaries are contained in F. S. Regs., Part II. and the Staff Manual respectively. Title pages will be prepared in manuscript.

Place	Date	Hour	Summary of Events and Information	Remarks and references to Appendices
X.10.c.b.2. Bouilly (SURRERY)	18/9/18		Major C.S.TENNANT, R.A.M.C. proceeded to VIII.² Do and & Penalty purposes in a.d.9. 1/Lt. I.E.HEMPSTID. I.E., U.S.M.O.R.C. 1/Lt. I.E.HEMPSTID, U.S.M.O.R.C. Major J.A.PRIDHAM, M.C., R.A.M.C. proceeded to O.P.2. to relieve Capt.T.H.HOUSTON. R.A.M.C. Remainder of day spent in examining and answering correspondence. Weather fine.	a.888
	19/9/8		Lt.Col. R.G.S.GREGG, R.A.M.C. and Major F.C.CHANDLER, M.C., R.A.M.C. visited O.P.2. Remainder of day spent in examining and answering correspondence. Weather fine.	a.888
	20/9/8		Lt.Col. R.G.S.GREGG, R.A.M.C. visited O.P.2. Remainder of day spent in examining and answering correspondence. Weather fine.	a.888
	21/9/8		Capt. J.N.L.BLAMEY, R.A.M.C. returned from leave in U.K. Weather fine.	a.888
	22/9/8		Major J.A.PRIDHAM, M.C., R.A.M.C. returned at O.P.2. by Capt. J.N.L.BLAMEY, R.A.M.C. Lt.Col. R.G.S.GREGG, R.A.M.C. and Major F.C.CHANDLER, M.C., R.A.M.C. visited O.P.2. Weather fine.	a.888

Army Form C. 2118.

WAR DIARY
or
INTELLIGENCE SUMMARY.

(Erase heading not required.)

Page 121.

Instructions regarding War Diaries and Intelligence Summaries are contained in F. S. Regs., Part II. and the Staff Manual respectively. Title pages will be prepared in manuscript.

Place	Date	Hour	Summary of Events and Information	Remarks and references to Appendices
X.113.C.b.2. 2 Dunkirk. CURRENCY.	23/9/8		1/Lt. W. HEMPSTID. I.E., U.S.M.O.R.C. rejoined. 2nd Major. F.C. CHANDLER, M.C., R.A.M.C. at O.P.2. No. 9 Ranger transferred on demand to U.S.A. ...	A.911
	24/9/8		...	A.911
	25/9/8		Lt.Col. R.G.S. GREGG, R.A.M.C. visited O.P.2. ... Relief of Reserves by another. Lt.Col. R.G.S. GREGG, R.A.M.C. and Major J.A. PRIDHAM, M.C., R.A.M.C. attended ...	A.911
	26/9/8		Lt.Col. R.G.S. GREGG, R.A.M.C. visited O.P.2. ...	A.911
	27/9/8		Lt.Col. R.G.S. GREGG, R.A.M.C. visited O.P.2. Capt. J.M.L. BLAMEY, R.A.M.C. ... at O.P.2. Capt. T.H. HOUSTON, R.A.M.C. ...	A.911

Army Form C. 2118.

WAR DIARY
or
INTELLIGENCE SUMMARY.
(Erase heading not required.)

Instructions regarding War Diaries and Intelligence Summaries are contained in F. S. Regs., Part II. and the Staff Manual respectively. Title pages will be prepared in manuscript.

[signature] 122.

Place	Date	Hour	Summary of Events and Information	Remarks and references to Appendices
X.16.c.6.2. 92nd MHB CARENCY	28/8		March Route.	R 888
	29/8		4 O.Ranks transferred to Divisional M.V.	R 888
			Major F.C. CHANDLER., M.C., R.A.M.C. relinquished O.P.S. & Major J.A. PRIDHAM, M.C. R.A.M.C.	R 888
	30/8		assumed O.C. M.D. 20 Brigade assumed O.P.S. 2 Divisional appendix sent with War Diary.	R 882 reff att of same OC 627q reff

Army Form C. 2118

WAR DIARY
or
INTELLIGENCE SUMMARY
(Erase heading not required.)

JL 38

140/3327

Confidential

War
Diary
of
62nd Field Ambulance

From 1st October 1918
To 31st October 1918

Army Form C. 2118.

62nd Field Amb[ulance]

123

WAR DIARY
or
INTELLIGENCE SUMMARY.
(Erase heading not required.)

Instructions regarding War Diaries and Intelligence
Summaries are contained in F. S. Regs., Part II.
and the Staff Manual respectively. Title pages
will be prepared in manuscript.

Place	Date	Hour	Summary of Events and Information	Remarks and references to Appendices
X.16.c.b.2. 28th H.A.B CARENCY.	1/8		Visits O.P.s and Posts. Weather dull.	a/d
	2/8		Visits O.P.s and 12 R.F.'s etc. Visits O.P.s.	a/s
			Capt. L. SATOW, M.C., R.A.M.C. and 15 O.Rs. from 15 Div. & one O.R. from 32 Div. Reception Centre attached for duty. O.P.s Longwood Tunnel B.16.c.4.2, R.O.Rs. and Reserve Posts B.12.d.4.5, B.11.a.2.5, B.10.c.8.9, B.16.c.2.7, B.9.a.8.8. Weather fine.	a/s
	3/8		Capt. J.N.L. BLAMEY, R.A.M.C. relieves Lt.T.E.HILL, R.A.M.C. as M.O. 1/12th K.R.R.C. Lt. I.E. HEMPSTID, U.S.M.O.R.C. attached. Carencières E.Coivres R.I.Rs. O.Ps and 32 Gen. Recep. Rep. Dist[illegible] Beaver attached. Weather fine.	R/s/s
	4/8		Visits O.P.s Weather fine	R/s/s
	5/8		Visits O.P. Rs. Weather dull. Regimental Stretcher Bearers returned to 20th Divisional Reception Camp	a/s

62nd Field Ambulance

Army Form C. 2118.

WAR DIARY
or
INTELLIGENCE SUMMARY.
(Erase heading not required.)

Page 124

Place	Date	Hour	Summary of Events and Information	Remarks and references to Appendices
X.M.C.C.62 Sheet H4B CARENCY	6/10/18		Bearers relieved in the line by 37th Field Ambulance and conveyed in buses to MARQUAY. Headquarters at CARENCY handed over to 37th Field Ambulance. Weather: Fine.	@ SBS
MARQUAY	7/18	4.0am	Headquarters and transport move off to MARQUAY arriving at 14-20. 1 O.R. proceeded on 14 days leave to U.K. Weather: Fair	@ SSS
	8/18	(tempst?) 10 am	4 WATER M.O.R.C. proceeded to medical charge (temporary) of 6 K.S.L.I. Weather: Fine	@ SSS
	9/18	10-00	3 Other ranks proceeded on 14 days leave to U.K. 1st Inspection of N.C.O.s & men by unit Weather: Dull	@ SSS
	10/18		4 Other ranks return from V.C.C. Bhn to unit. Weather: Dull	@ MS
	11/18	9-00	Major F.C. CHANDLER M.C. RAMC proceeded on 14 days leave to U.K. Bathing Parade Weather: Rainy	@ MS
	12/18	9-00	Route march Weather: Rainy	@ SS
	13/18		Weather: Rainy	@ MS

62 Field Ambulance

Army Form C. 2118.

Instructions regarding War Diaries and Intelligence Summaries are contained in F. S. Regs., Part II. and the Staff Manual respectively. Title pages will be prepared in manuscript.

WAR DIARY
or
INTELLIGENCE SUMMARY.
(Erase heading not required.)

Page 125

Place	Date	Hour	Summary of Events and Information	Remarks and references to Appendices
MARQUAY	14/10		3 Other Ranks proceeded on 14 days leave to U.K. Weather: Dull.	211
	15/10		Weather: Rained all day.	211
	16/10	9-00	Route March. Weather: Dull.	233
	17/10	9-00	Bathing Parade. 6 Other Ranks proceeded on 14 days leave to U.K. Weather: Dull.	211
	18/10	9-00	Company and Squad Drill. Weather: Dull.	211
	19/10		Capt. C.S. TENNANT, R.A.M.C. proceeded to temporary medical charge of 12th Kings Liverpool Regt on relief of Lieut NEAL M.B.E. granted 14 days leave. 1 Other rank granted 10 days leave to PARIS.	211
	20/10	10-00	Church Parade. 6 Other ranks proceeded on 14 days leave to U.K. Rained all day.	211
	21/10	9-00	Bathing Parade. Weather: Dull.	211
	22/10	9-00	Route March. Capt J.M.L. BRAMLEY, RAMC returns to unit from 12 K.R.R.C.	211

62 Field Ambulance
Page 126

WAR DIARY
or
INTELLIGENCE SUMMARY
(Erase heading not required.)

Army Form C. 2118.

Place	Date	Hour	Summary of Events and Information	Remarks and references to Appendices
MARQUAY	23rd		6 other ranks proceeded on 14 days leave to U.K. Weather fair. Route March.	A 233.
	24th	09-00	Bathing Parade. Weather fine.	A 233.
	25th	09-00	Capt. T.H. HOUSTON. R.A.M.C. proceeded to temporary medical charge of 12 R.13. Company and squad Drill. Weather fine	A 233.
	26th		Capt. L. SATOW. M.C. R.A.M.C. proceeded to report to A.D.M.S. 12 Division at SAMELON for temporary duty. 15 Other ranks proceeded on leave to U.K. Route march. Weather fine	A 233.
	27th	09-00	34571 Sgt. J.R. Farrell R.A.M.C. despatched to Reinforcement Camp ETAPLES for transfer to England for 3 months tour of duty on compassionate grounds. Weather fine. Church Parade	A 233.
	28th	09-30	Weather fine. Route March.	A 233.
	29th	09-00	Weather fine. Squad Company and extension drill.	A 233.

WAR DIARY
or
INTELLIGENCE SUMMARY

62 Field Ambulance

Page 124

Army Form C. 2118

Place	Date	Hour	Summary of Events and Information	Remarks and references to Appendices
MARQUAY	30/10		Weather Fine	
		1330	Unit moves to LIGNY. ST. FLOCHEL and entrains arriving at BAPAUME 2300	Q.S.S.S
		2300	Unit conveyed by Busses to CAMBRAI. Horse transport proceeding by road	
CAMBRAI.	31/10	0500	Unit arrives in billets at CAMBRAI. Transport arriving at 1700hrs Capt L. SATOW. M.C. R.A.M.C. returned to unit from 61st Field Ambulance. Weather Dull.	Q.S.S

R S Bragg
Lt Col. R.A.M.C.
O.C. 62 Field Ambulance

WAR DIARY
or
INTELLIGENCE SUMMARY

Army Form C. 2118

CONFIDENTIAL.

WAR DIARY

OF

62nd FIELD AMBULANCE

FROM 1st November 1918 To 30th November 1918.

WAR DIARY or INTELLIGENCE SUMMARY

62 Field Ambulance Army Form C. 2118

Page 128

(Erase heading not required.)

Place	Date	Hour	Summary of Events and Information	Remarks and references to Appendices
CAMBRAI	1/11		Weather Fine. Capt A. SATOW. M.C. RAMC in charge of one (1) Sub-division proceeded to relieve No 1 Field Centre (XVII Div) as collecting (my) for duty. Major F.E. CHANDLER. M.C. RAMC proceeded to Boulogne for local leave of England expiring on at 10.0/11.18. Lieut R.M. BURT proceeded on 10 days leave to U.K. and 1 O.R. proceeded on 14 days leave to U.K. and 1 O.R. proceeded on 14 days leave to U.K. and 1 O.R. proceed on 10 months reengagement leave.	R888
	2/11		Weather Showery.	
		9.00	Bathing Parades. Orders received from 61st Inf. Bde. to move to CAGNONCLES.	R888
	3/11		Weather Fine.	
		11.00	Unit moved by road with 61st Inf Bde & 9th Inf Brigade to Billets in CAGNONCLES.	R888
CAGNONCLES	4/11		Weather Fine.	
			4 O.R's proceeded on 14 days leave to U.K.	
		10.00	Unit moved by road with 2/8 of 9th Inf Bde. to Billets in ST. AUBERT.	R888
ST. AUBERT	5/11		Weather Ragged all day. Orders received from 61st Inf Bde to be prepared to move on 14 hours notice. Capt A. SATOW M.C. RAMC proceeded on 14 days leave to U.K. Capt F. McELHINEY RAMC admitted to hospital sick and transferred to 1 (60th) Field Ambulance	R888

62 Field Ambulance Army Form C. 2118

WAR DIARY
INTELLIGENCE SUMMARY
(Erase heading not required.)

Page 129

Place	Date	Hour	Summary of Events and Information	Remarks and references to Appendices
ST. AUBERT	6/11	10.45	Weather. Rained all day. Unit moves to VENDEGIES by road and arrives in Billets at 14.00 hours. Capt H.S. TENNANT, R.A.M.C. returned to unit from 12 hours of privilege.	A.388.
VENDEGIES	7/11		Weather. Dull with rain. (b.) O.R.s proceed on 14 days leave to U.K.	A.388.
		14.30	Unit moves by road to billets in SEPMERIES. Orders received from 61st Inf Bde to be prepared to move on 8th.	A.388.
	8/11	10.10	Weather. Rained most of day. Unit moves by road to Billets at LA. BOIS. CRETTE.	A.388.
LA.BOIS CRETTE	9/11 10/11	10.30	Weather. Fair. Unit moves by road to billets at ST. WAAST. LA-Vallée.	A.S.88.
ST. WAAST LA-Vallée	11/11		Weather. Fair. Unit attached to 59th Infy Bde. Orders received from of Division that hostilities will cease at 11.00 hours.	A.388.
	12/11	11.00	Weather. Fair. 4 O.R.s proceed on 14 days leave to U.K. Unit moves by road to Billets on TAISNIERES.	A.388.

WAR DIARY or INTELLIGENCE SUMMARY

Army Form C. 2118

60 Field Ambulance Page 130

Place	Date	Hour	Summary of Events and Information	Remarks and references to Appendices
THIRMEREZ	13th		Weather Dull. 1 NCO & 2 O.R's proceeded on 14 days leave to U.K. for duty.	A.S.88
"	14th		Weather fine. 4 O.Rs proceeded on 14 days leave to U.K.	A.S.88
"	15th/16th		Weather fine. Capt. E. Taylor RAMC. encamped at Major F.C. CHANDLER, M.C. proceeded to BELLIGNIES, Capt H.J.LUCK RAMC 50 Gen Hosp to date. Capt N.S. TEMPEST RAMC proceeded to report to O.C.BM 2nd Division for duty.	A.S.88
"	16th		Weather fine. 1 Gnr & 3 O.R's in returned to unit from 8 days trench training Amb & Conv.	A.S.88
"	17th		Weather fine. Frost at night. Capt. T.H. HOUSTON, RAMC. returned to unit from 12th N/Yorks Brigade and proceeded on 14 days leave to U.K.	A.S.88
"	18th		Weather fine. Revd. I.E. HEMPSTED, M.O.R.C. returned to unit from 2nd Scottish Rifles.	A.S.88
"	19th		Weather fine. Major J.A.PRIDHAM, M.C. RAMC proceeded on 10 days leave to PARIS. 4 Other Ranks proceeded on 14 days leave to U.K.	nil.

Army Form C. 2118.

62 Field Ambulance

WAR DIARY
or
INTELLIGENCE SUMMARY.

Page 131

(Erase heading not required.)

Place	Date	Hour	Summary of Events and Information	Remarks and references to Appendices
TAISNIERES	20/8		Weather fair. Lieut I. E. HEMPSTID M.O.R.C. proceeded on 14 days leave to U.K	R.S.S.S
	21/8		Weather fine. 3 Other Ranks proceeded on 14 days leave to U.K. 20th Division Warning Order received that this Division will probably move on 23rd inst.	R.S.S.S
	22/8		Weather fine. Orders received from A.D.M.S. 11th Corps to take over Corps sick station at BAVAY in relief of 1 Section of 60th Field Ambulance. Capt L. BATOW. M.C. R.A.M.C. returned from leave.	R.S.S.S
	23/8	1000	Weather fine. Unit less "C" Section moved by road to BAVAY.	R.S.S.S
		1200	"C" Section moved to MARGNIES-le-PETIT and establish a post for collection of sick from the Division.	
	24/8		Weather fine. Capt L. SATOW. M.C. R.A.M.C. and 1. O.Rks R.A.M.C. proceed to "R" Corps Siege Park for temporary medical duty. 1 Other Rank proceeded on 14 days leave to U.K.	R.S.S.S
	26/8	0000	Unit comes under administration of A.D.M.S XIII Corps. Weather fair.	R.S.S.S

WAR DIARY
or
INTELLIGENCE SUMMARY.

Army Form C. 2118.

62 Field Ambulance

Page 132

Place	Date	Hour	Summary of Events and Information	Remarks and references to Appendices
BAVAY	27/8		Weather: Rainy. "C" Section returns to HQrs from MARQNIES-LE-PETIT. 5 Other Ranks proceeded on 14 days' leave to U.K.	A 288
	28/8		Weather: Rainy. Visit by D.D.M.S. XIII Corps.	A 288
	29/8		Weather: Fair. Capt J.N.K. BLAMEY. RAMC in charge of one tent sub-division proceeded to VENDEGIES and establishes medical post for collection and treatment of local Corps Troops.	A 288
	30/8		Weather: Fine. Major J.A. PRIDHAM. M.C. RAMC returned from Paris leave.	A 288

R.M. Hogg
LT. COL. R.A.M.C.
O.C. 62ND FIELD AMBULANCE

Army Form C. 2118.

WAR DIARY
or
INTELLIGENCE SUMMARY.

(Erase heading not required.)

VOL 40

140/34+61

ORIGINAL

COMMITTEE FOR THE
MEDICAL HISTORY OF THE WAR
6 MAR 1919
Date

CONFIDENTIAL

WAR DIARY

OF

62nd FIELD AMBULANCE

FROM 1st December 1918.   TO 31st December 1918.

Army Form C. 2118.

62 Field Ambulance
Page 133

WAR DIARY
or
INTELLIGENCE SUMMARY.
(Erase heading not required.)

Instructions regarding War Diaries and Intelligence Summaries are contained in F. S. Regs., Part II. and the Staff Manual respectively. Title pages will be prepared in manuscript.

Place	Date	Hour	Summary of Events and Information	Remarks and references to Appendices
BAVAY	1/5/18		Weather: Fine. 3 O.R's proceeded on leave to U.K. for 14 days.	A.285.
	2/5/18		Weather: Fine.	A.285.
	3/5/18		Weather: Fine.	A.285.
	4/5/18		Weather: Dull with slight rain. Warning order received from O/C XIII Corps to prepare to move on 5th inst.	A.285.
	5/5/18	0900	Weather: Fine. Unit moves with transport to VILLERS POL and arrives in billets at 0200 hours. Capt. L. SATOW. M.C. R.A.M.C. proceeds for temporary duty as M.O./c 7th F.D. Capt. J. Major J.A. PRIDHAM. M.C. R.A.M.C. proceeds to report to O/C 7th M.S 20 Division as billeting officer for unit in New Divisional Area.	A.285.
VILLERS POL	6/5/18	0900	Weather: Fine. Unit moves with transport to SAULZOIR and arrives in billets at 1330 hours. Capt. J.M.L BLANEY R.A.M.C. and one send Sub Division return to unit from VENDEGIES	A.285.
SAULZOIR	7/5/18	0900	Weather: Fine. Unit moves with transport to CAMBRAI and arrives in billets at 1300 hours.	A.285.
CAMBRAI	8/5/18	0900	Unit with transport moves to GREVILLERS and arrives in billets at 1530 hours. Weather: Fine	A.285.
GREVILLERS	9/5/18	0830	Unit moves with transport to BERTRANCOURT and arrives in billets at 1430 hours. Major J.A. PRIDHAM. M.C. R.A.M.C. returns to unit. Capt L. SATOW. M.C. R.A.M.C. proceeds for temporary duty as M.O/C 17 Corps Heavy Artillery. Weather: Fine.	A.285.
BERTRANCOURT	10/5/18		Visit from O.M.S 20 Division. Weather: Fine	

(A5001) Wt. W17711/M2031 5/17 759,000 Sch. 58 Forms/C2118/14
D. D. & L., London, B.C

62 Field Ambulance

Page 134

Army Form C. 2118.

WAR DIARY
or
INTELLIGENCE SUMMARY.
(Erase heading not required.)

Place	Date	Hour	Summary of Events and Information	Remarks and references to Appendices
BERTRANCOURT	11/12		Weather: Rainy. 5 Other Ranks proceed on 14 days leave to U.K.	R.S.S.S.
"	12/12		Weather: Rainy. U/S MORE/Lt. I.E. HEMPSTID proceeds to 12th K.R.R.C. for temporary duty as M.O/c.	R.S.S.S.
"	13/12		Weather: Rainy. 5 Other Ranks proceed on 14 days leave to U.K.	R.S.S.S.
"	14/12		Weather: Rainy. 1 O.R. proceeded on 14 days leave to U.K.	R.S.S.S.
"	15/12		Weather: Fair. Capt. T.H. HOUSTON. RAMC. proceeds to 12th K.R.R.C in relief of U/S Lt.I.E.HEMPSTID U/S MORE Lt. I.E. HEMPSTID. U/S MORE proceeds to report to D.D.M.S. XVIII Corps for duty, and is struck off the strength of this unit.	R.S.S.S.
"	16/12		Weather: Fair. 1 Other Ranks proceed on 14 days leave to U.K.	R.S.S.S.
"	17/12		Weather: Rainy.	R.S.S.S.
"	18/12	0930	Weather: Rainy. 3 Other Ranks proceed on 14 days leave to U.K. D.D.M.S. XVII Corps arrives and inspects unit.	R.S.S.S.

62 Field Ambulance

Army Form C. 2118.

WAR DIARY
or
INTELLIGENCE SUMMARY.
(Erase heading not required.)

Page 135

Place	Date	Hour	Summary of Events and Information	Remarks and references to Appendices
BERTRAN- -COURT	19/12/18		Weather: Rainy. Lt-Col R.G.S. GREGG. RAMC proceeded to U.K. on 14 days leave. Major J.A. PRIDHAM. M.C. RAMC took over command of unit, during absence of Lt Col R.G.S. GREGG. RAMC. 3 O.Rks proceeded on 14 days leave to U.K.	1M
	21/12/18		Weather: Rainy. 19 Other Ranks proceed to U.K. for release as coalminers. 15 " " attached to 18 C.C.S. DOULLENS for temporary duty. 4 " " proceeded on 14 days leave to U.K.	2M
	22/12/18		Weather: Rainy.	2M
	23/12/18		Weather: Fair.	2M
	24/12/18		Weather: Fair. 4 O.Rks proceeded to U.K. on 14 days leave. 1 O.Rk proceeded on 10 days leave to PARIS.	2M
	25/12/18	11-30	Weather: Fair. Church Parade.	2M
	26/12/18		Weather: Fair.	
	27/12/18		Weather: Rainy. 3 O.Rks proceeded on 14 days leave to U.K.	2M Rk 2M M

62 Field Ambulance

Army Form C. 2118.

WAR DIARY
or
INTELLIGENCE SUMMARY.

(Erase heading not required.)

Page 136

Instructions regarding War Diaries and Intelligence Summaries are contained in F. S. Regs., Part II. and the Staff Manual respectively. Title pages will be prepared in manuscript.

Place	Date	Hour	Summary of Events and Information	Remarks and references to Appendices
BERTRAN-COURT	28/12		Weather: Rainy. 1 OR Pte proceeds to U.K on 14 days ordinary leave and 4 days King's leave.	JM
	29/12		Weather: Rainy	
	30/12		Weather: Rainy. 3 ORPtes proceeded on 14 days leave to U.K. 1 OR proceeds to U.K for release as coalminer.	JM
	31/12		Weather: Rainy	

Document 16   20 DIV   9.8.47
Confidential   14/3440
Box 1835

War Diary
of
G.O.C. Fourth Division entrance Rams
1st January 1919 – 31st January 1919

Army Form C. 2118.

67 Field Ambulance

WAR DIARY
or
INTELLIGENCE SUMMARY.
(Erase heading not required.)

Page 137

Instructions regarding War Diaries and Intelligence Summaries are contained in F. S. Regs., Part II. and the Staff Manual respectively. Title pages will be prepared in manuscript.

Place	Date	Hour	Summary of Events and Information	Remarks and references to Appendices
BURTAAM COURT	1/9		Weather: Rainy	app 183
	2/9		Weather: Fair. Lt/Col M.O. Wheeldon RAMC proceeded on 10 days special leave to HULT.	app 184
	3/9		Weather: Rainy. H. Other Ranks proceeded on 14 days leave to U.K.	app 185
	4/9		Weather: Rainy.	app 186
	5/9	9 am 11-30	Weather: Fair. R.C. Church Parade. C of E Church Parade. Lt/Col R.A.S. GREGG. RAMC returned from Leave. Major J.A. PRIDHAM. M.C. RAMC proceed on one months special leave to U.K. Capt. T.H. HOUSTON. RAMC returns to unit from 12/N.R.R.C. 10 Other Rank proceeds to U.K. for Demobilization	
	6/9		Weather: Fair	app 188
	7/9		Weather: Fair. Capt T.H. HOUSTON RAMC proceeds to take over permanent duties of M.O/c 117th R.I.	app 189
	8/9		Weather: Rainy	app 190
	9/9		Weather: Fair. slight rain.	app 191

62 Field Ambulance

Army Form C. 2118.

WAR DIARY
or
INTELLIGENCE SUMMARY.
(Erase heading not required.)

Page 138

Place	Date	Hour	Summary of Events and Information	Remarks and references to Appendices
BERTRAN-COURT.	10/9		Weather: Fair. 4 Other Ranks proceeded on 14 days leave to U.K.	AM1
	11/9		Weather: Fair. 2 Reinforcements R.A.M.C. reported for duty.	AM1
	12/9	9.0am 11.30am	Weather: Fair. R.C. Church Parade. C of E Church Parade. 5 Other Ranks proceeded to U.K. for Demobilization.	AM8
	13/9		Weather: Fair. 2 Other Ranks proceeded to U.K. on 14 days leave to U.K.	AM8
	14/9		Weather: Fair. 3 Other Ranks proceeded to U.K. for Demobilization.	AM8
	15/9		Weather Fair, slight rain.	AM8
	16/9		Weather. Fair.	AM1
	17/9		Weather. Fair. 1 Other Rank proceeded on 14 days ordinary leave, 4 days Kings Leave, to U.K. " " " to report to O/C R.A.M.C. Section, 3rd Echelon for duty.	AM1

Army Form C. 2118.

WAR DIARY
or
INTELLIGENCE SUMMARY.
(Erase heading not required.)

Place	Date	Hour	Summary of Events and Information	Remarks and references to Appendices
BERTRANCOURT	18/1/19		Weather Frosty. 9 Other Ranks departed to U.K. for demobilisation	appx
	19/1/19		3 Other Ranks proceeded on 14 days leave to U.K. Weather Frosty, fair later	appx
		09.00	R.C. Church Parade	appx
		11.30	C.E. Church Parade	appx
	20/1/19		Weather Cold & Frosty	appx
	21/1/19		Weather Cold & dull	appx
	22/1/19		Weather Cold & Bright. 4 Other Ranks proceeded on leave to U.K.	appx
		14.00	Lecture delivered by Major CHANDLER. M.C. R.A.M.C. on demobilisation	
	23/1/19		Weather Cold & dull. 2 Other Ranks were demobilized whilst on leave to U.K.	appx
	24/1/19		Weather Cold. Fair. 1 Other Ranks proceeded on 14 days leave to U.K.	appx
	25/1/19		Weather Cold & dull.	appx
	26/1/19		Weather Cold. Light snowfall	appx
		09.00	R.C. Church Parade	
		11.30	C.E. Church Parade	
		18.30	Wesleyan Service in YMCA Hut Acheux. German P.O.W. died early morning in the Hospital (Pte Arnold KUHNE. 402 Res. Inf. Regt) 205 P.O.W. Coy	

Army Form C. 2118.

WAR DIARY
or
INTELLIGENCE SUMMARY.

(Erase heading not required.)

Place	Date	Hour	Summary of Events and Information	Remarks and references to Appendices
BERTRAN- COURT	27/12		Weather Cold & Dull. Capt. & Dr. W. Kenshole and 16 other Ranks proceed on 14 days leave to U.K.	
	28/12		Weather Cold & Bright	
	29/12		Weather Cold & Dull	
	30/12		Weather Cold & Dull. Sergt Major Wheeler & 5 other Ranks proceed to report to A.D.M.S Abbeville. 1 O.R. reported at Depot R.A.M.C Blackpool & is struck off strength from 26-12-18	
	31/12		Weather Cold & Dull	

Army Form C. 2118

WAR DIARY
or
INTELLIGENCE SUMMARY
(Erase heading not required.)

ORIGINAL
Confidential

War Diary
of
62nd Field Ambulance
from 1st Feb. 1919 to 28th Feb 1919.

Place	Date	Hour	Summary of Events and Information	Remarks and references to Appendices
	Feb. 1919			

62 Field Ambulance
Page 141.

Army Form C. 2118.

WAR DIARY
or
INTELLIGENCE SUMMARY.
(Erase heading not required.)

Place	Date	Hour	Summary of Events and Information	Remarks and references to Appendices
BERTRAM COURT	1/2/19		1 O.R. R.A.S.C. M.T. proceeded to U.K. for demobilization	RSSS
"	2.2.19		R.C. & C. of E. Church parades.	RSS
"	"		1 O.R. R.A.M.C. proceeded on 14 days leave (special) to U.K.	
"	"		1 O.R. R.A.S.C.H.T. proceeded to U.K. for demobilization	
"	3.2.19		1 O.R. R.A.S.C. demobilized 14.1.19 writes on leave to U.K.	RM
"	5.2.19		Heavy snowfall	RSS RSS
"	6.2.19		2 O.R. O R.A.M.C. proceeded to U.K. for demobilization	RSSS
"	7.2.19		1 O.R. R.A.S.C.H.T. proceeded to U.K. for demobilization	
"	9.2.19		R.C. Church parade.	RSSS
"	"		1 O.R. R.A.M.C. proceeded on leave (14 days) to U.K.	
"	16.2.19		1 O.R. R.A.M.C. demobilized whilst on leave to U.K.	RSSS
"	"		2 O.R. R.A.M.C. proceeded to U.K. for demobilization	
"	17.2.19		1 O.R. R.A.M.C. proceeded on 14 days leave to U.K.	RM
"	"		No. 175 PTE MEICHSNER 109 Inf Regt German P.O.W. died - pneumonia	

62 Field Ambulance
Page 142

Army Form C. 2118.

WAR DIARY
or
INTELLIGENCE SUMMARY.
(Erase heading not required.)

Instructions regarding War Diaries and Intelligence Summaries are contained in F. S. Regs., Part II. and the Staff Manual respectively. Title pages will be prepared in manuscript.

Place	Date	Hour	Summary of Events and Information	Remarks and references to Appendices
BERTEAU-COURT	12.2.19		1. O.R. R.A.S.C.M.T. demobilized whilst on leave to U.K.	eee
"	13.2.19		8. Horses demobilized	
			Capt. J.W.L. BLAMEY R.A.M.C. and 2 O.R.s (R.A.M.C.) proceeded on 14 day leave to U.K.	eee
"	14.2.19		1 O.R. R.A.M.C. struck off strength whilst in hospital in U.K.	
			2 O.R. R.A.M.C. proceeded to U.K. for demobilization	eee
"	15.2.19		Capt. & Q.M. J.R. KEWSMOLE R.A.M.C. proceeded to return to R.D.M.S. RDEVILLE for duty.	eee
			R.C. Chuckhurst	
"	16.2.19		1 O.R. R.A.M.C. proceeded to return to O/C R.A.M.C. Sec'y dep.	eee
"	17.2.19		2 O.R.s R.A.M.C. proceeded to U.K. for demobilization	eee
"	18.2.19		1 O.R. R.A.S.C.M.T. demobilized whilst on leave to Base	eee
"	19.2.19		1 Horse Evacuated to Base	
			2 O.R.s R.A.M.C. proceeded on 14 days leave to U.K.	
			1 O.R. R.A.M.C. demobilized whilst on leave 25.1.19 in U.K.	eee

62 Field Ambulance
Page 143

Army Form C: 2118.

WAR DIARY
or
INTELLIGENCE SUMMARY.
(Erase heading not required)

Place	Date	Hour	Summary of Events and Information	Remarks and references to Appendices
BEATIAM COURT	20.2.19	09.30	Unit moved to MONDICOURT	RM
MONDI- COURT	"	13.00	Unit arrived MONDICOURT	RM
			1 O.R. R.M.C. proceeded to U.K. for demobilyto	
			2 O.R. R.A.M.C. reinforcements arrived for duty	RM
	21.3.19		Heavy rain.	
			6 O.R. R.M.C. & 1 O.R. "B" category proceeded to U.K. for demobyto	
			2 O.R. R.A.M.C. proceeded to U.K. for furlough & re-enlistment	
			CAPT R.A.W PROCTOR M.C. R.A.M.C. reported for duty & proceeded	
			to take over temporary medical charge of 92 Bde. R.F.A.	
			1 O.R. R.M.C. reported for duty from O/c R.A.M.C. See 3rd Feb.	RM
"	22.2.19		R.C. church Parade in village church.	RM
"	23.2.19		1 O.R. R.A.M.C. demobilyzed 26.1.19 whilst on leave in U.K.	RM
			1. "D" Hope proceeded to 32 Mobile Veterinary Section for	
			disposal	
"	24.2.19		3 Horses demobilyzed	RM

62 Field Ambulance

Page 144.

Army Form C. 2118.

WAR DIARY
or
INTELLIGENCE SUMMARY.
(Erase heading not required.)

Place	Date	Hour	Summary of Events and Information	Remarks and references to Appendices
MOBILIZATION COURT	1-25.2.19		2 OR of R.A.M.C/B Category proceeded to U.K. on 14 days leave	
"	26.2.19		Weather cloudy	
"	26.2.19		5 OR of R.A.M.C. proceeded to U.K. for demob.
2 OR of R.A.M.C. proceeded to U.K. on furlough & re-enlistment.
Total strength O.R. — R.A.M.C. 107 R.A.S.C. M.T. 20.
B category between 5, R.A.S.C. M.T. 12	

A.S. Shogg
Lt Col R.A.M.C.
O.C 62 Field Ambulance

Army Form C. 2118

WAR DIARY
or
INTELLIGENCE SUMMARY
(Erase heading not required.)

CONFIDENTIAL

WAR DIARY

OF

62nd. FIELD AMBULANCE.

From:- 1st.March,1919   to:- 31st.March,1919.

Army Form C. 2118.

62nd Field Ambulance
Page 145

WAR DIARY
or
INTELLIGENCE SUMMARY.
(Erase heading not required.)

Instructions regarding War Diaries and Intelligence Summaries are contained in F. S. Regs., Part II. and the Staff Manual respectively. Title pages will be prepared in manuscript.

Place	Date	Hour	Summary of Events and Information	Remarks and references to Appendices
MONDI- COURT	1/2/19		Summer time introduced at 23.00 hours.	
	2.3.19		C of E & R.C. services.	
	3.3.19		Unit received Case of SPARE PARTS ex MARIEUX.	
	4.3.19		1 O.R. proceeded on 14 days special leave to U.K. 3 O.R. rejoined from 221 Employment Company 1 H.D. & 1 L.D. proceeded for demobilization.	
	5.3.19		CAPT. L.L. SATOW. M.C. R.A.M.C. proceeded as A/D.A.D.M.S. 20th Division 2 O.R.s proceeded on 14 days leave to U.K. 5 horses to Amiens Collecting Camp for embark to England.	
	6.3.19		Whole Driver. Mock Trial held in billet.	
	7.3.19		Capt. J.W.L. BLAMEY. R.A.M.C. returned from leave in U.K. 9 O.R. R.A.M.C. proceeded for demobilization	
	8.3.19		1 O.R. R.A.M.C. rejoined from 18 C.C.S. Clothing & equipment by C.O.	
	9.3.19		A.D.M.S. 10th Division visited & inspected Hospital Church Service C of E & R.C.	
	10.3.19		1 O.R. R.A.M.C. proceeded on leave 3 O.R. R.A.M.C. (Army of Occupation) proceeded to No 6. Stat Hosp.	

62nd Field Ambulance
Page 146.

Army Form C. 2118.

WAR DIARY
or
INTELLIGENCE SUMMARY.
(Erase heading not required.)

Place	Date	Hour	Summary of Events and Information	Remarks and references to Appendices
MONDI- COURT	11/3/19		1. H.D. Posted to C.H.D.H.S. L.Cpl. STOKE & PESTELL attached Acting Corporal. 3 O.Rs joined from No. 6 Stat. Hosp.	Refs
	12.3.19		Conference of M.O.s of Field Ambulance Commands at 61 Field Ambulance MARIEUX.	MS
	13.3.19		2 O.R. 6/18 C.C.S. + 2 from 18 C.C.S. 3 O.R. R.A.M.C. (Army of Occupation) proceeded to No. 6 Stat Hosp., & 3 O.R. R.A.M.C. (demobilizable) received in exchange. 1 Horse ambulance wagon & one Mule Cart despatched to Railhead DOULLENS & the S.S.W. & 1 Limber S.S.W. to 1.0.M. CAM D.T.S. consequent on reduction of War Establishment, Motor Railway Details held.	MS
	14.3.19		3 O.R. R.A.M.C. & 2 O.R. R.A.S.C. proceeded for demobilization.	MS
	15.3.19		One O.R. R.A.M.C. proceeded to 3rd Army Infantry School. One O.R. R.A.S.C. (MT) proceeded to S. of G. Scene to PARIS.	Ross
	17.3.19		One riding horse sent to 3rd Army Remount Collecting Cent.	M3
	19.3.19		Lt. Col. R.C.S. Grey Mane proceeded on 14 days Special leave to U.K. Major A. Paintin M.C. R.A.M.C. took over Command.	M3

Army Form C. 2118.

62 Field
Ambulance
Page 147.

WAR DIARY
or
INTELLIGENCE SUMMARY.

(Erase heading not required.)

Place	Date	Hour	Summary of Events and Information	Remarks and references to Appendices
MON DIDOULT FRANCE	17/3/19		12 mules sent to 19 Veterinary Evac. Stn. Doullens. Capt. J.M.L. BLAMEY RAMC proceeded to Abbeville.	App
	18/3/19		Report to D.M.S. i/c C. 9 men sent away for demobilisation	App
	19/3/19	midnight	2nd Do Hd 10 closed. All tents & left end made a terminus hut. T 61 2nd Brigade Group.	App
	20/3/19		2 men sent away for demobilisation. S.M.O. 61st Bde opens office at Hd. Qrs 62 F. Amb. Lt. Col A.C. HAMMOND — DEANUS is acting S.M.O.	App
	29/3/19		Under authority A.G. circular 596 the following Officers are struck off the strength of 62nd F. Amb, Major J.A. PRIDHAM M.C. RAMC, S.R. & Major F.C. CHANDLER M.C. RAMC, & in both cases revert to rank of Captain	App
	30/3/19		Capt. J.A. PRIDHAM MC RAMC is Marked to No 2 F. Amb. & to command it pending return of Lt Col Surgeon GRECO RAMC from leave	App

Army Form C. 2118.

WAR DIARY
or
INTELLIGENCE SUMMARY.
(Erase heading not required.)

CONFIDENTIAL.

WAR DIARY

OF

62nd. FIELD AMBULANCE.

From:- 1st.April,1918.   to:- 30th.April,1918.

WAR DIARY
or
INTELLIGENCE SUMMARY.

Army Form C. 2118.

62nd Field Amb.
Page 148.

Place	Date	Hour	Summary of Events and Information	Remarks and references to Appendices
MONDICOURT	1st April 1919		Rev. E.V. Carter C.F. reported departure for U.K. for demobilisation	
	23/4/19	20.30	Brat Present Cadre Sports at PAS.	
	28/4/19		Lt.Col. A.G.S. GREGG R.A.M.C. is struck off strength of 62nd F Amb & ceases to command it. (Auth. D.N. M 34296 A.M. D.1. 15/4/19)	

J M Adams
Capt A.M.C.
a/o c 62 F Amb

105/3560

No. 62 Field Ambulance

28 JUL 1919

62 F. Amb.
Army Form C. 2118.

WAR DIARY
or
INTELLIGENCE SUMMARY.

Page 149.

Place	Date	Hour	Summary of Events and Information	Remarks and references to Appendices
DIONDICOURT FRANCE	3/5/19		All R.A.S.C. H.T. returned to Horses were struck off strength of unit & transferred to 161 Coy R.A.S.C. but retained on strength for rations etc.	
	7/5/19		20 R.A.M.C. O.R. posted for demobilisation who in turn to below establishment.	
	11/5/19		Capt J. A. PRIDHAM M.C. R.A.M.C. (S.R.) to O/Pct O.C. 62 F. Amb from 18/4/19. Auth (S.M.O. XVII Corps M.16/5 dated 7/5/19)	
	14/5/19		15 O.R. posted for demobilisation	
	17/5/19		Unit commenced to hand in stores behind sidearms	
	28/5/19		Remaining R.A.S.C. H.T. personnel that to Abancourt. All wagons handed in to Abancourt. Unit reduced to a medium for use apart of 150 O.R. none	
	30/5/19		Unit partly old personnel. Capt PRIDHAM R.A.M.C. transferred to 18 Cas Clearing Station	

M.R. ...
...
O.C. 62 F. Amb

62nd F. Amb.

Taken at Bertrancourt, France.

February 1919

www.ingramcontent.com/pod-product-compliance
Lightning Source LLC
Chambersburg PA
CBHW080917230426
43668CB00014B/2147